Perspectives Asia-Pacific

# Perspectives Asia-Pacific

## Navigating Changes in Society, Culture, Gender and Policy

*Editor*

Anasua Basu Ray Chaudhury

**Indian Association for Asian & Pacific Studies**

**Motilal Banarsidass Publications**

**MOTILAL BANARSIDASS**
**PUBLICATIONS**

4741/23, Ansari Road, Daryaganj, New Delhi - 110002 (India)
*Email: publications@mlbd.com | sales@mlbd.com | exports@mlbd.com*
*Indian Website: www.mlbdonline.com | Foreign Website: www.mlbd.com*



**Perspectives Asia-Pacific**
Navigating Changes in Society, Culture, Gender and Policy

*First Edition Published in 2025*



Published in India by
Motilal Banarsidass Publications
and
Indian Association for Asian & Pacific Studies

ISBN : 978-81-970870-2-8 (HB)

Printed and bound in India

# About the Editor

## *Anasua Basu Ray Chaudhury*

Anasua Basu Ray Chaudhury (Ph.D), a Senior Fellow at the Observer Research Foundation (ORF), Kolkata, specialises in South Asia's regional cooperation; Bay of Bengal and Indo-Pacific geopolitics; energy politics and forced migration. She is the Editor of ORF Bangla and serves on editorial boards for the *Journal of Indian Ocean Research* (Routledge) and *Borders in Globalisation Review* (University of Victoria, Canada). Dr. Basu Ray Chaudhury is a Visiting Fellow (2012) at Maison des Sciences de l'Homme, Paris and the recipient of prestigious awards such as the PSBT Senior Media Fellowship (2007) and the Kodikara Award (1998–99). She is also an alumna of the National Defense University, Washington, DC. Her recent publications include *India's Relations with Neighbouring South and Southeast Asian Countries: Perspectives on Look East to Act East* (co-edited, 2023); *Caste and Partition of Bengal: The Story of Dalit Refugees* (co-authored, 2022) and *New Futures of BIMSTEC: Connectivity, Commerce, and Security* (co-edited, 2021), among others. Her work explores key geopolitical, socio-economic, and security issues in South and Southeast Asia.

# List of Contributors

1. **S. D. Muni** is a Distinguished Fellow (Hon.) at the Manohar Parrikar Institute for Defence Studies, New Delhi.
2. **Debamitra Mitra** is a former Director, Satyajit Ray Film & Television Institute, Ministry of Information and Broadcasting, Government of India.
3. **Susmita Mukherjee** is an Associate Professor and Head of the Department of History, Syamaprasad College, Kolkata, India.
4. **Debarati Ganguly** is an Assistant Professor, Department of History, St. Xavier's College, Kolkata, India.
5. **Sulagna Som** is a Ph.D. Research Scholar, Department of History, Jadavpur University, Kolkata, India.
6. **Srabanti Basu** is a Professor, Heritage Institute of Technology, Anandapur, Kolkata, India.
7. **Soumya Bhowmick** is Fellow, Centre for New Economic Diplomacy, Observer Research Foundation, Kolkata, India.
8. **Aparna Bandyopadhyay** is an Associate Professor, Department of History, Diamond Harbour Women's University, West Bengal, India.
9. **Sayatri Dutta** is an Associate Instructional Designer, LearningMate Solutions Pvt. Ltd.
10. **Rajarshi Chakrabarty** is an Assistant Professor, Department of History, University of Burdwan, West Bengal, India.

11. **Sumana Bagchi** is a mental health professional and academic mentor, Legal Aid Services West Bengal, and a freelancer.
12. **Sumit Kumar Bar** is an Assistant Professor, Department of English, Prabhu Jagatbandhu College, Andul, West Bengal, India.
13. **Sayantani Sen Mazumdar** is an Assistant Professor, Department of Political Science, Diamond Harbour Women's University, West Bengal, India.
14. **Sohini Bose** is an Associate Fellow, Observer Research Foundation, Kolkata, India.
15. **Sohini Nayak** is a Ph.D. Research Scholar, Department of International Relations, Jadavpur University, Kolkata, India.
16. **Surajit Mahalanobis** is an Academic Counsellor (IGNOU), New Delhi; former Senior Consultant (Media), Vice Chancellor's Office, IGNOU, New Delhi, India.
17. **Lipi Ghosh** is a former Centenary Professor of International Relations, University of Calcutta, Kolkata, India.
18. **Ambar Kumar Ghosh** is an Associate Fellow, Observer Research Foundation, Kolkata, India.

# Preface

This book is a compilation of selected papers presented in the $11^{th}$ Biennial International Conference on *Asia Pacific from Past to Present: Bonding and Challenges*, jointly organised by the Indian Association for Asian and Pacific Studies and ASEAN Studies Centre, Chulalongkorn University, Thailand. The essays in this volume are incorporated in three broad areas: Emergence of the Indo-Pacific: Strategic and Economic Realignment, ASEAN Centrality, and Transition from Asia Pacific to Indo-Pacific.

While conceptualising this book, we felt it necessary to include only those essays that are being peer reviewed with satisfactory comments. We are indeed thankful to all these contributors, who were in the multiple panel discussion during the conference. We are very happy to have them on board. We acknowledge our debt to our Executive Committee members for their painstaking effort in editorial assistance.

This volume has been edited singlehandedly by Anasua Basu Ray Chaudhury, our Honorary Secretary of the Indian Association for Asian & Pacific Studies. She has given the volume an appropriate shape and true academic flavour and flow.

We take this opportunity to appreciate the efficient copyediting provided by Jehanara Wasi and Neena Abhyankar. We are thankful to all the authors who cooperated with us promptly. We express our sincere thanks to Pranav Jain of Motilal Banarsidass Publications, who agreed wholeheartedly to publish the volume.

We hope it will be an important addition in the domain of knowledge in Asian Studies.

Kolkata
2024

**Lipi Ghosh**
*President*
IAAPS

# Contents

## *Section II:*
## Gender Spectrum: Beyond Binary



## *Section III:*
## Foreign Policy Dynamics

## *Section IV:*
## Covid 19: The Pandemic of Our Time

# Introduction

*Anasua Basu Ray Chaudhury*

## Setting the Tone

The term 'Asia Pacific' has been in use since the mid-20$^{th}$ century, reflecting the increasing economic interconnectedness of East Asia, Southeast Asia, and Oceania.[1] During the post-World War II era, the Asia Pacific region became synonymous with the rapid rise of countries like Japan, South Korea, Taiwan, Singapore and later China. By the late 20$^{th}$ century, the Asia Pacific was widely recognised as the engine of global economic growth, driven by the unprecedented economic transformations of these nations, particularly through trade and integration into global markets.

The Asia Pacific framework emphasised the role of the Pacific Ocean as a conduit for trade and economic exchange, primarily between the United States (US), Japan, China and other East Asian nations. The region was largely defined by economic cooperation, with organisations such as the Asia Pacific Economic Cooperation (APEC) forum serving as platforms for multilateral discussions and trade agreements. However, it has been argued in due course of time that the Asia Pacific concept overlooked the growing strategic importance of the Indian Ocean and the emerging role of India in regional and global affairs.

The shift in terminology from 'Asia Pacific' to 'Indo-Pacific' reflects a significant change in global geopolitical and strategic thinking over the past decade. This transition represents more than just a rebranding of regional geography; it symbolises a transformation in the power dynamics, security concerns and economic engagements that define the contemporary world order. Understanding the reasons for this transition, its implications and the responses it has triggered provides valuable insight into the changing nature of international relations.

## The Emergence of the Indo-Pacific: Strategic and Economic Realignment

The transition to the term 'Indo-Pacific' began in the early 21st century, gaining significant traction around 2017 when the US, India, Japan and Australia—the so-called 'Quad' (Quadrilateral arrangement) countries—adopted it as a core part of their strategic thinking. The Indo-Pacific concept reflects a broader geographic scope, extending from the east coast of Africa to the western coast of the US. The term 'Indo-Pacific' refers to the geographical expanse combining the Indian and Pacific oceans. As Rory Medcalf (2015),[2] an early proponent of the term, notes, an 'Indo-Pacific definition of Asia lends further legitimacy to India's growing role as a strategic actor in East Asia, including the South China Sea and Western Pacific. It also offers a rationale for a stronger US–India relationship'. In other words, the term Indo-Pacific acknowledges the interconnectedness of the Indian and Pacific Oceans as a single strategic theatre, highlighting the increasing relevance of India as a major power and the growing competition between the U.S. and China.

The shift from 'Asia Pacific' to 'Indo-Pacific' has been driven by several key factors:

- China's Rise and Maritime Expansion: China's economic rise and assertive actions in the South China Sea and the Indian Ocean have prompted regional and global powers to rethink their strategies. China's Belt and Road Initiative (BRI)[3] and its efforts to develop ports and infrastructure across the Indian Ocean region have expanded its influence beyond East Asia, challenging traditional maritime powers like India, the US and Japan.

- India's Growing Influence: India's economic and military rise, combined with its strategic location at the heart of the Indian Ocean, has made it a pivotal player in the Indo-Pacific region. India's 'Act East' policy and its increasing engagement with Southeast Asian and East Asian nations have positioned it as a key counterbalance to China's influence. The Indo-Pacific framework recognises India's importance in regional security and economic networks.
- The Quad and Security Cooperation: The Indo-Pacific concept has been strongly promoted by the Quadrilateral Security Dialogue, or 'Quad', which includes the US, Japan, India and Australia. This grouping has emphasised the need for a 'free and open Indo-Pacific', with a focus on upholding the rule of law, freedom of navigation and respect for sovereignty. The Quad is widely seen as a response to China's increasing assertiveness in both the Pacific and Indian Oceans, particularly in relation to territorial disputes and trade routes.
- Economic Interdependence: While security concerns have driven much of the Indo-Pacific discourse, economic interdependence remains a critical factor. The region encompasses some of the world's busiest sea lanes, through which trillions of dollars in trade flow annually. The Indo-Pacific has become a central arena for global trade, investment and infrastructure development, with countries like the US, Japan, India and Australia seeking to promote alternative development models to China's BRI.

China's vision of regional governance with regard to the South China Sea and BRI has caused massive concerns to the Indo-Pacific nations. Japan was the first to propose, in 2007, a regional initiative to counter China's rising ambitions, engaging Japan, India, Australia and the US. That first 'Quad' failed to take off. Later, in 2016, Japanese Prime Minister Shinzo Abe launched the Free and Open Indo-Pacific (FOIP) initiative by highlighting the importance of the Indo-Pacific Ocean as an arena for 'international public goods'.[4] In the same year, the Asia Africa Growth Corridor initiative came into existence to engage Africa in the Indo-Pacific paradigm and compete with China's BRI.[5]

The Indo-Pacific concept has also become part of US national strategy. In May 2018, the US changed the name of the US Pacific Command to 'US Indo-Pacific Command',[6] and in 2019 two policy documents were released: the Indo-Pacific Strategy Report and A Free and Open Indo-Pacific: Advancing a Shared Vision,[7] all indicating the centrality of the Indo-Pacific in the US's strategic agenda. Former US Defence Secretary Jim Mattis has been quoted as saying: 'the Indo-Pacific region has many belts and many roads'.[8]

The term 'Indo-Pacific' was introduced by strategic thinkers in India and Australia around the mid-2000s. It gained traction in the early 2010s, particularly within the governments of New Delhi and Canberra. In India, the term aligned with Prime Minister Narendra Modi's 'Act East' policy, while Australia, geographically straddling the Indian and Pacific Oceans, has embraced the Indo-Pacific framework as central to its foreign and defence policies. It was first mentioned in the 2013 Defence White Paper as a 'framing device' or 'enabling metaphor' to describe Australia's strategic environment, focusing on its position between two oceans, with Indonesia at its centre.[9] Australia's engagement with the Indo-Pacific reflects its desire to balance relations with China, its largest trading partner, and the US, its key security ally.

## ASEAN Centrality

The BRI and the FOIP are two competing regional strategies, with Southeast Asia playing a pivotal role due to its control over critical sea lanes of communication (SLOCs). As a result, understanding Southeast Asia's perception of the Indo-Pacific is essential. Most Southeast Asian countries turn to ASEAN for guidance in their foreign policy objectives. The ASEAN Outlook on the Indo-Pacific (2019)[10] emphasises promoting cooperation within the Indo-Pacific region through ASEAN-led platforms, like the East Asia Summit (EAS), to foster dialogue and implement Indo-Pacific cooperation based on a rules-based order, international law, transparency, inclusivity and economic engagement.

This ASEAN vision aligns with India's inclusive Indo-Pacific strategy and seeks to expand partnerships with organisations like the Indian Ocean Rim Association (IORA) and the Bay of Bengal Initiative for Multi-Sectoral Technical and Economic Cooperation (BIMSTEC). As Indo-Pacific cooperation grows into a collective effort, India, as a key regional player, becomes a significant stakeholder in these discussions. Some see India as a counterbalance to China's rising influence, while others view India as a partner in maintaining stability and economic prosperity in the region. India, however, prefers to focus on enhancing regional connectivity and fostering collective growth, rather than acting as a counterweight.[11]

Southeast Asian countries, despite their national interests and relationships with other powers, generally favour a balanced approach to the Indo-Pacific rather than fully aligning with the US's vision of the region. For instance, Singapore seeks to avoid being drawn into competing interpretations of the Indo-Pacific, a stance shared by Thailand, Malaysia and Indonesia. At the same time, Southeast Asia's reservations about the BRI do not signal a decrease in economic cooperation with China. Instead, ASEAN countries aim to prevent over-reliance on China, striving for a more balanced relationship with other global powers. However, the absence of Southeast Asian nations in the FOIP framework led by Japan and the US has raised concerns, as many in the region associate the FOIP with the Quad.

## Transition from Asia Pacific to Indo-Pacific

The transition from 'Asia Pacific' to 'Indo-Pacific' represents a fundamental rethinking of regional dynamics in the 21st century. It reflects the rise of new powers, the evolution of economic and security challenges and the growing importance of maritime domains in global geopolitics. As countries navigate this new geopolitical landscape, the Indo-Pacific will likely remain a focal point for strategic competition, cooperation and economic engagement.

In a nutshell, the Indo-Pacific concept has significant geopolitical and strategic implications. First and foremost, it reflects a shift in focus from East Asia to a more expansive region that includes the Indian Ocean and South Asia. This reorientation places greater emphasis on maritime security and the protection of critical sea lanes, which are vital for global trade and energy supplies. Secondly, the Indo-Pacific framework underscores the increasing competition between the US and China. The US views the Indo-Pacific as a strategic arena in which to counterbalance China's influence and maintain its own presence as a Pacific power. US policies such as the FOIP strategy aim to strengthen alliances with regional partners and promote a rules-based order, with a particular emphasis on countering China's maritime ambitions.

For China, the Indo-Pacific concept is viewed with suspicion, as it challenges Beijing's regional aspirations and its efforts to establish itself as the dominant power in the Asia Pacific. China's response has been to continue its assertive actions in the South China Sea, increase its military presence in the Indian Ocean and expand the BRI to include maritime infrastructure projects that enhance its access to critical trade routes and strategic points.

## *About the Volume*

The vast region known as the Asia Pacific, though divided into nation-states by national boundaries, shares common challenges that must be addressed through cooperation—whether bilateral or multilateral—for the well-being of all involved. Historically, the seas and oceans have facilitated a network of communication, encompassing both trade and religion, which fostered extensive cultural exchanges. These interactions often included significant literary and linguistic exchanges. Connections were forged through the movement of people, goods and knowledge across land and sea routes. While debates persist over whether these connections resulted in influence or interaction, historical narratives reveal that many scholars emphasise the importance of social proximity. Following the period of decolonisation in much of the region, nationalism often took precedence over cosmopolitanism, leading to divergent paths of national development in the Asia Pacific.

Against this backdrop, with the historical changes in consideration, the collection of works presented in this volume explores the rich tapestry of Asia's social, cultural and political landscapes, with an emphasis on the dynamic interplay between tradition, modernity, identity and global forces. Thematically divided into four sections, this compilation delves into key aspects of Asia's evolving society, from its deep-rooted religious and cultural traditions to contemporary issues of gender, foreign policy and the impacts of the COVID-19 pandemic.

In this volume, special emphasis is put on India. *The volume is a collection of eighteen essays, which starts with the keynote address on* 'Pacific from Past to Present: Bonding and Challenges' delivered by S.D. Muni. Muni's deliberation sets the agenda of the book. The four major sections of the volume are: 'Society, Culture and Religion: A Continual

Interplay', 'Gender Spectrum: Beyond Binary', 'Foreign Policy Dynamics' and 'Covid-19: The Pandemic of Our Time'.

Section one, entitled 'Society, Culture and Religion: A Continual Interplay' contains six essays. The section starts with the essay on 'The Praxis of Cultural Pluralism under the Rubric of Religiosity and Religiousness' written by Debamitra Mitra. In her essay, Debamitra argues that the average Indian's daily life is deeply intertwined with religion, embracing multiple faiths without hesitation. India's religious diversity, far from being a source of conflict, is a natural and accepted reality. This diversity, however, does not imply assimilation, as maintaining distinct religious identities is crucial. The challenge lies in integrating these identities without erasing them. Indians, regardless of faith, are united by their shared 'Indian-ness', living harmoniously while respecting religious boundaries. This unique balance allows them to coexist, study, work and socialise together, enriching the nation's social fabric.

The second essay is by Susmita Mukherjee. In her essay on 'Priyanath Bose and the Great Bengal Circus: Performance Art and the Narratives of Nationalism', Susmita discusses the circus, a spectacle of trained animal acts and human skill which has roots in ancient Rome and Greece. However, the author argues that it was modernised by British ex-Sergeant Major Philip Astley. In India, Vishnupant Moreshwar Chatre (1840–1905) is credited with founding the Indian circus, inspired by a challenge from Western practitioners. This sense of emerging nationalism was echoed by Priyanath Bose, who established the Great Bengal Circus in 1887. Both figures played pivotal roles in shaping the Indian circus tradition, blending entertainment with a burgeoning national identity.

The third essay, 'The Literature Living Through the Ages, Ramakien: A Discussion on the Thai Version of Ramayana' by Debarati Ganguly focuses on *Ramakien*, a cornerstone of Thai classical literature. In this essay, Debarati opines that *Ramakien* is Thailand's unique adaptation of the Indian epic *Ramayana*. This rendition reflects the cultural exchange between India and Southeast Asia, evolving over time with new characters and incidents that give it an indigenous Thai identity. The *Ramakien* has been appropriated into shadow plays, offering fresh interpretations that differ from the original *Ramayana*. In modern Thailand, *Ramakien* and its related performances remain culturally significant, symbolising the lasting impact and relevance of this epic in Thai society. Her paper explores various facets of the *Ramakien* and its cultural importance.

The fourth essay has been contributed by Sulagna Som, '*An Alternative Story of the Arakan Front: Through the Eyes of an Indian Doctor, Shantilal Roy (1943–1944)'. In her essay, Sulagna* explores modern warfare and medical treatment during World War II through the lens of *Arakan Fronte*, a war memoir by Bengali doctor Shantilal Roy, who served in the British army in Burma. The study examines the harsh realities faced by Indian soldiers in the British forces, highlighting the horrors of the Arakan campaign against Japanese troops. By focusing on Roy's experiences and nationalistic sentiments, this research contributes to the evolving historiography of warfare, offering a non-European perspective on the brutalities of war and the role of Indian soldiers in global conflicts.

The next essay on 'Storytelling and Poetry Performance in ancient India and Thailand' by Srabanti Basu shows how oral literature has been vital in transmitting knowledge, values and societal norms across generations in ancient civilisations. This paper offers a comparative study of storytelling and poetry performance in ancient India and Thailand, focusing on presentation methods rather than content or societal impact. Despite the advent of written texts, the oral tradition persisted, with stories being memorised and orally transmitted across civilisations. The study examines how these oral techniques evolved and highlights the paradox of orality's fluidity versus the fossilisation that occurs when stories are written down.

The last essay in this section is by Soumya Bhowmick on 'Fast Fashion: The Sustainability Question for Asia', where he talks about the Indian fashion industry that is marked by the popular trend of fast fashion, which involves production of low-cost clothing that imitate luxury fashion trends with a quick turnover rate. While providing clothes at accessible prices, the true cost of fast fashion is quite high, especially for Asian countries like Bangladesh, where the production part of the fast fashion industry is quite prominent. It includes negative environmental externalities, gendered labour issues and exploitation, and the intellectual property rights (IPR) concerns that raise questions over the sustainability of the fast fashion trend. To be sure, this industry creates a variety of impediments to the UN Sustainable Development Goals (SDGs) and makes the achievement of these targets by 2030 even more difficult in the post-pandemic world. This paper explores the origin of the fast fashion trend, the various issues that arise and suggests possible paths for sustainable transformation in the industry.

The second section of the volume entitled 'Gender Spectrum: Beyond Binary' has five essays. The section starts with Aparna Bandyopadhyay's essay on 'Violence against Widows in Colonial Bengal'. Aparna argues in her essay that the Act for the Abolition of Sati (1829) and the Hindu Widows' Remarriage Act (1856) are often celebrated as liberating measures for Hindu widows in colonial Bengal. While the abolition of sati significantly reduced the practice, the legalisation of widow remarriage had limited success, with societal resistance prevailing. Despite these reforms, widows continued to face severe patriarchal control, deprivation and violence. Educated women reformers prioritised self-reliance over remarriage, advocating for institutional support.

This paper argues for a re-evaluation of male-led reforms, emphasising the need to focus on widows' lived experiences and women's initiatives for a more nuanced understanding of their plight.

In the essay on 'Space and Variation in Dalit Women's Lived Experience', Sayatri Dutta divides her argument into three parts. The first part gives a background of caste and what she means by space. The second part deals with interviews given by Dalit women across India to understand the spatiality of caste and gender. Finally, she talks about how solidarity could be built across spaces.

Rajarshi Chakrabarty has contributed the third essay of this section. 'Fighting Against Macaulay's Legacy: LGBTQ People's Struggle for Removal of Section 377 in South and South-East Asia' deals with the diverse gender identities and sexual orientations that have existed in South and Southeast Asia for centuries, with evidence of acceptance in ancient mythology, epics and religious texts. However, British colonial rule introduced repressive laws, such as Section 377 of the Indian Penal Code (1861), which criminalised homosexuality, reflecting Judeo-Christian and Victorian morals. While India decriminalised homosexuality in 2018, many post-colonial states like Pakistan, Bangladesh and Malaysia still enforce these colonial-era laws, perpetuating homophobia and transphobia. Aparna's paper documents the ongoing struggles of LGBTQ communities in these regions, analysing the impact of colonial legislation and the fight for its repeal.

The essay on 'Gender Issues in Asia through the Prism of Counselling—Adolescent Counselling' by Sumona Bagchi focuses on adolescence, as defined by the World Health Organization, spanning ages 10–19, which represents the transition from childhood to adulthood. The author argues that this period is marked by significant physical, biological and psychological changes, often leading to stress, confusion and insecurity. Adolescents face the challenge of developing independence and maturity, which can be difficult for some due to the pressures associated with this stage of life. While some young people navigate these challenges with resilience and effective coping mechanisms, others may struggle, highlighting the unique and varied experiences within this critical developmental phase.

The last essay of this section concentrates on 'Law for Women and Advocate Cornelia Sorabji's Vision of Women's Rights in Colonial India' written by Sumit Kumar Bar. In his writing, Sumit focuses on Advocate Cornelia Sorabji (1866–1954), who was a pioneering figure in advocating for the legal rights of pardanashin women in colonial India. Recognising the challenges faced by these secluded women, Sorabji focused on empowering them through education and legal assistance, particularly in matters of inheritance and property rights. Her work highlighted the systemic gender-based oppression embedded within the traditional legal and cultural frameworks. Sorabji's efforts were instrumental in challenging the status quo, laying the groundwork for women's rights in India and pushing towards a more modern, inclusive legal system. Her legacy remains a significant milestone in the history of women's empowerment.

The third section of the volume is entitled 'Foreign Policy Dynamic' which has four essays. The first essay is 'India and the ASEAN: The Logic of Partnership in the Indo-Pacific Region' by Sayantani Sen Mazumdar. In her article, Sayantani argues that under Prime Minister Modi, India's foreign policy has become more proactive, shifting priorities and enhancing global engagement. Key initiatives like the 'Act East' policy and 'Neighbourhood First' policy have reshaped India's approach to external affairs. The focus is on soft power, cultural ties and political connections with the diaspora. India's involvement in regional institutions like ASEAN, though not a member, is critical to its role in the Indo-Pacific, where its strategic interests intersect with China's, reinforcing India's global stature. These changes reflect a transformation driven by systemic and state-level shifts in foreign policy.

Sohini Bose in her essay on 'Deliberating Disaster Diplomacy in the Bay of Bengal: India's Interests and Imperatives' opines that disaster diplomacy has become a key strategy for countries, particularly in disaster-prone regions like the Bay of Bengal, where frequent cyclones and tsunamis occur. India has emerged as a leading provider and first responder in humanitarian assistance and disaster relief (HADR) in the region, enhancing its regional ties through collaborative disaster preparedness initiatives. This paper aims to: 1) examine the disaster risks in the Bay and the origins of India's disaster diplomacy; 2) assess India's effectiveness as an HADR provider, including factors behind its acceptance and rejection; and 3) explore India's future strategies in disaster diplomacy, focusing on BIMSTEC and the Quad.

Sohini Nayak in her article on 'India in the Indo-Pacific: Evaluating maritime strategies, envisioning strengthened analogies' indicates that the concept of the Indo-Pacific marks a strategic shift from the Atlantic to the Pacific, reflecting Asia's rising prominence in global economic dynamics. India's evolving maritime strategy has adapted to these geopolitical changes, aiming to enhance its role in the increasingly competitive global order. This shift has fostered multilateral collaborations and the emergence of regional dimensions in maritime security, underscoring the importance of a 'free and open Indo-Pacific Strategy'. This paper explores the development of key institutions in the Indo-Pacific, analysing India's ambitions and expectations within this new strategic landscape.

The last essay in this section is written by Surajit Mahalanobis. In his essay entitled 'Neo Symbiotic Reality in India's Foreign Trade: The Case of Thailand, 2014–2022', the author argues that India's refusal to join the Regional Comprehensive Economic Partnership (RCEP) hints at its preference for adopting a foreign trade policy on terms it considers fair. The earlier UPA governments' policies of looking towards the East and doing business idealistically through outreach bonding, resulted in giving up about 74 percent Indian market share to the ASEAN states and China, heavily tilting the balance of trade against India's interests till 2014. In contrast, the current Indian foreign policy has reached beyond soft power and symbiotic realism for the bilateral, to initiate norms of neo-symbiotic realism. Yet, there are challenges. This paper addresses the challenges to find out viable reactions that should ideally embolden a relation built upon neo-symbiotic realism between India and Thailand for a lasting ASEAN preference, in relations not shadowed by fear.

The last section of the volume is entitled 'Covid-19: The Pandemic of Our Time'. This section has two essays. Ambar Kumar Ghosh contributes the first essay in this section on 'Populist Political Communication in India during COVID-19: A Comparative Study of National and Regional Political Leadership's Messaging in Response to the Pandemic'. In his essay, Ambar argues that the rise of populist politics is crucial for understanding contemporary political discourse in democracies worldwide. Populism, characterised by its adaptability and lack of a fixed identity, thrives during socio-political crises such as the COVID-19 pandemic. This paper examines the populist political responses in India, focusing on the political communication of Prime Minister Narendra Modi and the leaders of two high COVID-19 infection states, Arvind Kejriwal (Delhi) and Mamata Banerjee (West Bengal). By analysing their leadership styles and messaging during the pandemic, the study aims to extrapolate key aspects of populism within India's federal political structure.

The last essay of the volume is written by Lipi Ghosh. In her article on 'Covid-19 and Asia Pacific in its Early Years Till the End of 2022', Lipi focuses on the Covid-19 outbreak that has brought the world to a standstill. The world faced a new 'Great Depression' and global panic as the virus toll largely mounted. The kind of undeclared cold war that had been gathering momentum shows its true face under the tedium of Covid-19, which had major impacts on international relations, especially in the Asia Pacific region for the contemporary period. Apart from the US and China's reciprocal allegations against each other about the origin of the coronavirus, relations among interregional powers have also become strained. The central directive of these relations are anti-Chinese feelings either at government or at civil society levels. This paper studies the issues of Covid-19 in the Asia Pacific and its impacts till 2022, the year when Covid-19 practically reached its end. This paper concentrates especially on the issue of vaccine diplomacy.

## Endnotes

1 Richard Stubbs, "ASEAN Plus Three: Emerging East Asian Regionalism?" *Asian Survey* 42, no. 3(2002): 440–55.

2 Rory Medcalf, *Reimagining Asia: From Asia–Pacific to IndoPacific*. The ASEAN Forum, 2015, http://www.theasanforum.org/reimagining-asiafrom-asia-pacific-to-indo-pacific.

3 President Xi Jinping's speech at the opening ceremony of the 'Belt and Road Initiative Forum for International Cooperation' at Beijing on May 14, 2017, http//www.xinhuanet.com/english/2017-05/ 14/c136282981.

4 Ministry of Foreign Affairs Japan, Diplomatic Bluebook, 2019, https://www.mofa.go.jp/policy/ other/bluebook/2019/html/chapter1/c0102.html#sf01.

5 "Asia Africa Growth Corridor," *The Economic Times*, September 3, 2017, https://economictimes. indiatimes.com/topic/Asia-Africa-Growth-Corridor/4.

6 U.S. Department of Defense, *Indo-Pacific Strategy Report: Preparedness, Partnerships, and Promoting a Networked Region*, July 1, 2019, introductory preamble by Acting U.S. Secretary of Defense Patrick Shanahan. https://media.defense.gov/2019/Jul/01/2002152311/-1/-1/1/ DEPARTMENT-OF-DEFENSE-INDO-PACIFIC-STRATEGY-REPORT-2019.PDF.

7 U.S. State Department, *A Free and Open Indo-Pacific: Advancing a Shared Vision*, November 2019, https://www.state.gov/wp-content/uploads/2019/11/Free-and-Open-Indo-Pacific4Nov2019.pdf.

8 George Varghese, "U.S. Pacific Command renamed U.S. Indo-Pacific Command," *The Hindu*, May 31, 2018, https://www.thehindu.com/news/international/us-pacific-command-renamed-usindo-pacific-command/article24043314.ece.

9 B. Sargeant, "The Pacific islands in the 'Indo-Pacific'," *Strategic Challenges* 16, no. 1(2020), 26–31.

10 ASEAN [Association of Southeast Asian Nations]. (2019, June 23). ASEAN Outlook on the Indo-Pacific. *ASEAN Statements & Communiques*. https:// asean.org/asean-outlook-indo-pacific.

11 Anasua Basu Ray Chaudhury, "The Indo Pacific: Counter Narrative," in *Mapping the Belt and Road Initiative: Reach, Implications, Consequences*, eds., Harsh V. Pant & Premesha Saha (New Delhi: Observer Research Foundation, 2021), 125–30.

# Asia Pacific from Past to Present: Bonding and Challenges

**Keynote Address by *S D Muni***

My sincere thanks to Professors Lipi Ghosh, Sarvani Gooptu and Piti Srisangnam of the ASEAN Studies Centre of Chulalongkorn University for this kind invitation. I also congratulate Prof. Partha Ghosh for assuming the Presidency of the Indian Association for Asian & Pacific Studies. I may not have much to share with you from my side but look forward to learning from stimulating ideas and insightful observations about a region which is stirring the global political and economic order.

Many academic concepts in political science and international relations spring out of strategic calculations of the great powers. 'Asia Pacific' is one such construct. I have, however, been somewhat uncomfortable with this construct. It emerged out of the (so-called) 'area studies' academic programmes emanating from the US, carved out to serve Western strategic interests during the Cold War. In these programmes, Asia was divided into various sub-regions. The post-partition Indian subcontinent was rechristened South Asia and separated from East Asia, which in turn, was split into Northeast and Southeast components. Initially, the US strategic interests in the region were institutionalised in the form of SEATO, the South East Asian Treaty Organization. But by the 1960s, the formulation had to be changed to 'Asia Pacific' to reflect the integrated US strategic interests in the Northeast and Southeast components of Asia, which also included Japan. This whole region was militarily secured under the Pacific Command of the US. This new term of 'Asia Pacific' made sense for the US because its Pacific interests extended to, and converged on, Asia's eastern front.

'Asia Pacific' was a strategically driven narrow geo-political construct. Someone described it as Pascal's horrific sphere 'with periphery indeterminable and a center that may be anywhere'. It excluded India and its immediate neighbours, except Myanmar. And yet it had an inherent strategic anomaly. Pakistan, though not included as a part of the 'Asia Pacific' construct, was strategically integrated into SEATO as a member. India was brought under the operational range of the Pacific Command. Recall the US military intervention in 1971 to stop the emergence of Bangladesh by sailing its naval task force under the aircraft career 'Enterprise' through the Bay of Bengal. India's exclusion from the 'Asia Pacific' was perhaps owing to India's refusal to participate in the US-led military alliances and follow the ideological lead of the Cold War to confront communism. India, then, also did not have enough economic clout to attract the region's interest. India's keenness to join ASEAN in 1967 was also rebuffed for strategic and ideological reasons. Even the communist regimes of Vietnam, Laos and Cambodia were kept out of ASEAN initially, though they were very much a part of the 'Asia Pacific' geopolitical construct.

In keeping India out, India's natural geographical span—marked by the presence of the Andaman and Nicobar islands right at the opening of Malacca Strait—and its physical contiguity with the region through Myanmar, were ignored. If 'Asia Pacific' represented the confluence of the Pacific and Indian Oceans, then the exclusion of India, which constitutes the principal anchor of the Indian Ocean and its Bay of Bengal, was a serious affront to the common sense of geography. Keeping India out of the 'Asia Pacific' also reflected the ignorance or calculated blinding of the builders of this construct towards the centuries' old huge civilisational and cultural spread of India into the region, which has been duly acknowledged in the Concept Note of this conference. Here I wish to compliment Prof. Lipi Ghosh and the organisers of this conference for establishing the 'Indian Association' of scholars for exploring India's civilisational and cultural binding, economic engagement and strategic proximity with the 'Asia Pacific'. You are doing an honour to the intellectual legacy of Rabindranath Tagore and scholars like RC Mujumdar, UN Ghosal, Kalidas Nag and many others who were celebrating the historic binding between India and the 'Asia Pacific' by exploring and documenting it under the banner of the 'Greater India Society'.

In the rapidly changing strategic and economic dynamics of the 'Asia Pacific', the irrational and unnatural exclusion of India was not sustainable. This exclusion constrained India's engagement with the region, but India never stopped getting itself involved in the region strategically. The end of the Cold War and economic opening and resurgence of India started eroding the strategic barriers erected unnaturally earlier. Doors were opened for India to creep into the region through what may be called the institutional back doors. India started partnering with ASEAN. It became a founding member of the ASEAN Regional Forum (ARF) and the East Asia Summit (EAS). And now, realising that the US 'rebalance' in Asia cannot succeed without active and extensive Indian involvement, the 'Asia Pacific' construct has been renamed 'Indo-Pacific'.

I disagree with the formulation 'Asia Pacific v/s Indo-Pacific', listed as one of the themes of the conference. Some other recent publications have also pitted these two constructs against each other. There is no hostility or incompatibility between the former and the latter. In fact, the former has been an artificial and short-lived aberration of the latter. 'Indo-Pacific' as a regional reality, conceptualised as such or not, has existed for centuries. The foundations of the Indo-Pacific were laid by the Maurya (322–185 BCE), Gupta (319–467 CE) and Chola (3 BCE–13 CE) empires of India. It has been nursed by the spread of Hinduism, Buddhism and Islam. Chinese scholars and travellers have been couriers of this civilisational transmission. The footprint and absorption of these civilisational spreads are distinctly visible even today in various forms. The Borobudur, Prambanan and Bali temples in Indonesia; Luang Prabang and Vat Phou in Loas; Angkor Vat in Kampuchea; Cham stone statue of Hindu Lord Ganesh in Da Nag Museum, Vietnam; Ramayana plays in the region in different forms; and Sanskritised names of persons and places all represent a rich civilisational assimilation between India and the 'Asia Pacific'. British India was an Indo-Pacific power in many ways, stretching its sway from the east of the Suez Canal to Hong Kong, Australia and the Pacific Islands. There was, however, an important difference between the British Indian empires' 'Indo-Pacific' character and that of pre-colonial India's. Culture and commerce constituted the founding pillars of India's engagement with the 'Asia Pacific' in ancient times. The British Empire destroyed these pillars and replaced them with economic exploitation and strategic domination. Indentured labour was sent to set up a plantation economy and Indian soldiers were used to ensure security of trade and economic stakes. Independent India had to pay for these colonial distortions in its engagement with the region for decades, though the Indian diaspora now stands as a valuable asset in diplomatic and economic cooperation with the region.

The credit for creating an 'Indo-Pacific' strategic construct is generally given to the Japanese Prime Minister Shinzo Abe, as he referred to the confluence of two seas, the Pacific and the Indian. But here, he was drawing a simile from Dara Shikoh, an Indian Mughal prince who was talking of the confluence of cultures in India. The strategic formulation of the 'Indo-Pacific' construct by Japan, supported by the US and Australia, cast primarily in the context of China's rise and assertion and the US strategy to contain China through rebalancing in the 'Asia Pacific' baffled the Indian policy makers initially. It was feared that accepting the 'Indo-Pacific' formulation would amount to following the US and Japan's lead and may bring India's strategic autonomy under a cloud and put India in confrontation with China.

It must not have been so. How could the mandarins in India's South Block ignore the rich civilisational connect between India and the region, so laboriously explored by the 'Greater India Society' scholars and French historians? Not only this, Nehru had, as early as in 1944 in his 'Discovery of India', proclaimed that the strategic significance of the Atlantic Ocean would decline, and then India would play an important role in the Pacific region. India's peace-making role in Korea and Indo-China during the 1950s and 1960s under the UN banner and later in Cambodia, even in the thick of the Cold War cold-shouldering of India in the region, reflected Nehru's vision. Thus, India always had pronounced strategic stakes and a deep-rooted civilisational presence in the region. The Look East Policy was the formal pronouncement of these stakes, which also opened the way for deeper economic engagement with the region. It may not be out of place to assert here that India has always garnered peace and prosperity in a close relationship with this region, except during the colonial and early independence period. It would always be essential for India's economic growth and strategic stability to remain productively and intensively engaged with this region. India's inhibition to accept the strategic projection of the 'Indo-Pacific' construct melted away soon under the weight of these considerations as well as the pressure of Chinese intrusion and assertiveness in Doklam (Bhutan) and Ladakh. The US also needed active Indian participation in its 'rebalancing' strategy and so was encouraging India to play a larger and more active role in the 'Asia Pacific' region. India has been considered a 'lynchpin' in the US 'rebalance'.

Prime Minister Modi has carried forward Nehru's vision for India's role in the 'Asia Pacific' in his own way by re-packaging the Look East Policy as the Act East policy. He has extensively travelled to the region, undertaking nearly three dozen visits in less than nine years of his Prime Ministership. While emphasising India's strategic and economic stakes in the region, Modi has also revived and reinforced civilisational and cultural links. He has organised Hinduism and Buddhism religious conferences, addressed large diaspora gatherings in the countries of his visits and come up with the concept of SAGAR (Security And Growth for All Region). India's trade during 2018–2021 with ASEAN, Australia, Japan and the US in the region has grown by 12.88 percent, 23.61 percent, 18.59 percent and 33.80 percent respectively. India's military exercises with regional major powers have increased in numbers and intensity, and India is claiming to emerge as an important security provider in the region. Modi has defined India's commitment to the overall peace and prosperity of the 'Indo-Pacific' by saying:

> We will promote democratic and rule based international order…We will work with others to keep our seas, space and airways free and open, our nations secure from terrorism; and our cyber spaces free from disruption and conflict. We will keep our economy open and our engagement transparent. We will share our resources, markets and prosperity with our friends and partners. (Shangri-La Address, August 2018).

In April 2019, India's Ministry of External Affairs established a separate division to focus on 'Indo-Pacific' affairs and Modi launched India's 'Indo-Pacific Oceans Initiative' (IPOI) at the EAS Summit in Bangkok in November 2019. India accords centrality to ASEAN in its 'Indo-Pacific' strategy and commits itself to working within the existing regional cooperative mechanisms to ensure maritime security and economic growth. ASEAN and other countries in the region welcome India's involvement but do not yet consider

India central to the unfolding regional developments. In a recently conducted survey in Southeast Asia, India's trust rating was only 16.6 percent as compared to Japan, the US and China at 54.2 percent, 52.8 percent and 26.8 percent respectively (State of Southeast Asia, 2022 Report). India, therefore, has a long way to go to enhance its credibility in the region.

All other important players in the region like ASEAN, Australia, Indonesia, Japan and the US have defined their respective visions of approaches to the 'Indo-Pacific' region. There are minor differences in these visions and approaches in terms of the conceived territorial span and proposed cooperative activities. However, broadly, every one stands for ensuring and promoting the freedom, peace, stability and prosperity of the region. Ideally, the territorial span of the 'Indo-Pacific' may extend from India's western front, leaving the Persian Gulf and the Arabian Sea aside, to the US Pacific front. China continues to express reservations on the 'Indo-Pacific' construct as it looks upon it from a narrow strategic perspective, assuming that it is an expression of the strategy of the US and its allies to contain China and restrain its emergence as a regional and global power. Russia supports China in this respect, considering the 'Indo-Pacific' construct an extension of US efforts to preserve and promote its global hegemony. Both of them seem reconciled, however reluctantly, to India's strategic integration with the region but prefer to retain the old *nomenclature of 'Asia Pacific' to oppose the US rebalancing strategy in Asia.*

The 'Indo-Pacific' construct is in the process of redefining itself in the context of the shifting global balance of power from the West to Asia. The old one was characterised by deep civilisational and productive commercial bonding. The new construct is wobbling in a deep flux on two counts: resetting strategic equations and coping with the socio-political implosions. The strategic front of the 'Indo-Pacific' has been stirred by the unfolding intense competition between China and the US for primacy and dominance. For its surged ambitions to acquire a great global power status and to realise its expanded territorial vision of the Middle Kingdom through massive military buildup, threats of the use of force, assertion, intrusions and 'wolf-warrior' diplomacy, China has strategically alienated itself from many of its neighbours in the region. This is despite China's extensive and mutually beneficial economic engagement with the countries of the region, including the US. To counter China's increasingly aggressive profile and to preserve its post-Second War dominance in the region, the US is reinforcing its traditional alliances and forging new strategic partnerships. The Quad (US, India, Japan and Australia), AUKUS (Australia, United Kingdom and the US), and a number of mini-lateral groupings represent new forms of strategic bindings. The rest of the region finds itself pushed into anxiety and concern for peace and stability, which is critical for economic growth and dynamism in the region. They fear that the histories of the rising powers challenging the established hegemons through war and disruption may be repeated in the 'Indo-Pacific'. There are a number of hot spots like the South China Sea, Taiwan issue, nuclear proliferation in the Korean peninsula, and India–China face off in the Himalayas. A somewhat distant possibility of the Ukraine war spilling over in Asia is also not being ruled out. All efforts, including US President Biden's summit meeting with the Chinese President Xi Jinping in Bali in November 2022, are geared to contain and resolve the hotspots and keep the possibilities of military conflict at bay. It is clear that the region cannot and will not be dominated by any single power. It never has been. Its future lies in a multi-polar power structure and multiple alliances or associations based on mutual interests and issues of common concerns. For example, the region is responsible for more than half of the global carbon emissions. The fuming cities and rising seas cannot be contained unless the countries of the region and the world cooperate sincerely in the spirit of give and take.

On the socio-political front, the 'Indo-Pacific' turbulence is not as threatening as on the strategic front, but there is a need for serious care and attention. The 'Indo-Pacific' is a pivotal region of the world. It accounts for 60 percent of the global GDP and two-thirds of global growth. It houses 60 percent of the global population, which is increasingly self-conscious, confident and aspirant, especially the younger generations. Its middle classes are growing and becoming more active and demanding through rapid expansion of social media and interactions. Urban spaces are expanding in the region, which already boasts 22 megacities out of a total of 33 in the world. Traditional identities are being revived, and new ones are being forged to be used as weapons in the fight for political rights, social justice and economic opportunities. While accepting strong and assertive leadership, people are disapproving of growing economic inequalities and shrinking democratic spaces. Recent developments in Myanmar, Thailand, Hong Kong and Sri Lanka have rudely reminded all of us that representative and responsive governance is the need of the day. There are constituencies of simmering discontent and alienation in many other 'Indo-Pacific' countries that may explode if left unattended for long. The 'Indo-Pacific' economies are struggling to adjust with the shifting supply chains and disrupted production lines, as well as implications of global economic headwinds. The challenges confronting governance have become more complicated and hardened by terrorism, cyber-crimes, migration and natural disasters.

The scholars and policy makers of the 'Indo-Pacific' region face the daunting task of decoding regional turbulence and finding credible solutions, both at the strategic and socio-political fronts. While doing so, it would be desirable to map out the regional order and its terms of mutual engagement that existed in the pre-colonial 'Indo-Pacific'. Bridging this knowledge gap may offer insights as well as cautions in dealing with the contemporary challenges. I hope and wish that this conference will make a bold and innovative contribution in this respect. I wish you all a grand success in your endeavour.

# *Section I*

# Society, Culture and Religion: A Continual Interplay

# The Praxis of Cultural Pluralism under the Rubric of Religiosity and Religiousness

***Debamitra Mitra***

## Introduction

The average Indian encounters God in a million daily interactions. Instead of steering away from religion, they steer towards it without hesitation, and 'religion' here does not always look the way Indians might expect it to. The idea that multiple faiths can peacefully intermingle not only does not shock Indians, it is actually taken for granted. The religious diversity that exists in India shows a lot of promise. But diversity is not assimilation. Rather, had it been assimilated, any discussion on diversity would remain meaningless without separate religious identities. So, the challenge for governance is how to integrate but not assimilate. In India, adherents to Hinduism, Islam, Christianity, Jainism, Buddhism, Zoroastrian and Judaism are all connected and united by virtue of their 'Indian-ness'. The religious minorities have figured out how to be the 'sugar in the milk', to quote from a Parsi story, as sugar dissolves in milk and adds sweetness, taking up space that is available for it to occupy. And what makes an Indian proud about being religiously observant in this country is how they continue to study together as students, work together as colleagues, live together as neighbours and eat together as friends, but do not stray outside the religious boundaries set for themselves.

## Debate of Tolerance and Intolerance

By celebrating India's ecumenism and religious diversity, however, I have no intention of ignoring India's history of sectarian violence and caste oppression or whitewashing India's history. But the texture of tolerance for India 'appears from a distance like a society where tolerance had grown organically, and has a far longer history, and was more deep rooted for that reason'.[1]

Girish Sahane says,

> While India's tolerance was deeper, though, it was not as wide as England's, for it was based on a respect for religious rights and customary rights but it did not extend to any modern conception of individual rights as a whole. In the established discourse of tolerance versus intolerance, the two categories are mutually exclusive, and yet a number of societies exhibit tolerance, or something deeper and more positive, within a limited sphere, without a wider universalist appreciation of human rights.[2]

The other view says, as Arvind P Datar argues, 'if one swallow does not make a summer, one Dadri or clamour over banning beef or the banning of the works of Taslima Nasreen and Salman Rushdie do not make a country of 1.24 billion people intolerant. These can be isolated, regrettable incidents but are not indicators of a nation's intolerance'. For example, the preamble of the Indian Constitution; the Supreme Court's declaration of secularism as part of the basic structure of our Constitution, denoting the positive concept of equal treatment of all religions as evident in cases such as Aruna Roy vs Union of India (2002) and S.R. Bommai vs Union of India (1994); Gandhiji's philosophy of 'sarva dharma samabhava' or equal respect for all religions; Article 25, which confers on all persons, including non-citizens, a fundamental right to freely profess, practice and propagate their religion; Articles

29 and 30 of our Constitution, which protect the language, script and culture of minorities and give them the right to establish educational institutions of their choice; the Right of Children to Free and Compulsory Education Act, 2009; and Mohd. Ahmed Khan vs Shah Bano Begum, the controversial maintenance lawsuit of India all demonstrate that the outcry against 'rising intolerance' is somewhere unjustified. 'Though, India has had an unfortunate track record of communal riots before and after Independence, but no one can deny that all endeavours have been taken by every Central and state governments to protect the rights and privileges of all minorities.'[3]

Yet another group of people who, in the actual sense, experience daily the respect for religious rights evident in Indian society, cannot understand why a few isolated and seemingly unexceptional incidents have led people to take such steps of renouncing their awards and titles. Though they might wish that the responses were less personal, at the same time they believe that their general reaction to 'go with the flow' is natural. Accepting the archetype of an absolute divide between tolerance and intolerance—rather than the complex mix of mutual respect and suspicion with the shadow of hatred that characterises relations between communities in India—is also happening in the discourse between Islam and Islamist extremism. Muslims who experience their religion as grounded in amity, goodwill and compassion respond to news reports of terror by saying, 'This is not Islam at all'. In this light, it is easy to understand the negative reaction of large sections of the public to intellectuals returning awards in protest against growing intolerance.

Nevertheless, in the debate between India's tolerance or intolerance, two precepts cannot be ruled out. First, we cannot ignore that, however praiseworthy our tradition of religious tolerance is, it has never extended to respect for human rights as a whole or for the rule of law, which any modern nation demands. Moreover, there is a parallel tradition of casteist abuse that needs to be taken into consideration as well in order to give a complete picture of our society. Not to mention the public interest litigation (PIL) raised against the developers of the location-based augmented reality game Pokemon Go, alleging that it hurts religious sentiments by showing eggs in places of worship or a 9-year-old Dalit boy in Rajasthan murdered for touching a drinking pot meant for the upper castes. Secondly, though no government will disturb the inter-communal respect that is woven into the fabric of Indian society, despite many skirmishes to prove Indian nationalism strong in the regimes of different political parties time and again, India will not witness a move overnight from its organic respect for religious customs to a wider comprehension of human rights. Hence, witnessing several examples of how quickly stable societies spiral into sectarian chaos, in India's case, it is sensible to err in overstating threats to freedom rather than staying contented about the resilience of our traditions of tolerance. This thus encourages one to probe into the rubric of Indian religiosity and religiousness, since religion in the country has manifold and manifest meanings, interpretations and vested applications.

## The Discourse of Religious Identity, Religiosity and Religiousness

Religious identity is a specific type of identity formation. As historian Romila Thapar says, 'Religion being the primary identity has gained strength over the years because it is an easy identity. It is easy to declare your religion and follow it, whereas with a national identity you have to work hard. Religion, for many people after all is a psychological necessity.'[4] The sense of group membership to a religion pertains to one's self-concept. As one's social identity is anchored in a system of guiding beliefs and symbols, religion serves as a uniquely powerful function in shaping psychological and social processes of the individual. 'To some, religious identification offers a distinctive "sacred" worldview and "eternal" group membership, unmatched by identification with other social groups'.[5]

Thus, an individual's religiosity can be explained by the marked cognitive and emotional value that religious group membership provides. Sociologically, the uniqueness of a positive social group imparts two-fold advantages: First, a belief system that offers knowledge, especially with regard to the methods, validity and scope of the group and the distinction between justified belief and opinion. Second, the individual gets the philosophical conception of his nature of being, his existence or reality and the basic categories of being and their relations. Religious group membership lends the individual a religious identity both epistemologically and ontologically for his well-being. Consideration of religion's dual function as a social identity and a belief system may facilitate greater understanding of the variability in its importance across individuals and groups, finally driving towards cultural pluralism. However, that uniqueness may have an equally negative impact when religious identity itself is threatened through intergroup conflict where identities range from religious fundamentalism to atheism or inter-sectarian fundamentalism. Extracting the essence from the book titled *Religion in South Asia: A Liberative Perspective* edited by Asghar Ali Engineer, B Varghese says that the 'problem with religion arises when it gets alienated from its deeper sources of inner life and is overwhelmed by customs, tradition, various social formations and superstitions. Such religion becomes a burden rather than a source of spiritual richness. It also becomes an obstacle for progress and change when it projects itself as an establishment'.[6]

Nevertheless, religious identity is not necessarily the same as religiousness or religiosity. Although these three terms share a commonality, religiousness and religiosity refer to both the value of religious group membership as well as participation in religious events like going to the church, temple or mosque and performing religious rituals and rites. It is almost like getting stamped and endorsed as a religious person. Religious identity, in contrast, refers specifically to religious group membership regardless of religious activity or participation. Here, the sense of belongingness to a religious group works more as an identity rather than idealising dogmatism or practices. It might work as a motivation factor for an individual to reach self-actualisation and self-transcendence, as Abraham Maslow tried to portray in the hierarchy of needs of individuals.

Stephen Gallagher and Warren Tierney, in the *Encyclopedia of Behavioural Medicine*, state that 'The terms religiousness or religiosity, used interchangeably are often defined as an individual's conviction, devotion and veneration towards a divinity. However, in its most comprehensive use, religiosity can encapsulate all dimensions of religion'. For instance, the concept can also be used in a narrow sense to denote an extreme view and over-dedication to religious rituals and traditions. After the Bangladesh hostage crisis, it has been inferred that recruiters who seek to radicalise young students feel that Islam is under attack and urge the younger generation to do their bit to defend their faith. The journalist-filmmaker Shahriar Kabir commented that 'the recruiters have identified [a] huge cultural void in society today. They are tapping a generation that has little knowledge about the history of Bangladesh. These young men have an identity crisis. The identity of many youngsters is primarily religious. It is this religious identity that the recruiters are zeroing in on. They look out for overly religious youngsters'.[7] In the current debate of 'tolerance' and 'intolerance' in India, this rigid form of religiosity can in essence be viewed as a negative side of the religious experience, typified by an overt involvement in religious practices which are deemed to be beyond the social norms of not only common society but one's faith as well. In other words, it goes against the political philosophy of pluralism that recognises and affirms diversity within a political body, permitting peaceful coexistence of different interests, convictions and lifestyles.

If we go by Emily Durkheim's view of religion, her four major functions of religion—disciplinary, cohesive, vitalising and euphoric social forces—merge the value of religiousness and religiosity. Religious rituals prepare men for social life by imposing self-discipline and a certain measure of asceticism. Religious ceremonies bring people together and thus serve to reaffirm their common bonds and reinforce social solidarity. Religious observance maintains and revitalises the social heritage of the group and helps transmit its enduring values to future generations. Finally, religion has a euphoric function when it serves to counteract feelings of frustration and loss of faith and certitude by reestablishing the believers' sense of well-being and their sense of the essential rightness of the moral world of which they are a part. Religion helps to reestablish the balance of private and public confidence. According to Durkheim, 'On the most general plane, religion as a social institution serves to give meaning to man's existential predicaments by tying the individual to that supra-individual sphere of transcendent values which is ultimately rooted in his society'. Durkheim was not concerned with the variety of religious experience of individuals but rather with the communal activity and communal bonds to which participation in religious activities gives rise.

Yet why is governance affected by the conflict between religiousness and religiosity? This paper tries to explore the phenomenon on the rationale of three arguments put forward by distinctions of Emily Durkheim's sacred and profane religion, Asish Nandy's religion of faith and ideology and, finally, the twisted relationship between secularism and communalism.

## Sacred and Profane Religion

Emily Durkheim, in *Sociology of Religion*, argued that religious phenomena emerge in any society when a separation is made between the sphere of the profane (the realm of everyday utilitarian activities) and the sphere of the sacred (the area that pertains to the mystical, spiritual, transcendental, extraordinary and supernatural). An object is intrinsically neither sacred nor profane. It becomes one or the other depending on our choice—whether we choose to consider the utilitarian value of the object or deem certain intrinsic attributes that have nothing to do with its instrumental value. For example, the wine at Christian mass has a sacred ritual attached to it. Though it is a beverage, in that context, it is considered by the believer to symbolise the blood of Christ. Sacred activities are valued by the community of believers not as a means to an end, but, because the religious community has bestowed their meaning on them as part of its worship. Religion being eminently a collective thing, society creates it by defining certain phenomena as sacred and others as profane. Those aspects of social reality that are defined as sacred are deemed forbidden and form the essence of religion. The sacred brings out an attitude of reverence, respect, mystery, awe and honour. It was perhaps thought to be sacred for Ram Vriksh Yadav, once a follower of the religious leader Jai Gurudev to form Swadheen Bharat Vividh Satyagrahi, a self-proclaimed revolutionary group under his leadership. But the strength of his leadership to occupy Jawahar Bagh in Mathura for the last two and a half years and demand an overhaul of administration on the lines of Netaji Subhas Chandra Bose till the court and police intervened, culminating in clashes and death, brings to the surface the profane attitude of the cult figure using religion as a means, inviting the state to repress it. According to Durkheim, distinctions between the spheres of the sacred and profane are always made by groups who band together in a cult and who are united by their common symbols and objects of worship, encouraging the clash between religiosity and religiousness.

## Religion of Faith and Ideology

In the context of the demolition of the Babri Masjid in December 1992, the direct connection between the BJP, VHP and the RSS led many people to think that the Ayodhya crisis had nothing to do with religion, and politics was the main determinant. Liberal newspapers repeatedly commented that the BJP was playing the Hindu card. The common people came to know that the *Hindutva* programme of Hindu nationalism was a travesty of real Hinduism. 'But most significantly, what emerged from the Ayodhya crisis was the popular distinction between real religion and unreal religion, that had been brought to the surface on a somewhat theoretical level by the Indian thinker Asish Nandy', stated Peter van der Veer.[8]

Considering Asish Nandy's arguments, religion in India, as the trend of belief and practice go, has been split into two: faith and ideology. By faith, he means: 'religion as a way of life, a tradition that is definitionally non-monolithic and operationally plural. I say "definitionally" because unless a religion is geographically and culturally confined to a small area, religion as a way of life has in effect turned into a confederation of a number of ways of life, linked by a commo1n faith and with some theological space for heterogeneity'. And religion as an ideology refers to sub-national, national or cross-national identifiers of population, that is contesting for or protecting non-religious, usually political or socio-economic interests. Nandy says,

> Such religions as ideologies usually get identified with one or more texts which, rather than the ways of life of the believers, become the final identifiers of the pure forms of the religions. The texts help to secure the ideologies in seemingly concrete and delimited, and in effect provide a set of manageable

> operational definitions. The modern state always prefers to deal with religious ideologies rather than with faiths.

Nandy cites two political decisions that best exemplify the comprehension of the two concepts by the then political leaders. According to him, while it was religion as faith that prompted two lakh Indians to declare themselves Mohammedan Hindus in the 1911 census, but it was religion as ideology that prompted Punjabi Hindus to declare Hindi as the mother tongue in the 1951 census. It implied that the post-colonial state used the census to communalise Punjab by using it as a pretext to eventually partition it along linguistic lines, thus, conveniently creating Hindu majority Haryana and Sikh majority Punjab.[9] It emphasised the differences between Sikhism and Hinduism, and thus sowed the seeds for the creation of a new minority as well. Though the modern state always prefers to deal with religious ideologies rather than with faiths, it is faith rather than ideology that has traditionally shown more malleability and liberality. For instance, the liberality of faith, also called 'catholicity of faith', prompted the Gujarati community of Mole-Salam Garasia Rajput to traditionally have two names for every member of the community, one Hindu and one Muslim.[10] (1) 'It is an example of the dynamic heterogeneity which evidently survived colonial conquest in the 1911 census, when nearly a quarter of a million Indians described themselves as 'Mohammedan Hindus', says John Keane.[11]

According to Nandy, three situations tended to reinforce religion as ideology. Firstly, the modern state both colonial and post-colonial had a bureaucratic imperative to divide the population into compartmentalised categories and thereby create an environment where the divided groups were pitted against each other. Secondly, Evangelical Anglican Christianity (2) 'had engendered an eurocentric perspective on the older faiths of South Asian region with few set polarities like centre vs periphery, true faith vs its distortions, civil vs primordial, and great traditions vs local cultures or little traditions'. Thirdly, in Nandy's views, secularism had an ethnophobic and ethnocidal force in South Asia that wanted to destroy religion as faith and religion as ideology, though it was more compatible to religion as ideology. 'Both are ideological forces that work against the fluid definition of the self as a configuration of selves that is prevalent in South Asia', says Nandy.[12] He further commented that, 'these two categories are not mutually exclusive; they are like two axes on which could be plotted the state of contemporary religions'.

Following Nandy, it can thus be inferred that religion as ideology was constrained by religion as faith. In other words, the ability of the religious and political elite to use religion for material ends was limited by the beliefs of their followers. Explaining further the difference between the two, according to Nandy, was to conceive ideology as something that needed to be constantly protected for individuals and people who believed in it, and faith as something that the faithful usually expected to protect them. This was because faith usually sanctions the experience of transcendence, whereas an ideology tends to bypass or fear theories and experiences of transcendence, except when they can be used for secular purposes. So, in the dilemma between religion as faith or ideology, the state's affinity for the latter and its provocation further nourished the tussle between religiosity and religiousness.

## Twisted Relationship Between Secularism and Communalism: The Reasons

Partition followed by independence involved a series of bloodshed between Muslims and Hindus, who had lived together as neighbours before British rule. The large-scale mass migration of religious groups was caused for two reasons: First, religion being linked with the modern territorial state and second, dogmatism that brought about religious confrontation, giving birth to 'communalism'. 'It was during the British colonial rule—that brought India into the modern age—that rigid boundaries were established between Hindus and Muslims. In other words, the unambiguous articulation of religious groups assumed primary importance under the modern governing system, and confrontation became palpable along those articulated lines'.[13]

Colonial rule brought unprecedented radical change and reorganisation in the Indian subcontinent, mostly influenced by three factors: Western secularism, internal conflict between Orientalist and Anglicist stances and Evangelical and Utilitarian movements. Indians were divided on the yardstick of religion and caste. The division of people on the basis of religion, especially, was the influence of Western-type secularism that implied separation of religion and politics, which originated from the separation of Church and State. Such a political stance gave rise to a rigid communalism that split Muslims and Hindus, thereby sowing the seeds of the twisted relationship between secularism and communalism in India. The internal conflict between the Orientalist and Anglicist stances was prevalent during the eighteenth-century enlightenment in Britain. The policy of non-intervention promoted by Orientalism affirmed the distinctiveness of Indian society and culture and ancient scriptures, thereby condoning the retention of indigenous structures. In contrast, the Anglicist stance of intervention in the 19$^{th}$ century sought to impose and apply the values of Western culture and society on India. Besides these, due to two British domestic movements of Evangelical and Utilitarianism (greatest happiness of the greatest number), the British colonial policy focused to intervene towards modernising and civilising Indian society. Hence, in the protracted Orientalist and Anglicist debate, the actual colonial policy vacillated between intervention and non-intervention. 'The governing policy, therefore, was a compromised mix of 'transcendental' and 'inherent' standpoints', stated Yasumasa Sekine.[14]

The colonial government's basic understanding of Indian society was the broad division of Indians into Muslims, Hindus and tribal people and further division of the majority Hindus into castes. Influenced by the 18th century sentiment of idealising the picture of 'nature's gentleman', the separation of tribal people from Hindus was due to the combination of the myth of the 'noble savage' (3) with anti-Hinduism. Social stratification on caste was on the basis of the Varna categories. 'In all these divisions, identity was provided through classification from above, the *transcendental* position of the ruler. Once the division was made, however, homogeneity of each group was assumed, its objectification led to the creation of 'an imagined community' within the *inherent* viewpoint of each group', stated Toshiyuki.[15]

There emerged a cultural pluralism in which standardised social customs were approved for each group as an immediate necessity to deal with the new situation; in 1772, it was decided that the European common law system would not be implemented in India. Hindus being ruled under their 'Hindu law' and Muslims under 'Muslim law' (*Sharia*) introduced the principle of personal law, respecting the customary law of each separate group. Hence, the contradictory structure of 'non-intervention within intervention' was incorporated on a practical level into the governing system. Moreover, relative independence was accorded to religious groups not only because of the introduction of personal law, but also by the political philosophy of secularism that separated state politics from religion. Serious contradictions thus became endemic, transforming religious groups into social units and, at the same time, building a ruling structure on the basis of separation of politics and religion. Second, since relative independence was officially provided to religious groups, potential communalism was inevitably involved. Such contradictions thus brought to the surface the twisted relations between secularism and communalism once again.

Unlike the rule of the pre-modern system when divinity of kingship ruled the state and religion pervaded people's daily lives, colonial rule in the modern period divided people's way of living into spiritual and secular. This was made possible as religion was separated from worldly affairs and was seen as forbidden, perhaps justifying Durkheim's concept of religion as sacred. But the irony was that when the system dividing the Indian population into Hindus and Muslims made religion seem the most important element of people's identity, the progress of secularisation of religion, when religion no longer coincided with the entire identity of the people, gave birth to 'diffusion of dualism', which finally made religion an object of conscious manipulation and choice. Thus people were placed in a 'double bind' religiously, as suggested by Yasumasa Sekine, affected the basic proposition of secularism since the latter reduced religion to just a part of life. The proposition that religion should withdraw from government implies that the state does not intervene in matters of religion. When religion is employed as the criterion for division of social groups, it implies that the state intervenes in religion. So in a secular state, the only solution to this irreconcilable situation was to divide the life of a person into private and public life and allot religion to private life. However such imposition of a clear distinction between his private and public aspects of life through the system of governance would infringe the people's right to life and freedom. In India, moreover, it would hardly work, because the official recognition of religious divisions has already been institutionalised. 'Thus, colonial rule in India brought into being a secular state system which used religion institutionally for its own ends where secularism paved the twisted path to communalism,' commented Yasumasa Sekine.

In the era of Indira Gandhi, communalism-prompted riots became widespread under the influence of the India-Pakistan wars in 1965 and 1971 as well as movements of secession of the Indian federal states in domestic politics on the one hand and strife between the Congress Party and the Janata Party on the other. Indian society was also gradually replacing the system of simple modernisation inherited from the Nehruvian period when Indians pursued a shared belief in socialism and modernisation. A type of risk society started to emerge, characterised by the progress achieved through reorganisation and reforms through technological processes, a constant flow of information, risky organisational activities and social relations[16] So the era of 'reflexive modernization' (4) contrasted with the 'simple modernisation' of the Nehruvian period. According to Yasumasa Sekine:

> In the uncertain period of reflexive modernisation, as people started to realise that their dreams were illusory, the insecure and delicate relationship between religion and politics began to take belligerent forms. In other words, the contradictory structure inherent in the twisted relationship between secularism and communalism began to resurface in new forms.

The series of communal riots provided a decisive turning point. Along with the legacy of Hindu-Muslim rivalry, an offensive by the Sikhs, a Hindu-Christian rivalry, deaths and miseries driven by parochial or ultra-nationalism all proved the wide arena of communalism in India. Following Dipankar Gupta's argument, Indian communalism of late is moving further and further away from religion. Offensives against 'peripheral' ethnic groups by the mainstream privileged class, not sparing even political factionalism among student unions in the country's university campuses are supporting evidence for Gupta. Additionally, communalism taking the dimension of terrorism cannot be ignored here either. Thus, Gupta rightly asserts that even nationalist fanatics who kill but avoid self-sacrifice should be distinguished from fundamentalists who are ready to die for great causes.

## Conclusion

It is very easy to suggest that India should promote real secularism by practicing complete separation of religion from public affairs and, at the same time, allowing people to live and let live. But against the backdrop of religion as compatible to the Indian scenario, to cite a few policies, to completely stop public funding of religion in any manner, complete removal of religious symbolism from the public sphere or the State, divested of any religious character whatsoever, till date has proved to be just next to impossible, though it is worth mentioning that the Supreme Court dissected the question of religion in electoral politics. A candidate cannot be prosecuted if an agent or a party sympathiser allegedly appeals for votes in the name of religion. Such appeals by agents and supporters warrant the disqualification of the winning candidate. The court has tried to establish that the purpose of the Representation of the People Act is to ensure that there is no basis for religion in politics. Religion should be separated from the political process. Justice DY Chandrachud said, 'the election agent is acting on behalf of the candidate. The law was enacted with an intention of stamping out communalism'.[17]

As a different instance, nobody can deny the spontaneous nationwide outpouring of sympathy for the people of Mumbai by all communities in those dark moments of the cataclysmic event of 26/11, when Mumbai was held hostage for more than 36 hours by terrorists sneaking in from Pakistan. Projected was a collective sense of 'we Indians', enduring a sense of national unity that helped the country tide over what could have been a deeply disintegrative challenge. The sense of humanity overpowered the divisions of caste, class and religion among the same Indians. People's experiential, ethical, practical and social cohesion undermined each of Indian's ritualistic, emotional, organisational, materialistic and political comprehension associated with religion. So, India's cultural pluralism is its best defence where, perhaps, religion and human life can be reconsidered. Class-based mobilisation can be a solution to proliferate cultural pluralism by shifting the focus from communal to class issues and by creating class identities so that mobilisation can take place on class lines. Religion can be relegated to the private sphere as a matter of personal belief.

The National Foundation for Communal Harmony (NFCH) already observes communal harmony campaigns. Can't it be entrusted along with its existing responsibilities to corroborate a platform where religion practically, experientially, ethically, socially, artistically and finally economically can be acknowledged? Difference should not be seen as a threat; rather, diversity should be celebrated.

The divergence between Gandhi and communalists was very deep ever since his entrance on the Indian political scene. 'The reason is simple', says Ramin Jahanbegloo 'for Gandhi the power of the nation was vested with the people, rather than religion. And the reason why Gandhi saw religion in the Indian intra-civilisational context rather in an ideological dimension was that he believed in the inherent harmony of the Indian cultural and social order, which had been disrupted by modernity'.[18] Gandhi was a pluralist in religious matters. His equal respect for all cultures and religions implied the idea of mutual learning and inter-faith dialogue. Religion for him was a matter of soft spirituality, rather than hard rituals and hard institutions. He believed that every religion can shed light on a seeker's path and realised that self-centredness in religious matters as in political matters created prejudice and misunderstanding. In an article in *Indian Opinion* in 1907, he wrote: 'If the people of different religions grasp the real significance of their own religion they will never hate the people of any religion other than their own…there may be many religions, but the true aim of all is the same.'

So unless people change their perceptions to awaken thinking having its impact on the institutions, it will be impossible to attain a forum of plurality. The 'dialogue to bridge the gap between the self and others' is one of the keys to attain plurality. Kojin Karatani's analytical concepts, 'individuality as particularity' ('I' that can be compared with others) and 'individuality as singularity' (the 'none other than I' that cannot be compared with others) show the path to bridge the gap between the 'self and the others'. (5) Following Yasumasa Sekine, it can be inferred that 'it is possible to make a distinction between "religion as particularity", in which religions can be compared and often used as a means of discrimination, and "religion as singularity", in which the differences of the secular "costumes" worn by religions are meaningless, and only deep faith in the absolute other, regardless of religious differences, can be focused upon'. Explaining his concept of 'religion as particularity' and 'religion as singularity', Karatani says:

> The latter, or 'religion as singularity,' can only exist on the peripheral border of the social space of secular modern society, where religion as ideology is dominant. Only there, does the world of faith open to others, and, this should be the core of religion that unfolds. This is because, that place borders on the outside (the other). On the surface, the place seems to be where 'traditional' or 'indigenous' culture is being lost under the impact of a dominant culture. But in fact, the place is where the closed space of modern secular society borders on the outside. It is the scene of plurality where 'dialogue' is possible between the self and others, and 'tolerance' (not that advocated by modern humanism) that belongs in Nandy's 'religion as faith' can be materialised. The passions of communalism are erupting on the oppressive periphery of the modern secular social space dominated by reason. This is occurring in reaction to the act of attempting to immediately

> throw into the secular prison of reason (closed space) all encounters with the outside (the other of reason), which results in violence and sacrifices of the other. At the same time, this volatile peripheral place is the very place where it is possible to reform the modern, a place suitable for thinking about the 'other of reason.' In other words, the place where communalism is occurring can become a place where a homicidal religion can be transformed into religion that brings people alive. When violence that sacrifices others in the name of religion is transformed into acts of the self-sacrifice which is the core of faith, it will become a force that makes people spontaneously accept others. Nowhere except at this border (periphery) where reason encounters the outside, can such genuine faith emerge.[19]

Gandhi's critique of an ideologised religion led him to a concept of the spiritual, which found its expression in the 'spiritualisation of politics'. For Gandhi, religion was a morally conscientious and socially responsible exercise of spirituality; instead of politicising religion, the aim of spiritualising politics is to construct the future of 'human living together'. He believed that every social and political opportunity must be made use of to forge harmony among communities. Believing in a plural political and religious society, 'his vision of communal harmony and his critique of religious fanaticism went hand in hand with his theory of participative democracy and shared sovereignty', continued Jahanbegloo. Thus in the case of Gandhi, religious pluralism and a struggle against fanaticism were not merely a political agenda, but a matter of faith in the dynamism and potentiality of Indian society to tackle the evil of communalism at the structural and mental levels. For him, a culture or religious tradition that denies individual freedom in the name of unity or purity are coercive and unacceptable.

(1) The Molesalams are a Muslim Rajput community in Gujarat, India. They refer to themselves as Molesalam Thakur and sometimes Molesalam Garasia (Grasiya). They are scheduled tribes living mainly in the Pali, Sirohi and Udaipur districts of Rajasthan. They are divided into Rajput Garasia (being descendents of the Rajputs), Dungri Garasia and Bhil Garasia. Their group heterogeneity also supports a stratified order. Constant contact with Bhils and Hindus has led to several changes in their social order.

(2) The evangelical movement that began within the Church of England in the $18^{th}$ century emphasised biblical faith, personal conversion, piety and the Protestant features of the Anglican Communion. Their followers were referred to as low churchmen, because they demanded reforms and liberalisation in the English church and its structure, undermining the episcopal form of church government, the sacraments and rich worship experiences. Anglicanism was one of the major branches of the 16th-century Protestant Reformation and a form of Christianity that included features of both Protestantism and Roman Catholicism.

(3) The concept of an idealised indigene, outsider or 'other' who has not been 'corrupted' by civilisation, and therefore symbolises humanity's innate goodness. The idea that humans are essentially good is often attributed to the 3rd Earl of Shaftesbury, a Whig supporter of constitutional monarchy. In his *Inquiry Concerning Virtue* (1699), Shaftesbury postulated that the moral sense in humans is natural and innate and based on feelings, rather than resulting from the indoctrination of a particular religion.

(4) The concept of reflexive modernisation or reflexive modernity was enunciated by three leading European sociologists: Anthony Giddens, Ulrich Beck and Scott Lash. It stresses how in reflexive modernisation, modernity directs its attention to the process of modernisation itself. It deals

with the changes brought by the ideals of modernity, such as universal suffrage, education, the welfare state, civil and political rights, all changes that marked the shift to the second modernity. The authors considered it a reflexive modernity because it opposed the first modernity in the same way as the latter opposed feudal traditionalism. The features of reflexive modernity are: The state started to lose its importance with the rise of transnational forces (corporations, NGOs). The family structure has been splitting apart with rising divorce rates encouraged by the flexibility of work and women's liberation. Religion is reduced to a cultural artifact. All previous sources of solidarity lost momentum with the rise of individualisation. Ulrich Beck especially promotes that amid all types of uncertainties, a new type of solidarity has emerged on the face of the human-made dangers of a 'risk society', exacerbated by the inherent limits being discovered by all forms of social knowing.

(5) Singularity, as the Japanese philosopher and literary critic Kojin Karatani suggests, is the difference between 'I' the individual subject and the 'I' that belongs to the general category of everybody. It is precisely the difference between 'this I' and all the 'I's that must be distinguished. The attachment of the 'this' to the 'I' does not mean that 'this I', or the 'me' is special. Rather, it is taking the ego, the individual subjectivity and the persona out of the 'me' to make 'this I'. Thus, 'this I' begins to distinguish the idea of singularity from the idea of particularity and individuality. This implies that even though I know that I am like everyone else, I am not anyone else. What is at stake here is the 'this' in 'this I' and not the 'I' as consciousness. It is the qualification of 'I', the naming of the 'this I' that is important in this context. Karatani says that 'this-ness' of the subject and object, of 'this I' has nothing to do with its formal or physical features and characteristics. The 'this-ness' of 'this I' is singularity, which distinguishes it from particularity. So it is the 'ness' of

the 'this-ness' that is the condition of singularity as opposed to 'I'. Singularity does not mean that a thing is unique. As opposed to particularity and individuality, which are seen as unique when seen in relationship to generality; singularity is an individuality which does not belong to the realm of generality. The attempt is to move the question of 'I' and the individual outside a metaphysical discourse. The singularity of a thing is inseparable from the act of calling it by a proper noun. Thus the nomination of 'this thing' also begins to separate singularity from particularity.[20]

## Endnotes

1 Girish Sahane, "Shades of Grey: How India is Both a Tolerant and an Intolerant Society," June 27, 2016, http://scroll.in/article/771636/shades-of-grey-how-india-is-both-a-tolerant-and-an-intolerant-society

2 Sahane, "Shades of Grey: How India is Both a Tolerant and an Intolerant Society".

3 Arvind P Datar, "The Myth of Intolerance," *Indian Express*, December 4, 2015.

4 Smitha Verma, "History is not Fantasy; It is Based on Rational Analysis," *The Telegraph*, July 10, 2016.

5 R Ysseldyk, K Matheson and H Anisman, "Religiosity as Identity: Toward an Understanding of Religion From a Social Identity Perspective," *Personality and Social Psychology Review* 14, no. 1(2010): 60–71.

6 B Varghese, "Screening Culture, 'Hiding' Religion - Positioning of Religion in Malayalam Cinema 1970s–90s," 2012, http://shodhganga.inflibnet.ac.in/bitstream/10603/4420/12/12_chapter%205.pdf

7 Sonia Sarkar, "Who's that Man?" *The Telegraph*, July 10, 2016.

8 Peter van der Veer, "The Politics of Devotion to Rama," in *Bhakti Religion in North India: Community Identity and Political Action*, ed. David N Lorenzen (Albany: State University of New York Press, 1995), 291–2.

9 Giorgio Shani, *Sikh Nationalism and Identity in a Global Age* (Routledge, 2008), 12.

10 ST Lokhandwala, "Indian Islam: Composite Culture and Integration," *New Quest* (1985): 87–101.

11 John Keane, *Global Civil Society?* (Cambridge University Press, 2003), 37.

12 van der Veer, "The Politics of Devotion to Rama".

13 Sekine Yasumasa, "Religion and Politics in Contemporary India, The Complexities of Secularism and Communalism," *Faultline* 11, (2002): 1, The Institute of Conflict Management, South Asian Foundation, New Delhi.

14 Sekine, "Religion and Politics in Contemporary India, The Complexities of Secularism and Communalism".

15 Mise Toshiyuki, "Changes in the Theory of Classification of Castes in National Census' in India during the Colonial Period," in *Collected Summaries of the Reports at the 11th* Conference of the Japanese Association for South Asian Studies, (1998): 34–9.

16 Ulrich Beck, *Risk Society: Towards a New Modernity* (Sage Publications Limited, 1992): 153–4.

17 "SC Questions Religion in Politics," *The Telegraph*, October 21, 2016.

18 Ramin Jahanbegloo, "Gandhi and Religious Fanaticism," *Indian Express*, June 12, 2014.

19 Peter Eisenman, "The Affects of Singularity AD, Nov-Dec 1992," in *The Digital Turn in Architecture 1992–2012,* ed. Mario Carpo (John Wiley, 2013): 19–25. The article has also been published in Andreas C Papadakis, ed., *Theory +Experimentation, AD Profile 100, AD 62, Nov-Dec 1962* (New Haven: Yale University Press, 2007).

20 Eisenman, "The Affects of Singularity AD, Nov-Dec 1992".

# Priyanath Bose and the Great Bengal Circus: Performance Art and the Narratives of Nationalism

***Susmita Mukherjee***

## Introduction

A circus is an entertainment or spectacle usually consisting of trained animal acts and exhibitions of human skill and courage. Circus is a Latin word derived from the Greek word *kirkos* meaning 'circle', 'oval' or 'ring'.[1] It relates to the distinctive situation or setting in which such entertainment is presented—the ring, a circular performance area usually bounded by a short fence (or 'curb'). The ring may be enclosed in an arena, in a building designed for circus performances or in a tent generally surrounded by tiers of seats for spectators.

The circus as we know it today is inseparably linked to an ex-Sergeant Major of the British army named Philip Astley. Philip Astley, who fought in the war against France (1757–63) conceived the notion of the modern circus in 1768 in London. He brought his considerable skill with horses to an equestrian entertainment in Lambeth, between Blackfriars and Westminster Bridges, in an area called Halfpenny Hatch.[2] It was the first circus to stage its events in a ring with the audience seated all round. Top billing went to a star horse that could execute complex movement and tricks like those associated with military parades.

We can trace similar shows and performances of wild beasts exhibited in the Circus Maximus and the amphitheatres of Ancient Rome.[3] Troupes of various sizes and strolling jugglers made their living through feats of acrobatics, doing magic shows or exhibitions of trained animals. They were known as 'circulators'.[4] Roman audiences enjoyed acrobatics, performances by trained animals, and clowning on a large scale. The animal acts were numerous, like elephants playing musical instruments or having dinner. However, the most sensational feat was the tightrope-walking elephant, an act that was well-attested by eye witness and performed many times. Women performers were also prevalent. They had healthy bodies and nice smiles, and after their spectacular performance behaved as if nothing much had happened. Julius Caesar was fully aware of the potentiality of circus entertainment in increasing his popularity and used it with great confidence.[5] Bread and Circus was to remain an imperial maxim for winning the hearts of the Roman people.

The Greeks had no place for gory spectacles, although bull-fighting and cock and quail-fighting was prevalent. In Crete, Minoan bulls were used in a display of acrobatics which had its origin in religious rites.[6]

## Origin of the Circus in India

Following the establishment of the modern circus in London and Paris during the latter decades of the eighteenth century, the circus began its steady dispersion around the world. From the later decades of the 19th century, the circus was one of the most popular and profitable entertainment ventures in the Indian subcontinent. Three geographical regions, namely the Bombay Presidency, Bengal and the State of Travancore (Kerela) around the late 19th century were the breeding grounds for early circuses owned and operated by Indians. The performance of foreign circuses left an indelible mark on the origin of the Indian circus. The earliest examples of foreign circus companies touring India were Wilson's Great World Circus (1880) and Giuseppe Chiarini's Great Italian

Circus (1882). The latter brought the Royal Italian Circus to Mumbai, camping out at Maidan near what is now Mumbai›s Victoria Terminus. Chiarini's circus visited India, Malaysia, Burma, Ceylon (today's Sri Lanka) and Singapore. At the end of his Indian tour, in March 1882, Chiarini and his company set sail for Manila and the Philippines.

The history of the Indian circus is characterised by the stories of outstanding performers both men and women who came from modest and humble backgrounds and attained success. Vishnupant Moreshwar Chatre (1840–1905) is generally considered to be the architect of Indian circus.[7] Born in the village of Ankalkhop in Sangli, Maharashtra, Chatre was in charge of the stables of the Rajah of Kurundwad, in the district of Kolhapur. Here, he occasionally performed 'feats of horsemanship' of English riding masters such as Philip Astley. As the story goes, Chatre and the Rajah visited a performance of the Royal Italian Circus in Bombay. The director of the circus Giuseppe Chiarini, who had already performed in various parts of the world, visited Bombay for the first time in 1879.

Chatre was greatly impressed by his performance and show. However, in a conversation with Chatre and the Rajah, Chiarini said that India didn't have a proper circus and that we'd have to wait quite a few years to develop one. Then he laid down a reward of 'one thousand British Indian rupees' and one of his horses to anyone who managed to replicate his daring stage acts within six months. Chatre took up the challenge and promised to perform the same daring acts with his own horses in Kurundwad in three months. If he failed, Chatre promised the Italian 'ten thousand British Indian rupees and ten horses of the best breed'.[8] Chatre decided to organise his own circus, of which he would be the star equestrian and his wife would become a trapeze artist and an animal trainer. He probably used some of his pupils in the equestrian department as well. The first performance of Chatre's Great

Indian Circus was held on 20 March 1880 in the presence of a selected audience, among which was the Rajah of Kurudwad who may have helped him in starting his venture, and the Governor of Bombay James Fergusson. His wife Arudas Bai Parulekar was the only woman artist who appeared in Chatre's ring as well as in the history of the Indian circus ring.[9] Chatre travelled extensively with his Great Indian Circus visiting the vast regions of North India, then further South, to the large east-cost city of Madras, and down to the island of Ceylon. In 1884, Chatre embarked on a tour of Southeast Asia to cities like Singapore and Jakarta. According to Indian circus lore, he thereafter crossed the ocean to conquer the United States. But here, Chatre failed to apprehend the prowess and skill or size of the giant American circuses, returned to India facing defeat. No record exits of Chatre's performance in the United States.[10] But he performed before the Emperor of China, who was very impressed and gave him valuable gifts. Thus, the first Indian circus originated from a sense of being challenged by a Western imperial power. Probably a sense of nascent nationalism prompted Chatre to accept the challenge and prove his masculinity. In Bengal, a similar sense of nationalism seemed to motivate Professor Priyanath Bose who established the Great Bengal Circus.

## Priyanath Bose and the Great Bengal Circus

In Bengal, the genesis of circus acts with trapeze, gymnastics, jugglery and shows with trained animals dates back to the melas or fairs organised on the outskirts of towns or cities. In the Hindu Mela (1867) programme, the promotion of physical culture was recognised as an important element. This organisation illustrated the attempt of the Western educated middle-class at self-assertion.[11] During this period, a muscular nationalism was gaining ground. Bengalis were being stigmatised as a frail and effeminate race. Ramchandra Guha writes that to overcome the colonial stereotype Bengalis strenuously sought to promote physical cultures.[12] John Rosselli also noted the connection between the 'effeteness' of educated Bengali men and the consequent revival of physical cultures as part of nationalism.[13] Pushed to the corner, both men and women began to participate in various kinds of physical culture ranging from martial arts to gymnastics, trapeze acts and hot air ballooning. With the rise of Swadeshi movements, akharas or gymnasiums mushroomed all over North Calcutta. Men like Suresh Chandra Biswas (1861–1905) who ran away to join a circus in London at the age of seventeen and later became a Colonel in the Brazilian army, or Ramchandra Banerjee who rose in a hot air balloon in April 1889, were the new generation who protested against the stereotype of the submissive, docile and deceitful or untrustworthy babus. Jyotindranath Tagore states that Nabagopal Mitra the founder of Hindu Mela 'pioneered the National Circus with [a] few ill-nourished horses and the famous Bose's circus was the culmination of that'.[14] It may be regarded as the beginning of circus acts in Bengal, the precursor to the highly renowned and successful Great Bengal Circus founded by Priyanath Bose, a gymnast trainer in 1887.[15]

P.N. Bose's son Abanindra Kishore Bose writes that when Wilson's Great World Circus or Chairny's Great Italian Circus came to Calcutta Bose would often visit and say 'I have to make a circus troupe with Bengalees and show that if Bengalees tried then they could show their valour and techniques and thereby absolve themselves from the stigma of being a weak race.'[16] During his visit to these circuses, he would often make sketches of some special movements of the body or instruments used. He was a very good gymnast teacher and among the Bengalis he was perhaps the first to perform the pyramid act, juggling act, parallel and horizontal bars.

In 1885, Priyanath was invited to a fancy fete event at the Zoological Gardens in Alipore where he exhibited the gymnastic feats of his students before Lord Dufferin Viceroy of India. Lord Dufferin was very impressed with the performance and he supposedly asked 'Who is the professor?'. He expressed his interest in meeting Priyanath, and when they met, Lord Dufferin addressed him as Professor Bose. After that Priyanath became popular as Professor Bose.

At this point of time, a very important incident happened. In his village, P.N. Bose came across a very frail young horse. This strengthened his determination to form the circus and prove to the world that Bengalees too could rise to the occasion. With this vision, he started training the horse. He believed in the maxim 'Where there is a will there is a way'. Money was an important factor in setting up the circus. He procured some from the female members of his family and from his father's friend Gurudas Chattopadhyay. He left Calcutta and formed the Great Bengal Circus in 1887 on a small scale.

## Rising Popularity of the Circus

Very soon, the Great Bengal Circus became immensely popular and he embarked on a tour of Bengal. He first toured Dacca, Jhalokati and Barisal. Then on his second tour, he visited Shantipur, Dainhat, Katwa and Murshidabad. In December 1888, the Great Bengal Circus was invited to perform equestrian and gymnastic feats at the Tajhat palace of Gobindalal Roy, the zamindar of Rangpur. The zamindar was so impressed with their performance that he retained them two more nights and presented the team 25 pairs of shawls and certificates of excellence. Soon the Great Bengal Circus began to be invited by the zamindars of Bengal. Many of the zamindars gifted them equipment and horses in addition to the stipulated payment. Later on, it was patronised by the rulers of the princely states of Tripura, Rewa, Kashi, Kashmir and Jhalwar. Some of them gifted tigers and elephants to the circus. Priyanath Bose had to constantly reinvent new games to hold the attention of the people. His performances were highly appreciated and apart from cash money he received valuable gifts as well as animals. The contemporary newspapers also highly praised his performances.

*Lahore Tribune* writes on 10 November 1897,

> The Great Bengal Circus has taken the Lahore public by storm. No other show had such a hold on popular fancy here within living memory. People have gone what may be called circus-mad and laudatory ejaculations with reference to the performance of the members of the troupe are heard on every side.[17]

As the news of success of Great Bengal Circus began to be published in the newspapers, the people of Kolkata longed to see its performance in the city of its birth. In November 1899, the Great Bengal Circus came to the Calcutta for the first time since its inception. Priyanath Bose set up the tent at the Maidan. His shows were graced and patronised by eminent dignitaries, including the Maharajas of Kapurthala and Cooch Behar and the zamindar of Burdwan. After a spectacular performance at Calcutta Maidan, he went to Ceylon and came back again to Calcutta in 1900–01. The Lt Governor visited the circus and was highly impressed.

Next, Bose went to Rangoon. There he attained fame and money and went to Penang, Singapore and Java. In these places, the performance of his circus was highly appreciated. Apart from wealth, he also received animals as gifts for his circus. After touring Southeast Asia, he came back to his roots in Calcutta again in 1901–02. The Straits Time[18] stated that 'Singapore has had many visitors in the way of circuses but rarely has a cleverer show visited the town that now performing on the Raffle Reclamation Ground. Last evening there was a good attendance and judging from the applause the circus is likely to have a most prosperous season before it'. Priyanath Bose camped in Kolkata each winter till the 1911–12 season.

## Incorporation of Swadeshi Ideas in Great Bengal Circus

After 1905, when the Swadeshi movement was sweeping Bengal, the Great Bengal Circus attained a new dimension. His son Abanindranath writes when the audience assembled at the Maidan it seemed as if they had come not to see just a circus but to participate in a public function or meeting where Mother India was being venerated. Interestingly, during the breaks, Priyanath Bose came to the ring and interacted with the audience, where he inspired them with his fiery oration and requested them to firmly strengthen the Swadeshi Brata or mission. When he ended his speech with Vande Mataram, the audience reciprocated it and it reverberated throughout the tent inculcating a strong feeling of the Swadeshi movement.[19] During this movement, for some time songs and dance were accommodated during the circus. Prof. Bose composed Swadeshi songs where he called upon the young men to take up gymnasium or athletic in order to save the country from perishing. Men like Lala Lajpat Rai visited his circus. He wrote songs in honour of Lala Lajpat Rai.[20]

During the Swadeshi era, the press heaped praise on Prof. Bose for his continued efforts to absolve the Bengalis from the disgrace of being categorised as an effeminate race by the colonisers. In this context, Mrinalini Sinha discusses the image formation of the athletic, chivalric, hunting ‘manly Englishman’ as opposed to the bookish, grave, disorderedly ‘effeminate Bengali’ self.[21]

The *Amrita Bazar Patrika* wrote on 1 March 1909,

> Bengalees are said to be worthless people, who can only talk, with no manliness or power of organisation and only a race of imitators. Bose’s Circus gives lie to this statement.[22]

The *Hindu Patriot* wrote on 1 March 1909,

> It makes a Bengalee proud to think that such daring feats are performed by his own class on whom wanton insult has been poured as weak and lily-livered. The fact that Bengalee young men, women and children do such daring acts gives the lie direct to such malicious accusations.[23]

The *Indian Mirror* wrote,

> Professor Bose has made a promising start and it is very fervently hoped that his patriotic efforts at wiping out the unjust stain of physical cowardice, cast on the Bengali community, will be amply appreciated and substantially supported.[24]

During the Swadeshi era, and even later, the press heaped praises on Prof. Bose for his continued efforts to absolve the Bengalis from the disgrace of being categorised as an effeminate race by the colonisers. In this context, Mrinalini Sinha discusses the image formation of the athletic, chivalric, hunting 'manly Englishman' as opposed to the bookish, grave, disorderedly 'effeminate Bengali' self.[25] Prof Bose's courage and prowess to break the stereotype of the 'effeminate Bengali self' and establish them as a powerful race endeared him to the Bengalis.

## Role of Women Performers

Women performers also played an important role in invoking a sense of patriotism through their performance. Most important among them was Sushila Sundari. 'Her physical acts were locations, where battles of nationalism, masculinity and regional prowess were waged.'[26] She was an expert gymnast and captivated the audience with her deft double trapeze and double bar act. At the opening of the show, she and her sister Kumudini appeared on the stage riding a horse amidst rapturous applause. Kumudini was also an accomplished equestrian. However, Sushila Sundari captivated the audience with the tiger act. In November 1896, the Great Bengal Circus performed before the Raja of Rewa, who in turn gifted them a pair of tigers in appreciation of their performance.[27] The tigers were named Lakshmi and Narayan in keeping with Hindu identity. In 1901 the Great Bengal Circus would show Sushila Sundari in daring acts with the two tigers. She would enter the cage with elan, make them growl, wrestle with them and show their open jaws to the audience. Thereafter, she would recline on them and pose for photographs. She performed with utmost grace, fearlessness leaving her audience spellbound. Sreedhar Champad mentions that the popularity of these female acts placed the Indian and international women performers on equal footing in terms of skill; the Indian bodies were now seen as ‘equally strong’ as the white bodies and the Indian performer acquired a certain equality and self-identification.[28]

In 1902, the *Muslim Chronicle* wrote, ‘Who ever could think before that a saree and slipper wearing timorous Bengali lady whose face is seldom seen outside the limits of the zenana can make herself bold enough to coax and play with two large man-eaters like domestic dogs. Thanks to the skill of Professor Bose who has shown the world that smews (sic) of the Bengali ladies who are known to be so delicate are capable of performing such wonderful feats as will unnerve the bravest of the brave’.[29]

Mrinmoyee, another performer from the Great Bengal Circus, was coded with a goddess image (which was quite literal; she was publicised in circus posters as the Mother Goddess riding the lion) and was the star performer of the show. She was publicised as the ‘mother who is no longer in chains but the free ‘Mother India’ controlling beasts as her destiny and power has ordained her’.[30] Astha Gandhi observes, ‘the visual dominion of these women over tigers thus epitomises a particular image of Mother India and is emblematic of the maternal roles imposed on women within this nationalist narrative’.[31]

However, there was a contradiction regarding the image of Mrinmoyee. On the circus front she was projected as a strong and powerful woman but in reality, she was given the worst wagon and when her husband died, she was made to follow a strict vegetarian diet. Charu Gupta remarks, 'Female icons, particularly of the mother as a national symbol, have been shown to coexist uneasily within masculinist ideologies of the nation, so that women occupy an unstable position within the imagined community'.[32]

Another performer of the Great Bengal Circus in Calcutta around the early years of the $20^{th}$ century was a Filipino acrobat called Antonita. Not much is known about her background except for a few anecdotes, which makes an interesting read. Antonita was a bareback rider and a gymnast with the circus. These acts bought her little fame; however, her other acts were more striking. After her daily performances in the circus, Antonita was famous for portraying the 'Great Chinese Sorcerer, Shen Shooi' and the 'incredible Japanese swordswoman, Nakota'. The circus utilised her 'South-East Asian' physical features to the fullest. Parading her as Chinese, Japanese and other southeastern nationalities, she sought to represent and stereotype the versions of 'Chiney' (Bengali derogatory term for a Chinese person). Anirban Ghosh writes that the contemporary Bengalis did not have a very positive impression of China because of the prevalence of opium dens in Calcutta. So, when a 'Chinese' person performed, the audience enjoyed it thoroughly.[33]

The women performers in the circus were mainly fallen women or helpless women abandoned by their husbands or families. But unlike the theatre, the circus was an entertainment where people came with their families. Hence the public image of the women performers constituted a very important part of the circus. They were depicted as powerful women representing the image of Mother India. However, as mentioned earlier, they were discriminated against within the four walls of the circus tent. The strong patriarchal domination was prevalent in the circus industry.

## End of a Great Era

Men like Priyanath Bose or Krishnala Basak[34] exhibited a masculine identity through the circus in Bengal. The stereotype of the 'effeminate' Bengali babu, much promoted in the colonial official and semi-official discourse, provoked a reaction among middle-class Bengalis. They tried to prove the falseness of this perception by promoting physical culture among Bengali youth. Akharas or gymnasiums became very popular in Bengal. This nascent feeling of nationalism was reflected in contemporary literature and theatres in Bengal. The circus was another such arena in which physical and acrobatic feats could be displayed. Priyanath Bose and his contemporaries appropriated this medium to challenge European practitioners. He toured various parts of India and Southeast Asia with his grand circus and received accolades everywhere. The beginning of the First World War hit the circus industry too. Priyanath Bose decided to go to Singapore with his troupe. But suddenly he fell ill. While his troupe was performing in British Malaya, he went to Singapore for medical attention. At the age of 55, he passed in Singapore on 21 May 1920, leaving his family in faraway Bengal.

## Endnotes

1 P.R. Nisha, *Jumbos and Jumping Devils: A Social History of Indian Circus* (New Delhi: OUP, 2020), 33.

2 For details see Peta Tait, *Fighting Nature: Travelling Menageries, Animal Acts and War Shows (Animal Publics)* (Sydney: Sydney University Press, 2016), 38.

3 Rupert Croft-Crooke and Peter Coates, *Circus: A World History* (Great Britain: Paul Elek Ltd., 1976), 7.

4 *Paul* Bouissac, *Circus and Culture: A Semiotic Approach* (Bloomington and London: Indiana University Press, 1976), 11

5 Croft-Crooke and Coates, *Circus: A World History*, 17.

6 Croft-Crooke and Coates, *Circus: A World History*, 14.

7 Anirban Ghosh*, The Tropic Trapeze: Circus in Colonial India* (Inaugural diss, Kolkata, 2014), 35–6.

8 Rachel Lopez, "Mumbaiwale, How Mumbai's Circus Acts Took to the Stage," in *Hindustan Times,* 17 November 2018.

9 Sreedharan Champad, *An Album of Indian Big Tops*, (History of Indian Circus) (Houston: Strategic Book Publishing & Rights Agency, 2013), 4–6.

10 T Shameerdas, "Past and Present Economic Conditions of Circus Workers in Kannur district - A Glimpse," in *International Journal of Advanced Research*, 11, no. 05B(2022): 889–90.

11 Indira Chowdhury Sengupta, "Colonialism and Cultural Identity: The Making of a Hindu Discourse," Bengal 1867–1905, (doc. thesis, University of London, 1993), p. 2.

12 Ramchandra Guha, *The States of Indian Cricket: Anecdotal History* (New Delhi: Permanent Black, 2005), 36

13 John Rosselli, "The Self-Image of Effeteness: Physical Education and Nationalism in Nineteenth-Century Bengal," in *Past & Present*, no. 86 (Oxford: Oxford University Press, 1980), 121–48.

14 Sukla Das, *Fabric Art, Heritage of India* (New Delhi: Abhinav Publications, 1992), 129.

15 *Carey Watt,* "Physical Culture and the Body in Colonial India, c. 1800–1947," in *Routledge Handbook of the History of Colonialism in South Asia,* eds., Harald Fischer-Tiner and Maria Framke (London: Routledge, 2021).

16 Abanindra Krishna Bose, Bangaleer Circus (Kolkata: Publicity Studio Press, 1938), 10–12. After the National Circus, the son-in-law of Nabagopal Mitra, the physical instructor of Hindu

School along with Syamacharan Ghosh, physical instructor of Hooghly College, Dinanath Ghosh, Jogindranath Pal and S.O. Abel, the elephant instructor of Wilson's Circus, opened the Great Indian Circus in the Raja Bazar area of Calcutta. A few months later, the grandson of Rammohun Roy bought the circus and the shows were held in an Amherst Street house. Abel went to Chittagong and opened a circus with a German named Olmann called Abel Klaer Olmann Circus and toured Southeast Asia. Later, Jogindranath Pal owned the Great Indian Circus and sold it to P.N. Bose when he came to Calcutta to hold his shows (pp. 13–5).

17 Bose, *Bangaleer Circus*, 25.

18 *Straits Time*, 2nd May, 1903, 5.

19 Bose, *Bangaleer Circus*, 35.

20 Bose, *Bangaleer Circus*, 36.

21 Mrinalini Sinha, "Colonial Masculinity: The 'manly Englishman' and the 'effeminate Bengali'," in *The Late Nineteenth Century* (*Studies in Imperialism*) (New York: Manchester University Press, 1995), 1–32.

22 Bose, *Bangaleer Circus*, 38.

23 Bose, *Bangaleer Circus*, 39.

24 Bose, *Bangaleer Circus*, 29.

25 Sinha, "Colonial Masculinity: The 'manly Englishman' and the 'effeminate Bengali'," 1–32.

26 Ghosh, *The Tropic Trapeze: Circus in Colonial India*, 86.

27 'That His Highness very gladly offered two tiger cubs' addition to the reward is due only to the brilliant success gained under the supervision of Professor P.N. Bose'. Bose, Bangaleer Circus, 48.

28 Champad, *An Album of Indian Big Tops*, 19.

29 Ghosh, *The Tropic Trapeze: Circus in Colonial India*, 86–87.

30 Ghosh, *The Tropic Trapeze: Circus in Colonial India*, 90.

31 Astha Gandhi, "From Postcolonial to Neoliberal: Performing the 'Other' Body in Indian Circus," *Performance Matters* 4, no. 1–2(2018): 86.

32 Charu Gupta, *Sexuality, Obscenity, Community: Women, Muslims, and the Hindu Pubic in Colonial India* (Delhi: Permanent Black, 2001), 202.

33 Ghosh, *The Tropic Trapeze: Circus in Colonial India*, 96.

34 Krishnalal Basak was the owner of the Hippodrome Circus.

# Literature Living Through the Ages, Ramakien: A Discussion on the Thai Version of the Ramayana

*Debarati Ganguly*

## Introduction

In India, perhaps no other legend has found such prolific and diverse representations and expressions in literary and performing arts as the story of Ramayana. The popularity of the Ramayana is associated with various significant factors. Besides being an inseparable part of the religious sentiment of Indian people, the Ramayana 'can be seen as the expression of a certain historical consciousness...' as the veteran historian Romila Thapar describes.[1] She has discussed how different versions of this epic provide 'validation for the monarchical states' in a 'changed historical situation'.[2] Apart from this interesting manifestation of the text, Thapar seeks the reason for its popularity in the mythological character, literary appeal, connecting 'the classical tradition and literature' and, most importantly, the propagation of ethical values emphasising the victory of good over evil.[3] All these undoubtedly explain the long-term continuity of this epic in our country. But what is fascinating is the presence of constant admiration and acceptance for this narrative among the local inhabitants of Southeast Asia. This is a fine example of cultural interaction between two regions and consequent exchanges which have captivated scholars' attention for a long time. Nationalist historians have always seen such prevalence of Indian epics because of 'Indianisation' generated from an all-inclusive deep impact of the Indian culture. But like all other socio-cultural-religious aspects, the adaptations of the Ramayana in Southeast Asia are characterised by the presence of local/ indigenous features within the epic's familiar storyline. The inclusion of new characters, events and interpretations along with 'selective absorption' of the original Ramayana resulted in its various versions under different names in Southeast Asian nations.[4] In Thailand, such a retelling and modifications of the Rama legend are discernible in the Ramakien tradition through adaptation of local customs and beliefs, which gave the text its own distinctive identity.

The story of the famous Ramakien and its characters have become integral parts of Thai life. The representation of events and characters in literature, images, sculptures, dance, theatrical performance and shadow-play practices explicitly show the close emotional connection that people have developed with the text over a long time. Such immense admiration for Ramakien indicate how thoroughly the Rama story has been absorbed there, which historians see as a part of the 'universal acceptance of Ramayana theme' which, in the words of G. Coedes, 'tugs at the heart of audiences from one end of Asia to another..'[5] Rabindranath Tagore, Sunitikumar Chattopadhyay and Shantidev Ghosh on their visit to Southeast Asia in 1927 were also impressed with the popular presentation of the narrative in the literary, visual and performing arts of Java, Bali, Siam and Sumatra.[6] Interestingly, they all considered how the Ramayana heritage was localised in those regions and evolved through time by accommodating new features.[7] What remained unchanged, they believed, was the story's appeal of human values and fairness.[8] Such principles were seen as an inseparable part of eastern heritage, and India was hailed for teaching other nations ethical and moral values through these narratives.[9] Himansu Bhusan Sarkar, who has done detailed research on the Javanese Ramayana, kakawin and other recensions, also supported this aspect of localisation of the epics, especially after the coming of Islam when various Islamic features entered narratives.[10] Yet, the scholars' primary objective was to show the continuation and validation of the Ramayana story in Southeast Asian countries. This, they asserted, undeniably pointed to the deep impact of the Indian epic. For example, while discussing how or by whom the influence of the Ramayana tradition was disseminated into Southeast Asia, Sarkar reinstated the familiar idea associated with the 'Greater India' theory about the media through which Indian culture spread, that is, the relevant roles of priests or Brahmanas, adventurers or Ksatriyas, traders or Vaishyas and others.[11] With these people, according to him, 'the earliest stream of the Rama saga flowed towards Southeast Asia'.[12] Sarkar assumed that in the early phase, the story 'developed in those areas which lay on the routes of communication to Far East'.[13] He might not have been very wrong to assume that the trade routes, halting stations and port centres played an important role in dispersing the Rama saga to Southeast Asia, because in these places there grew inhabitations of Brahmins and traders as well as Indianised royal courts, which provided the initial stimuli behind this process. Places like Takuapa, Langashuka, ports in the Malaya region, etc. are significant examples of this process.[14] Sarkar referred to the sixth century letter of the Langashuka king Bhagadutta to the Chinese ruler mentioning the incident of the uprooting of *Gandhamadana* by Hanumana, as narrated in the Ramayana.[15] This he referred to as 'the only valid reference to the Ramayana in pre-Islamic Malaya'.[16]

The scholars not only considered the relevance of Valmiki's Ramayana in evaluating the narrative's popularity among indigenes of Southeast Asia, but also investigated how various Indian local versions and oral traditions were accommodated in those Southeast Asian recensions.

Himansu Bhusan Sarkar's discussion about the Javanese and Balinese versions of Ramayana texts is a fine example of this approach.[17] Dutch archaeologist W Stutterheim identified that the sculptural reliefs of Candi Prambanan showed 'the localization and indigenization of the Ramayana story and its visual composition based on the 9th century art and possible oral translations'.[18] Sachchidanand Sahai's argument in this case is considerably meaningful. He noticed, 'From a careful analysis of the diffusion of the epic theme it appears that, while reinforcing the process of Indianisation, the Indian epic was gradually indigenised leading to the growth of oral tradition and re-created story-forms, expressing the world view of the Southeast Asian people'.[19] Prof. S Singaravelu dedicated such inclusion of local features to the *dalang* or puppeteers, dance-drama storytellers, visual artists and sculptors 'for their creativity in adaptation, diffusion and acculturation of the Ramayana tale's motifs, place names and forms as per their own local contexts'.[20] India's Sahitya Akademi's significant effort in collecting data, publishing research works, organising conferences, etc. regarding the spread and variations of the Ramayana story across Asia uncovered reliable evidence of the adaptation of the story and its characters through the localisation process. The Akademi has undertaken a massive work to publish volumes on different Ramayana versions prevalent in the Southeast Asian countries, the first volume of which deals with Ramakien, the Thai Ramayana. Published in 2020, this volume was composed by Satya Vrat Shastri, who has surveyed various aspects of Ramakien, helping us to form a thorough understanding of the text.[21] He studied all ten versions of Ramakien, providing readers a detailed idea about different features and evolved elements of the same storyline. This research has very ably shown the distinctive traits of the text independent from the Valmiki Ramayana. However, this difference had also encouraged the writer to search for other Indian sources of the Ramakien, including Hindu, Buddhist,

Jain and folklore writings. This approach is not new in the related discussion, but Shastri's credit lies in the fact that he has tried to understand how the Rama story has been absorbed into Thai society and created an assimilated impact on the social matrix.

## Evolution of the Rama Saga in Thailand: From Ancient Origins to the Chakri Dynasty

The vibrant Rama saga of Thailand manifested in literary, inscriptional, sculptural and other artistic forms, evolved over a very long time and underwent considerable alterations. Written forms of this story emerged much later in Thailand compared to other parts of Southeast Asia and obviously, India. Proofs are very meagre about the Rama story's prevalence in the ancient period, but evidence referring to this tradition in sculptures, paintings and inscriptions can be noticed from a much earlier time. For example, sculptural remains of the stone shrine of 'Parasart Hin Pimai' in Nakhon Rachasima Province and King Ramakhanhang's inscriptions mention Rama's cave, Depiction of the Rama story in the Lopburi epoch's temples and certain similarities with geographical localities around Lopburi, capital of Dvaravati in ancient Siam, like Thanon Fra Rama road or Kidhkin (possibly derived from Kishkindhya), etc. might suggest the prevalence of the Rama story in as early as in the last centuries of the first millennium. It was the Sukhotai period, in approximately 1250–1450 CE that the story found great popularity among the masses. Prior to that, Siam was part of the vast Khmer empire, from which she gained freedom under the leadership of king Ramkhamhaeng. His successors followed the tradition of using Rama in their names and took the title of 'Dharma Racha' or 'Dharma Raja', bespeaking their belief in King Rama's ideal character comprising righteousness and high morality. According to historians, the influence of the Ramayana in the Sukhotai period can be regarded as a part of the Indian impact spread due to the Khmer dominance and was visible through the widespread effect of Sanskrit, Bengali and Tamil on Sukhotai culture. It is even assumed that the name of their capital Ayutthaya was inspired by the name of Ayodhya, the mighty capital of Lord Rama. This period saw various literary references to the Ramayana and the name of Rama indicating immense impact over and popularity among Thai society. But the earliest literary work on the Rama legend was Ramayana composed during the time of King Taksin of the Lopburi period. It had 2012 verses, but did not cover the full story.[22]

Ramakien was the first complete and standard version of the Thai Rama story produced under king Chao Phaya Chakri, who became popular under the name Rama I of Bangkok. Inspired by the Sanskrit name Ramakirti or the glory of Rama, Ramakien's composition was started in 1797 and completed in 1809. It is worth mentioning that this text was based on an old Rama story prevalent in the days prior to the sack of Ayutthaya and then was lost. It primarily followed Valmiki's Ramayana, starting with the incarnation of Phra Narai (Vishnu) as Phra Ram (Rama) to destroy the demonic forces of the world. It portrays the war between Phra Ram assisted by a divinely created simian army and the demons led by Thotsakan (Ravana). The text narrates the major familiar episodes of Valmiki's Ramayana, such as the exile of Phra Ram to the forest along with his younger brother and wife Nang Sida (Sita); the abduction of Nang Sida by Thotsakan (Ravana); Hanumana's courageous acts; the long-drawn war; the death of Thotsakan (Ravana) and the other demons; the return of Phra Ram (Rama) and Nang Sida (Sita) to Ayutthaya and the later banishment of Nang Sida (Sita) by Phra Ram (Rama) who doubted her loyalty; the birth of their two sons, Lava and Kusha; and Nang Sida's disappearance into the ground. But the uniqueness of the story lies in the episode where Phra Ram and Nang Sida are both reunited by Phra Isuan (Shiva), which in fact has made it independent of the

Valmiki Ramayana. Later rulers King Rama II, III, IV, V and VI refashioned the tale by accommodating songs, prose and dialogues. As Rama I's Ramakien was too huge to perform on the stage (which was the main aim behind the story's composition) because of its 50,286 verses, it was further brought down to 14,300 verses by King Rama II. However, his version, not updated till now, was not a complete story. Instead, it was a compilation of episodes adapted from Rama I's text as well as Valmiki's Ramayana. His successor Rama VI took the initiative to publish these episodes in three volumes in 1913. Rama IV himself composed several episodes taken from the standard version of Ramakien of 1793 to perform on stage. He described the episode of Rama's exile to forest and his adventures in 1664 verses. It is assumed that this episode was an indirect reference to King Rama IV's journey to monkhood before his rulership started. Rama VI's composition was not only a literary accomplishment, but also based primarily on Valmiki's Ramayana. Nevertheless, certain independent incidents have been accommodated, providing a distinct character to this narrative. It should be noted that all kings of this Chakri dynasty (coming from the name of king Chao Phaya Chakri. Chakri means one who holds the chakra. In other words, this indicates the rule of Vishnu in Thailand) were regarded as incarnations of Rama. Rama VI chose the name 'Ramathibodhi' or 'King Rama' for the kings of this dynasty. An interesting example of this could be seen during the period of king Chulalongkorn or Rama V. After his return from England in 1897, the court staged a masked play named 'Phra Ram returns to Ayutthaya'.[23]

## Ramakien: The Thai Transformation of the Ramayana

The adaptation of the Ramayana tradition in various forms clearly demonstrates the popularity of the story among the masses. But at the same time, this process is responsible for introducing altered features regarding the story, events and characters having less or no similarity with Valmiki's Ramayana, which is very normal for a narrative tradition after its adaptation on foreign soil. This becomes clear when we go through the Ramakien version produced during Rama I's era. Written in Klon verse, in the form of recitations and helpful for singing in classical dance performances, Ramakien can be regarded as a long story having no divisions into acts or scenes. Instead, it consists of three narrative episodes. This characteristic has made it different from the Sanskrit Valmiki Ramayana, which is divided into seven kandas. Both versions of Kings Rama I and VI retained seminal features of the Sanskrit Ramayana, yet accommodated interpolations showing the influences of South Indian and local traditions. Historians are not certain about the sources Rama I used for his literary reconstruction of the Rama saga. They have assumed that the king showed an urge to collect all available materials relating to the Ramayana story, including those from the southern part of Thailand, which received considerable influence from southern India, especially from the Tamil region. For example, the first section of Rama I's Ramakien mentioned a South Indian sea-goddess, Mekhala.[24] Interestingly, some episodes of the second section that had been traced to non-classical Ramayana traditions of India, were moulded according to indigenous storylines.[25] A description of the Lanka war in this work was reshaped in such a way that main features and characters of the story were represented in a new light mixed with indigenous traits.[26] Here Phrot or Bharata became the generalissimo, not Rama, and the role of Ravana was attributed to the king Cakravat of Malikan.[27] Another very significant feature of Ramakien was the identity of Sita, who was described as the daughter of queen Mantho (Mandodari) of Lanka.[28] She buried her daughter due to her inability to accept the child, as she was living a life of celibacy. Later, the girl was brought up by king Chonok (Janaka) of Mithila.[29] Some Indian non-Sanskrit versions of the Ramayana also stated similar explanations about Sita's birth. Advuta Ramayana mentioned Sita as Mandodari's daughter, who was conceived after she drank the blood of rishis killed by Ravana. In the Jaina tradition, Gunabhadracharya's Uttara Purana of the eighth century also described Sita as Ravana's daughter. Hanumana's romantic engagement with the queen fish and birth of their son, Macchanu, who was later brought up by Maiyarab, the demon king of Badan (Patala), was another part of the story that cannot be seen in Valmiki's Ramayana, where Hanumana was described to have been practicing celibacy. Even after winning the war against Thotsakan, Hanumana was given a new state by Phra Rama that was identified as near modern Lopburi (Navapuri in Sanskrit). The Thai Ramakien portrayed a long series of wars between Phra Ram and Thotsakan. This feature could be seen in the Cambodian Reamker also and made both distinct from the Indian standard version of Ramayana. In the versions of both King Rama I and VI, episodes of floating Benjakay and Phrommat arrow were included, apart from the familiar events based on the Valmiki Ramayana. There were more such new and independent episodes to which scholars should pay attention. For example, the episodes of Anomatan, Chiuha, Benjakay or Binayaki, Mahipanthebasun (Mahipaladevasura), the quarrel between Nilasphad or Nila and Hanumana, the segments dealing with Maiyarab and the abduction of Rama, the birth of Sita's sons, the destruction of Ravana's soul kept in a cage with Khobut (Goputra), insurrection of Lanka, etc. Apart from these new inclusions, Ramakien's striking deviations from Valmiki's Ramayana are visible in altered and modified descriptions of various incidents such as the birth of Rama and Ravana, Balin's fight with Mayavin, Manthara's role, Sita's abduction, Jatayu's fight with Ravana, etc.[30] Do such variations and new features indicate the influence of other Indian non-classical Rama story versions, oral folk traditions and non-Indian versions' impact like that of the Khmer's? Here, comparative and minute research is desired. But what is not hard to understand is that the Thai Ramayana tradition, like all other versions of Southeast Asia, cannot be seen only in the light of Valmiki Ramayana's influence, or for that matter, the all-inclusive Sanskritised influence. Indian regional and Southeast Asian indigenous factors' roles are hard to ignore.

Ramakien's independent and indigenous attributions are visible in the depiction of characters; the existing characters have been reshaped, whereas fresh ones have been accommodated. This could be a valid reason why Ramakien has the features of a literary work but without the 'sacred character of Ramayana'.[31] This became evident when King Rama I said, 'This royal writing, the Ramakien, has been written in accordance with a Hindu tale. Not being a matter of substantial import, merely an offering from his Majesty (to Buddhism), it should lead nobody astray in leading it, for nothing material is permanent'.[32] Such distinctiveness invited scholars' minute analysis of the characters, enforcing the worldly nature of the narrative. Unlike the Indian version, here Rama was not merely a divine figure and not beyond the reach of mortals. Besides the divine origin, the portrayal of the Rama character in Ramakien, focusing on his virtues and achievements, could relate to the image of a just and ideal ruler.[33] Author Satyavrat Sastri even criticised the character for not being good to his wife, Sita, which made him no different from any common man.[34] Thus, here Rama was shown as having the greatest humanly qualities; especially a hero and ideal king. The eternal virtues of Rama were the significant thread that bound the reverence for the character in both India and Thailand, leading to explore his image in reconstructing the nations. Ramakien's Sita was also projected as having her own original characteristics, including both Indian and indigenous elements.[35] She was innocent and faithful and could be very aptly posited within the structures of ideal womanhood, an idea which contributed to her popularity and reverence in India. Yet, in Ramakien, Sita's strong character was reflected through her condemnation and criticism of Rama's behaviour.[36] She remained unmoved by Rama's repeated pleas and denounced him for his actions. The problem could be solved only when Shiva intervened.[37] Thus, Sita here was showered with some modernised traits, and this combination of traditional and modern virtues could be a possible reason behind her acceptance for a long time in Thai society. Another interesting character of Ramakien was Hanumana. His familiar valour, energy, leadership qualities and dedication to Rama and Sita were unmissable in the narration. But along with this, Ramakien's Hanumana was a very colourful character who, instead of spending life in celibacy and idealism like his Indian counterpart, preferred the company of beautiful women.[38] Hanumana's relation with Benjakay and Suvarnamatsa was an excellent example of Hanumana's mortal nature.[39] Thus, his character in Ramakien had various shades, making it more multifaceted than Ramayana. Such transformative features could be seen regarding other important characters like Ravana and Vibhishana. These characters had preserved their basic traits along with the inclusion of new elements, and this was a natural outcome for a narrative that had been evolved and reproduced into various versions for a long time. While Ravana's prowess, knowledge, anger and arrogance were portrayed beautifully, his efforts to avoid direct confrontation with Rama could leave us bewildered.[40]

## Conclusion

Ramakien is a wonderful example of a literary living tradition which, having preserved the basic ideologies of the Rama saga, successfully welcomed new approaches and alterations. This undoubtedly made the Thai tradition popular among all sections of people, as the story's appeal could connect them on an ideological plane. The morals and values emphasised in the Rama saga are universal, and hence can attract people irrespective of nations, languages and cultures. This is a natural explanation of why the Rama tradition produced so many versions, including in India itself. Accommodation of local traits is an important reason for the story's long existence, which proves its dynamism and flexibility as well as fulfilling a general principle of history, that is, interactions and assimilations are helpful in thriving cultures. It is thus not very surprising to note how Ramakien has become a major influential force in Thai politics, society, religion and culture. The presence of the story and its characters is visible in all aspects of Thai life. It teaches how to achieve qualities for ideal kingship, helps in a philosophical quest and offers values important for society. In the cultural field, Thailand's paintings, sculptures and performing arts show the valuable impact of Ramakien. Mural paintings or frescos depicting episodes and characters of Ramakien can be found in Wat Pho or the Bodhi Temple, on the walls of Wat Suthat, Wat Phya Nang and in the galleries of Wat Phra Kayeo or the temple of the emerald Buddha, as it is popularly known. Numerous sculptures and woodcarvings showing Ramakien's influence have become part of various architectural designs. The performance of Khon and Nang Yai, a kind of mask play, betrays the adaptations of events and characters from Ramakien. Its strong influence is visible in Thai folklore as well. Ramakien, thus, is a significant aspect of India and Thailand's cultural interaction. As intangible evidence of such collaboration, Ramakien should be assessed and highlighted accompanied by a parallel discussion of the tangible evidence. It presents the power of adoption of the Thai people, culture and society. Assimilation with and inclusion of the Thai localised characters in Ramakien challenged the idea of a homogeneous adaptation of the Ramayana. The text thus questioned the idea of 'Indianisation' as well, which was emphasised over an extensive spread of the Ramayana story. It also upholds the idea of cultural convergence and acculturation across regions.

## Endnotes

1 Romila Thapar, "The Ramayana: Theme and Variation," *Cultural Pasts: Essays in Early Indian History* (New Delhi: Oxford University Press, 2000), 647.

2 Thapar, "The Ramayana: Theme and Variation," 670.

3 Thapar, "The Ramayana: Theme and Variation".

4 Gauri Parimoo Krishnan, "Mighty Messenger: Adaptation and Localization of Hanuman and the Ramayana in Southeast Asia," in *The Multivalence of an Epic: Retelling the Ramayana in South India and Southeast Asia*, ed. Parul Pandya Dhar (Manipal: Manipal University Press, 2021), 123.

5 Krishnan, "Mighty Messenger: Adaptation and Localization of Hanuman and the Ramayana in Southeast Asia".

6 Rabindranath Tagore, "Java Jatrir Patro," *Vishvabharati*, Kolkata, Falgun, 1392 BS (in Bengali); Suniti Kumar Chattopadhyay, "Rabindra Sangame Dvipamay Bharat O Shyam-Desh," *Prakash Bhaban*, Kolkata, 2002 (in Bengali); Shantideb Ghosh, "Java o Balir Nrityagit," *Vishvabharati*, Kolkata, Baishakh, 1401 BS (in Bengali).

7 Tagore, "Java Jatrir Patro,"; Chattopadhyay, "Rabindra Sangame Dvipamay Bharat O Shyam-Desh,"; Ghosh, "Java o Balir Nrityagit".

8 Tagore, "Java Jatrir Patro,"; Chattopadhyay, "Rabindra Sangame Dvipamay Bharat O Shyam-Desh,"; Ghosh, "Java o Balir Nrityagit".

9 This particular idea of India being the source of Asian culture and heritage became popular in the heyday of nationalism, though its prevalence can be seen among Indian intellectuals from an early time.

10 Himansu Bhusan Sarkar, *Indian Influences on the Literature of Java and Bali*, (Kolkata: Greater India Society, 1934); *Dvipamay Bharater Prachin Sahitya* (Kolkata: Firma K.L. Mukhopadhyay, 1968, in Bengali).

11 Himansu Bhusan Sarkar, "The Ramayana in Southeast Asia: A General Survey," in *Asian Variations in Ramayana*, ed. K.R Srinivasa Iyengar (Madras: Sahitya Akademi, 1983), 207.

12 Sarkar, "The Ramayana in Southeast Asia: A General Survey".

13 Sarkar, "The Ramayana in Southeast Asia: A General Survey".

14 Sarkar, "The Ramayana in Southeast Asia: A General Survey".

15 Sarkar, "The Ramayana in Southeast Asia: A General Survey," 208.

16 Sarkar, "The Ramayana in Southeast Asia: A General Survey".

17 Sarkar, *Indian Influences on the Literature of Java and Bali.*

18 Krishnan, "Mighty Messenger: Adaptation and Localization of Hanuman and the Ramayana in Southeast Asia," p. 125.

19 Sachchidanand Sahai, ed., *The Ramayana in South East Asia* (South East Asian Review Office, 1981), 1.

20 S Singaravelu, "The Rama Story in the Thai Cultural Tradition," in *The Ramayana in South East Asia*, ed. Sachchidanand Sahai (South East Asian Review Office, 1981).

21 Satya Vrat Shastri, *Ramayana in South East Asia Vol. I: Ramakien* (New Delhi, Sahitya Akademi, 2020).

22 For details, see Shastri, *Ramayana in South East Asia Vol. I: Ramakien*. Also, Chamlong Sarapadnuke, "The Ramayana in Thai Theatre," in *The Ramayana Tradition in Asia*, ed. V. Raghavan (New Delhi: Sahitya Akademi, 2017).

23 For details, see Shastri, *Ramayana in South East Asia Vol. I: Ramakien*; Sahai, *The Ramayana in South East Asia.*

24 Shastri, *Ramayana in South East Asia Vol. I: Ramakien*, 30.

25 Shastri, *Ramayana in South East Asia Vol. I: Ramakien*, 31–8.

26 Shastri, *Ramayana in South East Asia Vol. I: Ramakien.*

27 Shastri, *Ramayana in South East Asia Vol. I: Ramakien.*

28 Shastri, *Ramayana in South East Asia Vol. I: Ramakien*, 47–8.

29 Shastri, *Ramayana in South East Asia Vol. I: Ramakien.*

30 For a detailed discussion of all the changed characters, see Shastri, *Ramayana in South East Asia Vol. I: Ramakien.*

31 Shastri, *Ramayana in South East Asia Vol. I: Ramakien*, 29.

32 Shastri, *Ramayana in South East Asia Vol. I: Ramakien.*

33 Shastri, *Ramayana in South East Asia Vol. I: Ramakien*, 55–7.

34 Shastri, *Ramayana in South East Asia Vol. I: Ramakien.*

35 Shastri, *Ramayana in South East Asia Vol. I: Ramakien*, 57–9.

36 Shastri, *Ramayana in South East Asia Vol. I: Ramakien.*

37 Shastri, *Ramayana in South East Asia Vol. I: Ramakien*, 59.

38 Shastri, *Ramayana in South East Asia Vol. I: Ramakien*, 59–60.

39 Shastri, *Ramayana in South East Asia Vol. I: Ramakien.*

40 Shastri, *Ramayana in South East Asia Vol. I: Ramakien*, 61.

# An Alternative Story of the Arakan Front: Through the Eyes of an Indian Doctor, Shantilal Roy (1943–1944)

*Sulagna Som*

## Introduction

From 1757 to 1900, when Britain ruled India, there were significant socio-political shifts and scientific advances that had an impact on India's medical systems, institutions and practitioners. Historians have also argued over whether the colonial government utilised Western medicine as a tool to expand and justify its authority. Army Medical Department (AMD) physicians provided care wherever the British army stationed its troops. In contrast to the all-European British army, the Indian Medical Service (IMS) hired officers to provide care for the Indian Army.[1] The practice of *daktari* or the Western medical profession achieved popularity in India then among Western-educated people. The subordinate medical service was staffed by many Indians who had received Western medical training, while the superior medical service was predominately reserved for Europeans.[2]

The first Indians to receive medical care from British doctors were Indian troops who had been hired by the East India Company. British doctors recommended the company engage Indian practitioners for new Indian regiments as compounders and to deliver medicine to the patients.[3] To coordinate them, Subordinate Medical Services (SMS) were established in each presidency starting in 1760. Until 1947, these services coexisted with 'superior' medical services. 'Native doctors' was the title given to British-trained Indian assistants.[4]

One of the greatest British achievements during the colonial period was importing the European infantry system and teaching the Indians to be sepoys.[5] Out of the 1.27 million men who served in the British Indian army during the First World War, approximately 50,000 Indians and 947,000 British soldiers died.[6] From then, the number of Indian soldiers in the British Indian army increased gradually, which can be seen in the Second World War in 1943, in which nearly two million Indian soldiers were appointed.[7] Up from 577 at the beginning of the war, there were almost 8000 Indian commissioned officers (ICOs), 220 lieutenant colonels and four temporary or acting brigadiers at the end of the war, among them 140 medical officers. By 1945, the ratio became 4.1 British officers for every ICO, down from 10.1 in 1939.[8]

One of the most interesting phases of the history of the Second World War was the Burma campaign. Along with the official records of this campaign, the medical history of the Burma campaign was well discussed by the British official medical historian Francis Albert Eley Crew in his book *The Army Medical Services*. Dirom Gray Crawford's *A History of the Indian Medical Service, 1600-1913*; the official records of the Royal Army Medical Corps; Queen Alexandra's Imperial Military Nursing Service; *Nursing Journal of India*; *British Medical Journal* and many other official records nourished the Eurocentric view on the medical history of the war, which could compromise the neutrality of the historical narrative. An alternative version of the Indian nationalistic view on the affairs of the Burma campaign can be traced in *Arakan Fronte* by Shantilal Roy, a Bengali medical officer of the British Army in the Burma campaign.

At the end of the First World War, in April 1937, Burma got its independence from the British and established a semi-autonomous nation, reporting directly to the Colonel's Office. At this point, Burma Command broke away from the Indian Army. On 12 December 1941, four days after invading Malaya and officially starting the Second World War, Japanese troops made their first incursion into Burma at Victoria Point. Thailand, supposedly autonomous and known for its neutrality, supported Japan in that war and became a major threat to southern Burma. On 31 January 1942, the Japanese overran Moulmein and left toward the north. After crossing the Bilin River, the $17^{th}$ Indian Division was forced to run over the River Sittang. The lone railway bridge in the area that crossed the river was destroyed on 23 February 1942 by British soldiers. Two of the division's brigades were regrettably still on the river's eastern bank. The $17^{th}$ Indian Division was severely diminished as a result, yet did not surrender. The $7^{th}$ Armoured Brigade arrived in Rangoon with help. The $7^{th}$ Indian Division and the $5^{th}$ Indian Division, under the command of the $15^{th}$ Indian Corps, launched a modest offensive in Arakan in January 1944. While the Japanese $28^{th}$ Army was starting its significant attack at the same time, the main drive of the $15^{th}$ Army was to seize the Imphal Plain and then move into India. According to F.A.E. Crew, the most important point in British success in Southeast Asia can be attributed to the Battle of the Admin Box in February 1944, when the Japanese attack failed and they were forced to back off.

The big onslaught in central Burma started shortly after that. The IV Corps was cut off on the Imphal Plain, forcing the $17^{th}$ Indian Division to retreat along the Tiddim Road. On 29 March 1944, the route between Kohima and Imphal was blocked, and Kohima was put under siege from 8 April to 20 April 1944. The Japanese were pursued by the $14^{th}$ Army, which eventually forced them back to the River Chindwin. Crossing the Chindwin, the $14^{th}$ Army moved closer to the Irrawaddy. In the meantime, Akyab was taken by the $15^{th}$ Indian

Corps, which was commanded by the Allied Land Forces South-East Asia (ALFSEA). As if moving toward Mandalay, formations from the 14th Army crossed the Irrawaddy River, while a silent advance force from the 4th Corps was moved up the river from below. As a result, Operation Extended Capital officially began with the 4th Corps attacking Meiktila. After Meiktila was taken and held, the Japanese resistance gave up. With the 4th Corps and 33rd Indian Corps moving into Rangoon, Central Burma was reclaimed. The 15th Indian Corps defeated them after fighting in a valiant amphibious battle to gain Rangoon.[9]

According to Jeremy Black, the study of military history is largely Eurocentric,[10] as it primarily focusses on the armies and conflicts of Western powers. More intensive research on non-Western military experience as well as the spread of Western military systems into the non-European globe and the hybrid forms that evolved from that, such as the great social histories of colonial armies, are currently gaining importance in the research.[11] In more contemporary war historiography, the non-European perspective has taken the place of the Eurocentric approach. The experiences of soldiers who fought on the front lines deliver us an alternative story of the war and bring us to the realities of war and its detrimental effects on people's lives, society, politics and culture. These are living documents of war history. Understanding the brutality of the battlefield requires more intense investigation through the war literature. Among all the British colonies, only the Indian native army was allowed to fight overseas. The details of the war, the relationship of the Indians with their *sahibs* (upper ranks), caste and racial differences at the front, war crises, psychological trauma, etc. all come up in their memoirs.

*Arakan Fronte* was written by Bengali doctor Shantilal Roy, who served the British Indian Army in the Burma campaign during the Second World War as a military surgeon.[12] The book was published with the constant encouragement of

Dr Nihar Ranjan Gupta, one of his colleagues at the Arakan war front. Dr Gupta validates that this book is not mere fictional or imaginative war literature; it is indeed a real war history, which will eradicate the scarcity of real war literature in Bengali.[13]

In this book, Shantilal Roy briefly discusses the war history of the British and Japanese forces that met in the mountainous region of the Arakan province in Burma in late 1943 and early 1944. Shantilal joined the British military force as a surgeon in mid-1940, when Japan in the far east had started conquering countries and destroying the British glory and prestige that had been established for so long. The defeat in 1941 at Burma of the so-called 'invincible' British forces was a shameful chapter for the British Empire.

Shantilal Roy was appointed to the civil service of the IMS after returning from the battlefield of Malay. From March 1942 to April 1944, he worked in various military hospitals known as 'Peace Stations'.[14] Though he wanted a peaceful life after witnessing huge destruction, death and blood, within four months he got bored and applied for a front-line job, which got approved after his serious, meticulous efforts. After leaving Calcutta, he led the advance party of the troops from the northeastern part of India and reached Comilla of Bengal, the headquarters of the 14$^{th}$ Army.[15] From Comilla, they started their journey to Arakan.

He stated that 'our motor carriage is joined to the passenger carriage, and we go with all the other passengers, but we are completely separated from them'.[16] They had old, dry bread, tinned fish and meat, but little opportunity to bathe. After reaching Mainamati, they started for Arakan through the mountains, forests and dusty, muddy road. During his five years of employment, Roy met a few Bengali co-workers. On this long, tiresome journey, he met two or four Bengali men for a short period. After a week, they crossed the Arakan border of Burma and reached Chota Mangdana, just beside the Mayu range of mountains. They set up camp in the valley.[17] The whole hospital was inside the tent, with provisions to accommodate 250 to 500 patients. Their *palton* (group) was a small mobile surgical unit. The number of officers was three—a surgeon, an assistant specialist and an anaesthetist. He was the only Indian doctor among them. Along with that, they had 15 assistants for the hospital work.[18]

They had stocked all kinds of dressing tools and battery-operated electric lights. For quick moves with short-term notice, they had four motor vehicles. Their job was to stay connected with the field ambulance, perform surgery on the wounded men and transfer them to safe hospitals quickly. Two or four such field ambulances and other casualty clearing stations had been brought there.[19]

It was the duty of everyone to build their accommodation tents in the shade of the forest, in the hills or in the dry stream. They built this set-up near the battleground. The trench was surrounded by wire fences and guarded by soldiers. No lights were allowed outside after it was dark to keep the trench safe from enemies, and even smoking cigarettes was prohibited.[20] Roy gave a brief description of his daily routine.[21] Their day started with 'stand to'; then pushing injections or blood to the wounded soldiers; surgery and treatment; then transferring them to the relatively safe, larger, rear hospital. The field hospitals needed to be ready for the next batch of wounded. For emergencies, the patients were evacuated by air to large hospitals. In the afternoon, they took baths in filthy canal water, if available. They had to finish their meal before night. Then again, 'stand to' and a long, frightful night at the mudhole.[22]

Modern artilleries like tanks, armoured cars, machine gun mortars and various types of firearms were used at the battle. Two or three times a day, enemy aircraft circled over their heads to make them frightened. He recalled once that they constructed the tent along one of the routes of the Japanese pre-planned three-pronged drive. In that emergency, two wounded soldiers arrived for treatment. The surgeon began his procedure in the tent with battery and electric lights, and a torch on their headgear for the operation theatre. Suddenly, with the sound of shooting (according to the order), they left everything and took positions with firearms. The trench was almost filled with army men, and Roy didn't dare to raise his head, because he was not wearing an iron cap. The soil of the trench started falling.[23]

After spending over two hours there, unable to bear the cold, he decided to go to his shelter tent, which was about six hundred yards from the trench. He crawled slowly out of the trench and reached his goal through the canal. He lay down there like a mummy and experienced the lighting and tremendously horrifying sounds of the firearms. However, he could not stay there for long; a burst from a Bren gun abolished his tent. He took shelter in the cave of Captain Tote (probably an Indian) and spent the rest of the night there. In these descriptions, Roy hasn't shown any extra heroic image of himself. He has depicted a picture of an ordinary doctor's life at war.

Roy described a horrifying picture of the next morning when he found the lifeless body of the half-operated patient last night lying under the operation table, which was also turned over. For a long time, he was haunted by the horrifying image of that patient.[24] Shantilal remembered that the Japanese air fleet started bombarding that very day, and it became a daily routine. After tidying up everything as per orders, at 10 am, the order came to attend to the soldiers and hold the position. The surgical unit started building the tent again, even though they were tired. Mental and physical health were ignored at the front. Roy felt sorry for the doctors because they were not allowed to show feelings, emotions, momentary weakness, happiness and sadness like ordinary people.[25]

A similar situation came up when a wounded patient came in the same condition as the previous night. Major Ives received a signal message and ordered Roy to leave the place within two hours with all the surgical tools and the whole unit, because the Japanese had attacked the 7th Division, the headquarters of the British army, and mentioned that the 'situation [is] serious but not hopeless'. It was assumed by Major Ives that the Japanese would kill the British men brutally but not the Indians, as they were collecting the Indian men for Subhash Chandra Bose's Indian Independence Army. Interestingly, Major Ives left for Bawli Bazar with Captain Ward and Captain Hutton and took the station staff car. Three motor lorries were left for Roy and the unit.[26] This act of weakness on the part of the major created huge discontent among the white men in the unit.

Roy could not leave this patient again. He finished the surgery and handed him over to the rear party with other patients.[27] After a long, nerve-breaking journey, they reached Bawli Bazar. On that journey, he experienced the tremendous brutality of the war.[28] He portrayed the unbearable pain of the Bawli camp. Some of the soldiers arrived in only their pants or inner garments. Some of them were so traumatised that they lost their sanity. Roy distributed his personal belongings to his fellow soldiers; the pain of the war made him a selfless person.[29]

Shantilal and his unit got shelter in a casualty clearing station.[30] The Japanese air fleet distributed leaflets to mark the Red Cross area. According to the Geneva Protocol, no army men or firearms can get a room within 800 yards of the Red Cross area.[31] Roy mentioned that the Japanese air fleet never bombarded that marked region.[32] Shantilal described the unnecessary misery of the innocent village people who lost everything in that war.

An important part of Roy's commemoration was the Japanese soldiers' advertisement for the Azad Hind Fauj (Indian National Army; INA). Roy witnessed a discouraging attitude toward the Indian Independence Army by the British officers which, according to him, created a huge misconception about the INA among the Indian soldiers. The Japanese fleet distributed books on the Azad Hind Fauj and urged Indian army men to join the INA if they were working under the British unwillingly. British people call them JIFFS (Japanese Indian Fighting Force). Roy mentioned that the British intelligence department reported weekly on the movements and workings, number of soldiers and exact location of the brigades of the Azad Hind Fauj (Nehru Brigade, Azad Brigade, Jhansi Brigade and Subhash Brigade) to their higher authorities. Roy mentioned that even though he may not have been able to publicly show respect for the INA, he felt proud as a Bengali and hoped that just as the Turks got independence under the leadership of Kamal Pasha, India would gain independence from the British under the leadership of Netaji Subhas Chandra Bose.[33]

Their next destination was Gopi Bazar, which could be reached through the dangerous Gopi Pass. They were not allowed to use the Red Cross flag while moving with the army group. The 'Dakota' supplied aid in the Gopi Bazar Camp area through parachutes.[34] The uncertainty of life on the battlefield is clear in the writing of Roy. As the situation was getting worse, they started living in suffocating 'foxholes'.[35] The beds of the patients were made of branches of the forked tree and bamboo sticks from the forest, and stretcher lines were placed on them. The canopy was made of foliage. There was a blood transfusion unit and a surgical room in the field hospital. The surgical room was built by digging five or six cubits deep underground. For emergency surgery at night, the commander was to be informed before lighting up the lamp, or they would be shot by the soldiers stationed around the perimeter. There was a 'Pass and Counter Password' for any kind of emergency movement at night.[36]

Roy praised the dedication and devotion of stretcher-bearers for their work. They carried the wounded on their shoulders and passed seven to eight miles from the battlefield to the field hospitals through the Japanese sniper bullets from the roadside jungles. They served selflessly without any acknowledgment. He didn't exaggerate the unnecessary heroism of the soldiers while the enemies were approaching closely. Though being a part of the surgical unit, Roy had to be ready with his gun in emergencies. He described his terrifying escape from the enemy's den after inadvertently getting too close to the enemy camp. He was called an 'idiot' by Commander General Lomax of the 26$^{th}$ Division for taking a wrong turn towards the enemy camp. He was saved from the punishment by giving information regarding the location of the enemy.

Racial discrimination towards Indians in the army camp has also been reflected in Roy's writing. He mentioned the cultural gap between Indian and European soldiers in the army.[37] The white masters were always disrespectful toward Indian culture, cooking methods, food habits, dietary rules, etc. Indian soldiers were forced to follow British etiquette at every moment. They were not allowed to talk in their mother tongue in the presence of any white men. Maintaining European decorum was another problem for Indians in the army—limited talk, expressing verbal politeness, fake smiles, waving to greet people and eating and drinking quietly with a knife and fork.[38] However, to get acknowledgment from their white masters, some of the Indian soldiers, deliberately acted like sahibs. Roy expressed his anger for those Indians who had no faith in their religion, nationality, culture or civilisation.[39]

He described the British high-rank officers as womanisers and addicted to alcohol, which was also not the culture of

Indians. According to Roy, racism and imperialism were in their blood. They always tried to prove their racial superiority by saying *kala aadmi* does not come in qualities.[40] This encounter of caste and racial discrimination was also observed in the hospital by Roy. This disparity between Indian and British wounded soldiers was evident in their provision of food, accommodation and special allowances. He mentioned a tragic case of discrimination against Indian soldiers. Many wounded Indian soldiers lost their fingers or hands while fighting for the British. They were taken care of by the white nurses (sisters and VADs).[41] They requested Roy for a couple of spoons to feed the patients, because poor patients had to wait for a long time due to the unavailability of spoons during their meal time.[42] Roy wrote about the same to the quartermaster. The request was rejected, because Indians were not entitled to have spoons.[43] Roy felt sorry and angry for his fellow Indian soldiers who lost their limbs to those cruel British colonisers. He again requested the authorities not for Indians but for the white nurses who fed them with their hands. But the officer in charge immediately rejected the proposal by showing him the rule book.[44] Later on, Roy and the ward sister appealed to the higher authority at a party unofficially, and the spoons arrived in two days.[45] In another case, the requirement to change the blood-soaked dirty mattresses of Indian soldiers at the hospital was denied by claiming that the Indians were provided beds, which was enough.[46] He hopes for a better future when young people would devote their lives to free India.

With the changing course of the war, the Japanese army was moving back. Roy was moving forward, passing through the war-ravaged area. He saw the destruction, blood, dead bodies, ashes, bullet shells, the boxes full of firearms and grenades, love letters, 'love knots', 'forget me not' handkerchiefs, etc. Not only humans but wild animals also lost their lives.[47] He depicted the emotional side of the war.

He reached a field ambulance hospital and heard the painful story of a Japanese attack on the hospital. One Japanese doctor and soldiers surrounded the hospitals and demanded a long list of medicines and surgical tools. Unfortunately, one patient there started firing at them, which resulted in a catastrophe. All the patients and doctors were killed by the Japanese army before the British rescue team reached the place. However, one Bengali doctor was saved, as he fainted the moment the bullets were shot.[48] Roy realised that the Red Cross badge could not save them on that night. After that tragic incident, the 7$^{th}$ Division of the Indian army created the famous 'admin box', a defence perimeter within which the field hospitals were being built.[49] Later on, this system was followed by other camps as well. However, that system deprived them of the right to use the Red Cross, as it was violating the Geneva Protocol. The doctors were being trained in using the revolver, Tommy gun, grenade and Sten gun.[50] While visiting the deserted camp areas of the Japanese army, Roy mentioned the booby trap, where explosives were hidden in the beautiful, lucrative, precious things.[51]

During his three-month halt at Ngekydak pass, Roy met two Bengalis from the field ambulance and three Bengali doctors from other units (*paltons*). He mentioned a few names of his fellow Bengali doctors: Paritosh Roy, Uma Mukherjee, Nihar Ranjan Gupta, Nalini Choudhury and Pritthish Choudhury, with whom he had a great acquaintance.[52] After two months of staying there, they went in different directions. Roy came to Redwame Bin, which was located near the river Nuff. The river Nuff indicates the border between India and Burma. Arakan was on its eastern side, and Bengal was on its western bank. They waited there for a few days and then started their journey back to India.[53] The majority of the field forces used by the Allies in Burma—where Japan waged its largest land war outside of China—were supplied by the Indian army. After experiencing some setbacks, Indian forces were able to stand their ground against the 'fanatical' Japanese on the battlefields.[54] Each company in the majority of the Indian army's infantry battalions was distinguished based on race or religion. Due to the awkward 'class' structure, logistics (different meals for each class) and replacements, in particular, were severely hampered.[55]

Roy's writings demonstrate how the pain of modern war tactics and of losing friends, personal belongings and attachments become insignificant in the face of death. He described himself as a machine with no emotions, not a human being. He protested from within the system. His mind became rebellious with intense resentment and hatred towards British apartheid. He tried his best to get Indian soldiers their fair dues. Despite this, Roy's writings revealed his devotion to his work, his sense of duty and his hardworking, courageous mind that did not give up on the battlefield. Although he served in the British army, he never accepted the British as his master. His identity always made him proud to be a Bengali and an Indian. Exhausted, Roy wanted to return home and dreamed of an independent India. This diary of his during the war brings alive those war days. Therefore, the role of this book in the study of war history is immense. Along with this, the infinite importance of writing a diary is also proved in the present time for the study of social history.

## Endnotes

1 Dirom Grey Crawford, *A History of the Indian Medical Service, 1600–1913* (London: W. Thacker, 1914).

2 David Arnold, *Colonizing the Body: State Medicine and Epidemic Disease in Nineteenth-Century India* (New Delhi: Oxford University Press, 1993), 55.

3 T Patterson, "The Interaction of Indian Medicine and Modern Medicine (Colonial Period)," in *Medicine and Life Sciences in India*, ed. BV Subbarayappa (New Delhi: Centre for Studies in Civilizations, 2001), 574–605. [DP Chattopadhyay, gen.

ed., *History of Science, Philosophy and Culture in Indian Civilization*, Part 2. Vol. IV].

4 Poonam Bala, *Medicine and Medical Policies in India: Social and Historical Perspectives* (Lanham: Lexington Books, 2007).

5 Nelson D Lankford, "The Victorian Medical Profession and Military Practice: Army Doctors and National Origins," *Bulletin of the History of Medicine* 54, no. 4(1980): 511–28.

6 David Omissi, *Indian Voices of the Great War. Soldiers' Letters, 1914–18* (London: Penguin Books Limited, 1999), 4; FW Perry, *The Commonwealth Armies. Manpower and Organisation in Two World Wars* (Manchester: Manchester University Press, 1988), 96–7.

7 Perry, *The Commonwealth Armies. Manpower and Organisation in Two World Wars*, 116.

8 Pradeep P Barua, *Gentlemen of the Raj. The Indian Army Officer Corps, 1817–1949* (Westport: Praeger, 2003), 130; Apurba Kundu, *Militarism in India. The Army and Civil Society in Consensus* (London: IB Tauris, 1998), 50; Lt. Col. Gautam Sharma, *Nationalisation of the Indian Army (1885–1947)* (New Delhi: Allied Publishers Pvt. Ltd., 1997), 174, 184.

9 "'Burma 1930–1947: Overview Burma Campaign,' British Indian Army and Britain's Allies," *British Military History,* https://www.britishmilitaryhistory.co.uk/docs-burma-1930-1947-overview-burma-campaign/

10 Jeremy Black, *Rethinking Military History* (London: Routledge, 2004).

11 Jeremy Black, *War and the World* (New Haven: Yale University Press, 1998); Timothy Parsons, *The African Rank-and-File: (Social History of Africa)* (Portsmouth: Heinemann, 1999).

12 Shantilal Roy, *Arakan Fronte* (Kolkata: Bengal Publishers, 1946).

13 Roy, *Arakan Fronte*, II.

14 Roy, *Arakan Fronte*, 2.

15 Roy, *Arakan Fronte*, 2–5.

16 Roy, *Arakan Fronte*, 6.

17 Roy, *Arakan Fronte*, 8.

18 Roy, *Arakan Fronte*. In every theatre of the war, there were tiny, mobile surgical units that were deployed flexibly based on the nature of the battle and that operated closely behind the fighting. They performed abdominal, thoracic, head and neck and limb surgery in tents, bunkers and requisitioned buildings using equipment that was transported by truck, van or mule. They had two responsibilities: saving lives and making sure injured soldiers were stable enough to be transported back to a base hospital.

19 Roy, *Arakan Fronte*, 9.

20 Roy, *Arakan Fronte*, 10–1.

21 Roy, *Arakan Fronte*, 46.

22 Roy, *Arakan Fronte*, 47–9.

23 Roy, *Arakan Fronte*, 14–7.

24 Roy, *Arakan Fronte*, 18.

25 Roy, *Arakan Fronte*, 18–9.

26 Roy, *Arakan Fronte*, 20.

27 The soldiers in the rear party were assigned to all the menial tasks and were constantly on alert. The worst part is that they were abandoned at the camp, while the rest of the regiment engaged in what we refer to as the 'real work' of combat in deadly war zones.

28 Roy, *Arakan Fronte*, 22–4.

29 Roy, *Arakan Fronte*, 23–5.

30 Roy, *Arakan Fronte*, 27.

31 The mission of the Red Cross Society was to raise funds and gifts from the public to provide medical care for the sick, injured and war victims, among other needs.

32 Roy, *Arakan Fronte*, 27–8. The Indian Red Cross Society (IRCS) was founded in 1920 as a result of the passage of Parliament Act XV and became incorporated under that Act.

33 Roy, *Arakan Fronte*, 29–31.

34 Roy, *Arakan Fronte*, 37. Developed from the commercial Douglas DC-3 airliner, the Douglas C-47 Skytrain or Dakota (RAF, RAAF, RCAF, RNZAF, and SAAF name) is a military transport aircraft. During World War II, the Allies made great use of it, and for many years afterward, different military operators employed it in combat. These aircrafts were used to send aid to the camp area of the battlefield.

35 Roy, *Arakan Fronte*, 40–2.

36 Roy, *Arakan Fronte*, 48.

37 Roy, *Arakan Fronte*, 50–7.

38 Roy, *Arakan Fronte*, 92–4.

39 Roy, *Arakan Fronte*, 98–101.

40 Roy, *Arakan Fronte*, 102.

41 Roy, *Arakan Fronte*.

42 Roy, *Arakan Fronte*, 103.

43 Roy, *Arakan Fronte*.

44 Roy, *Arakan Fronte*, 103–4.

45 Roy, *Arakan Fronte*, 104.

46 Roy, *Arakan Fronte*, 104.

47 Roy, *Arakan Fronte*, 57–61.

48 Roy, *Arakan Fronte*, 63–5.

49 Roy, *Arakan Fronte*, 66. Also see, Alan Jeffreys, *The British Army in the Far East 1941–45* (Oxford: Osprey Publishing, 2005), 33. From 5 February to 23 February 1944, on the southern front of the Burma campaign, in the Southeast Asian theatre of World War II, the Battle of the Admin Box took place. The fight is named after the 'administrative area' of

the 7th Division of the Indian Army, which served as Major-General Frank Messervy and his staff's temporary defensive position when their divisional headquarters was captured on 7 February.

50 Roy, *Arakan Fronte*, 66.

51 Roy, *Arakan Fronte*, 78.

52 Roy, *Arakan Fronte*, 87–91.

53 Roy, *Arakan Fronte*, 115–23.

54 John W. Dower, *War Without Mercy. Race and Power in the Pacific War* (London: Pantheon, 1987).

55 Tarak Barkawi, "Culture and Combat in the Colonies: The Indian Army in the Second World War," *Journal of Contemporary History* 41 no. 2(2006): 325–55.

# Storytelling and Poetry Performance in Ancient India and Thailand

*Srabanti Basu*

## Introduction

Oral literature plays an important role in human civilisations. Information, knowledge and wisdom were passed on from place to place and from generation to generation through verses and stories. They inculcated values in humans, discussed societal norms and guided people to handle social, economic and even political crises. At the same time, they entertained people as well. This paper will make a comparative study of the storytelling and poetry performance in ancient India and Thailand.

Both India and Thailand have old civilisations and a long oral tradition. Moreover, the Thai culture was influenced by India. This is why I have chosen these two countries as the area of my study. In this study, an attempt has been made to compare the practices of oral tradition in India and Thailand. It is to be noted that more emphasis has been placed on the way of presentation than the texts and their societal contexts or influence.

The oral art of passing on knowledge did not die down even after books came in. Most of the materials on which books were written did not last long and had to be copied afresh several times. Therefore, most of the contents were remembered, memorised and taken to others orally by storytellers. Stories were passed on to other civilisations through trade routes. The oral techniques retell stories over generations and countless revisions. A paradox is obvious to anyone interested in oral tradition. As discussed by Baker and Baker, the basic orality of language is permanent. However, it fossilises when it is written down. Till then it remains in a fluid state and changes its form.[1]

## Oral Tradition in Ancient India and Thailand: General Information

The oral tradition of India can be traced back to the Vedic period. The Vedas were recited. Listening was the only way of learning the knowledge of the Vedas. Though rich in poetic elements the verses of the Vedas were considered religious hymns and not 'poems', as they were recited only on religious occasions. The two epics, Ramayana and Mahabharata, and the Puranas played significant roles in oral literature and storytelling in India. There was a specific notation for reciting the Vedas but for the two epics and the Puranas there were no such instructions or practices.

Most of the ancient Thai poems were lost with the fall of the Ayutthaya dynasty in 1767. There is evidence which shows that Thai poetry dates back to the Sukhothai period (13$^{th}$ and 14$^{th}$ century) and flourished in the Ayutthaya period (14$^{th}$ to 18$^{th}$ century). After the fall of the Ayutthaya dynasty by the Burmese, the art of Thai poetry was revived by subsequent kings, especially Sunthom Phu (1786–1855). Considering the periods of composition of the Ramayana and Mahabharata, it can be stated that Thai poetry is relatively young compared to Indian poetry. In Thai poems, there are notations and the ups and downs of the voices are specified. The poems have to be recited following that pattern. In that way, the rendition of Thai poems is similar to the rendition of Vedic verses.

There are five types of Thai poems, Khlong being the oldest. There are three tones in the language, and they are marked in the text of Khlong poems. This is quite similar to the rendition of Vedic verses. It has been a common practice of the rendition of Thai poems long after the Vedic period (in the Sukhothai and Ayutthaya periods).[2]

## Texts for Storytelling

Indian storytellers mostly used the stories of the Ramayana and Mahabharata. In addition to that, parables, religious stories and stories of wisdom were common materials for storytelling sessions. *Panchatatra*, written by Bishnu Sharma in the third century BCE in a combination of verse and prose, was one of the most popular books for storytelling. The beginning of *Panchatantra* was that King Amarshakti had three sons who were not intelligent. The king failed to educate them in conventional ways and requested one of his ministers to take care of their education. The minister told them a story every day and asked them to interpret it. After one year, the boys gained knowledge; they also developed analytical and societal skills. The *Panchatantra* was so popular that by the early 11$^{th}$ century, it had reached Europe and by the 17$^{th}$ century, it had been translated into several European languages including Greek, Latin, Spanish, German and Saxon, to name a few. The stories were also popular in the Far East. There are 200 different versions in more than 50 languages of the tales of *Panchatantra*. The book shared some common stories with *Jataka*, stories of previous lives of Lord Buddha. Most of the stories were a combination of verses and prose. It is a collection of fables with humans and animals describing the wise ways to lead life and also to understand the statecraft.[3]

*Kathasaritsagara*, written by Somdev in the 11$^{th}$ century, was also popular. It contains 18 books with 124 chapters and 22,000 slokas (verses) and prose sections. The principal narrative is the adventure of Naravahanadatta, son of king Udayana; other tales are connected to the central narrative. The stories of the Panchatantra and Kathasaritsagara were a combination of prose and verses.[4]

In Thailand, Ramakien was one of the most popular texts for storytelling. It is the Thai version of the Ramayana. Thailand bears a great similarity to India in this respect. In Ramakien, some practices of animism and Buddhism were also reflected by the characters (unlike India's Ramayana). Both Hinduism and Buddhism influenced the texts of Thai folk stories. Jataka tales consist of a part of their folk stories. Other Thai folk stories have their origins in Thailand.

Some of the epic Thai poems need to be mentioned in this regard. *Thao Hung Thao Cheuang* is an epic poem written in the Thai language. Though it is not Thai and often Laos claims it, it is one of the oldest and most important epic poems of Thailand. It was passed down orally from generation to generation, eventually it was written down and only one surviving copy exists today. It is considered as important as the *Illiad* to the West and the Ramayana to India. It gives glimpses of the pre-Buddhist period with details of religious rites, rituals and praise of Gods. It also gives information about Thai migrations. *Yuan Phai* is another epic poem. It is one of few pieces of literature that survives from the early Ayutthaya period. *Mahachat Kham Luang*, translated as 'The Great Birth', is another Thai epic that tells the story of Siddhartha Gautama's life before he became enlightened as the Buddha. It was written in the 1490s, possibly by a team. The poem spans 13 books. Some books were destroyed during the Burmese invasion and were rewritten afterwards (in the 1800s). Therefore, there are several versions of the book. There are several sections which are written in Pali. All the old texts mentioned here were written much later than the Indian epics and the *Puranas*.[5]

## Storytellers of Ancient and Medieval India

The purpose of storytelling was to inculcate values and ethics in people and, at the same time, to entertain them. However, the duties of the storytellers were far more diverse and intricate. They were entertainers, genealogists, praise poets, announcers in the king's court and so on.

## *Bhats and Charanas*

Bhats and Charanas were two classes of bards in the northern part of ancient India. The Bhats were famous for creating and reciting poems at marriages and other social occasions. In the *Mahabharata*, there is a description of a group of bards, who marched in Yudhisthira's procession—right in front of him—during his journey from Kurukshetra to Hastinapur. The word Bhat originates from the Sanskrit word *Bhatta* meaning 'The Lord' or 'The Scholar'. The

Charanas did the same job as the Bhats. In addition, they went to battlefields with the kings to create battle poems describing the heroic deeds of the warriors. Charanas were distinguished for their laudatory discourse and praise poems of battlefield bravery, victory, royal generosity and sacrifice. Charanas had distinct literature on their praise poems of battle fields—*Bira-kavya.*[6]

## *Kathak*

The Indian dance form of kathak is believed to have originated in storytelling. The virtual stance and subtle gestural vocabulary of the dance are quite different from the other classical Indian dances, which originated from temple dances. The choreographic forms of kathak are so distinct that researchers searched for its origin through etymological rather than choreographic routes. The term 'kathak' originated from the word *kathaka*, meaning storytellers. According to researchers, the origin of the dance form lies in the art of storytelling and oral performance. There were *kathaka* communities in Vedic times that moved from village to village entertaining people with poetry, stories, music and dance.[7]

The word *kathaka* has been used in the Mahabharata several times. In the *Adiparva*, we get a sloka describing the associates of Arjuna on his departure to the forest. It states that Arjuna was accompanied by narrators of sacred stories, by devotees, by Brahmanas reciting celestial history while going to the forest.[8]

The profession of a kathaka was mentioned in literatures of a much later period. In *Kathasaritsagara*, there was one *Kathaka Sangataka,* who used to entertain King Sahasranika with long love stories. *Sangitaratnakara*, a text of the 13th century, mentioned the word along with music and dance for the first time. In the section 'The Seating Assembly', the book describes the seating positions of the scholars and entertainers in a king's court. It states that the storytellers, bards, scholars, flatterers, those 'clever in praising and /or clever in words of song' are to be seated on the king's left. Texts like *Ganapatha, Ganesha Purana, Amarakosa* and *Sabdakalpadruma* contain the word *kathaka*. It is clear from these sources that there were people in pre-Mughal India who told stories and were called *kathakas*. In *Sangitaratnakara*, there are descriptions of two desi (related to common people) dances, one of which had expressive gestures illustrating a poem or *Kavita.*[9] However, researchers think that *kathaka* was a common word to describe storytellers in general rather than specify a particular group of storytellers.[10] Apart from the professionals, there were people in villages and towns who had expertise in narrating stories and verses, who were the regular entertainers in their native places.[11]

## *Scroll Narrators*

Storytelling with scroll painting is one of the oldest practices in India. The profession of storytelling using a scroll was mentioned in Patanjali's *Mahabhashya* and in Vishakadatta's play *Mudrarakshasa*. In *Harshacharita*, Vana mentioned Yamapata, which is a single picture containing several scenes highlighting the picture of Yama, God of death. The narrator described with pictures, stories and verses the sufferings of hell and rewards of heaven. This form was practised all over India. The painter and the narrator carried his picture on a pole with his left hand and narrated it, pointing towards relevant portions during his performance.[12]

R.V. Russell mentioned a caste, Chitrakathi, belonging to Maharashtra in his book *Tribes and Castes in Central Provinces of India*. The name originated from the two words *chitra* (picture) and *katha* (story). The name indicates that the group were travelling storytellers who told stories with pictures. They used wooden puppets as well to enact the stories, sometimes with ventriloquism. However, storytelling with pictures was more common and popular than with the puppets. Stories were told with a series of pictures (*pothi*). Chitrakathi paintings are stylistically closely related to the shadow puppets of Karnataka, Andhra Pradesh and Kerala.[13] The puppeteers narrated the legends with dramatic visual presentation with the puppets. The puppets were made of leather, sometimes life-sized, and designed to give effective and dramatic shadows when moved from the outside. The shadow puppeteers of Karnataka and Andhra Pradesh, called Killekyatas and Killekothus respectively, speak corrupt Marathi which links their origin to Chitrakathis. Killekyatas' performances were accompanied by music and dance, and the narrators memorised songs and verses by heart.

The scroll painters of West Bengal, mostly known as Patua or Chitrakar, specialised in painting narrative scrolls, known as *patachitra* or *pata*. They painted a series of scenes of a story on a scroll and composed a song for each story they illustrated. They narrate the stories with songs, which they sang in a monotonous tone. The Patuas have been performing and plying their trades since the 13$^{th}$ century or even before. The word *patachitra* is mentioned in the *Puranas*, other ancient literature and ancient documents.[14]

Little information is available on the classes of storytellers or poetry recitalists in ancient Thailand.

## Forms of Storytelling

In India, stories were told in temples, during weddings and other social functions. The performance was either a one-person performance or in a group. There were several forms of storytelling in ancient and medieval India.

One form was *Pravachana* or *katha*. It consisted of discourses on religious stories and sacred texts usually narrating the life of a saint from an epic. It often involved professional storytellers who recited a text with music in places. People who heard *Pravachana* regularly were believed to be more tolerant and patient. The narrators were usually well-versed in different languages and were held in high respect in the society. The texts were not only narrated but also explained and judged from different angles. Stories from the *Ramayana*, *Mahabharata* or *Purana*s were popular texts.[15]

Another form was *Kathakalashepa*. Any tale (*katha*) narrated with music, dance and elements of acting (*kalaskhepa*) belonged to this category. Anecdotes were mostly narrated in this form. The narrator, who was usually a classical vocalist, interwove the main story with music, dance and digression. It was a way to make the literary texts reach the common people in a comprehensive and entertaining manner. The narrator had to have a good command over literature and theology. Most importantly, they had to possess an overall competence to project the subject through music, acting and spoken words.[16] The dance form kathak might have arrived from the form *kathakalakshepa.*[17]

The Ramakien is performed with dance, music and, sometimes, mask and shadow puppets.[18] The form, however, is more like a dance drama than poetry performance, and it is rightly categorised under the category of dance instead of poetry reading or poetry performance. However, it is similar to the Indian form *kathakalshepa*, which consists of poetry reading, music and dance. There is a possibility that the form *kathakalakshepa* gave birth to the kathak dance and eventually lost its identity as a form of storytelling. A similar possibility for Thailand cannot be ruled out. Thai storytelling or poetry rendition might have taken the shape of dance recital and is no longer classified as a form of storytelling. Texts of Thai stories are not very frequently available. How the stories of Ramakien were performed in ancient time is not well-documented. It is, therefore, difficult to state whether the present dance form of Ramakien has its origin in storytelling. Puppets and paintings are also used in some presentations of Ramakien. The use of shadow puppets in Ramakien reminds us of a similar practice by the storytellers of Karnataka.

The third form practised in India was folk narratives. Folk narratives were about kings and queens or brave persons, war heroes or clever animals. The stories were to preach values and ethics like not to tell lies, not to steal, not to be greedy and many others. Usually the locals narrated these stories; even in the households, mothers and grandmothers told these stories to children. Sometimes, these stories were accompanied by musical instruments. Folk stories were centred on common men, local kings and queens and local heroes. They had animals as characters. The folklore particularly flourished in kingdoms that followed Buddhism (like the Pala dynasty in Bengal). This is supported by the fact that those stories rarely contain the concept of Brahmins as a very high class of society, and common people held the centre stage of the story.[19,20]

Thai folklore include stories with mythologies and traditional beliefs by Thai people. They include stories from ancient kingdom, legends and ghosts. Many of the stories were originated from rural Thailand. Many of the Thai folklores had materials from Buddhism. This is similar to and at the same time, slightly different from India. In India, Buddhist philosophy influenced the contents and orientation of the folk stories. However, direct inclusion of Buddhism was not much evident. Animals were also important parts of Thai folklores as in India. In Thailand, there were stories based on geographic location and local practices. The story of *Doi Nang Non* or the story of the sleeping mountain can be stated as an example. Spirits or ghosts are generally known as phi and they are very important parts of Thai storytelling. There are concepts of spirit houses in Thai Buddhist temples and even some residences. The spirits are not drawn in figures in pictures; they exist only in the oral depiction of folklores. Thais used to narrate folk stories to instil beliefs, teach young generations the importance of following traditions and show respect to elders. Stories were told by elders. Even today, these stories are told in traditional festivals.[21,22] This is quite different from India. In India, stories with animals and common people were not told in traditional religious festivals. This may be because the Buddhism-based dynasties eventually gave way to Brahminism-based dynasties. So in traditional Indian festivals and celebrations, stories from the Puranas and other religious texts are recited instead of folklore.

## Conclusion

Thus, storytelling and poetry recitals were part of both Indian and Thai civilisations. Ancient India and Thailand had some similarities in this respect. Popular texts for storytelling in both the countries were similar. The Ramayana and the Jataka tales can be cited as examples. The dance recital of Ramakien might have originated from storytelling, as kathak has its origin in storytellers. Some forms of storytelling used paintings and puppets as props in both countries. Both places had storytellers, apart from professional entertainers, who told stories to the locals. Thai poems were marked with symbols for different tones for a long time, unlike India. In India, fixed notes were followed only for Vedic verses. Different forms of storytelling and different types of storytellers were mentioned in several Indian texts. Limited information is available in Thai literature and history in this regard. The purpose of the storytelling was the same in both countries. Stories were used not only to entertain people but also to inculcate values and ethics in the society.

## Endnotes

1 Rosalie Giachinno-Baker and Fredrick J. Baker referred to the books by E. Havelock and W. J. Ong, both published in 1982 in their article titled "Cultural Values in Thailand and Mexico: Oral Tradition, Folk Tales and Proverbs: East and West," archived in California State University.

2 Alexandra R. Kapur-Fic, *Thailand: Buddhism, Society and Women* (New Delhi: Abhinav Publications, 1998).

3 The cited books were the most common texts for the storytellers, as mentioned by Dhara Kothari in her article, "Travelling Bards or Ballads of India," https://www.academia.edu/4177758.

4 Kothari, "Travelling Bards or Ballads of India," https://www.academia.edu/4177758.

5 Margaret Walker, "Kathak Log Ya Kathak Nrtya: The Search for a Dance Called Kathak," *Journal of the Indian Musicological Society* 2009–2010: 168–90.

6 Kothari, "Travelling Bards or Ballads of India," https://www.academia.edu/4177758.

7 Walker, "Kathak Log Ya Kathak Nrtya: The Search for a Dance Called Kathak".

8 The original sloka is *kathakascapare rajan sramanasc banaukasah/divyakahani ye capi pathanti madhuram dvijah.*

9 In a text S*angitasamayasara* (1250 AD), five types of whirling movements (Bhramari) were described related to kathak. Another text, *Nrtyabali*, composed in the same period, also illustrated the whirling movements. Neither describes the dance forms as 'kathak', but various types of spin and footwork are central items of kathak and rendering of the poetic form 'kavita' is still a part of kathak dance.

10 Walker, "Kathak Log Ya Kathak Nrtya: The Search for a Dance Called Kathak".

11 In *Meghadutam* (The Cloud Messenger), Kalidasa mentioned them; he called them *kathakobid* (expert in storytelling). Their description came in context of describing Avanti. His sloka in this context reads *Prapyaavanti-udayana kathakobidaan gramabriddhaan*, which means 'there you will get old villagers, who are expert storytellers, narrating Udayana stories'.

12 Jeffery Snodgrass, "The Centre Cannot Gold: Tales of Hierarchy and Poetic Composition from Modern Rajasthan," *The Journal of the Royal Anthropological Institute* 10, no. 2(2005): 261–85.

13 Eva Ray, "Documentation for Paithan Paintings," *Artibus Asiae* 40, no. 4(1978): 239–82.

14 Sourabh Datta Gupta, "Village of Painters: A Visit to Naya, Pingala," *Chitralekha International Magazine on Art and Design* 1, no. 3(2011).

15 The forms may be classified with some other names. But the *katha/parvachana*, *kathakalahshepa* and folk narratives are mostly stated forms of presentation. This classification was stated by Dhara Kothari in her article "Travelling Bards or Ballads of India". It is also found in https://allgoodtales.com/storytelling-traditions-across-the-world-india/.

16 Kothari, "Travelling Bards or Ballads of India," https://www.academia.edu/4177758.

17 The evolution of katha and *kathakalakshepa* to kathak in Bengal and kathak in North India is the author's hypothesis.

18 Anuman Rajadhon, *Essays on Thai Folklores, Thai Inter-Religious Commission for Development & Sathirakoses* (Bangkok: Nagapradipa Foundation Bangkok, 1988).

19 Kothari, "Travelling Bards or Ballads of India," https://www.academia.edu/4177758.

20 Sandip Bandyopadhyay, *Katha Brittanta* (Dhansiri, 2006).

21 Rajadhon, *Essays on Thai Folklores, Thai Inter-Religious Commission for Development & Sathirakoses*

22 https://allgoodtales.com/storytelling-traditions-across-world-thailand/.

# Fast Fashion: The Sustainability Question for Asia

*Soumya Bhowmick*

## Introduction

The fashion industry is marked by the popular trend of fast fashion, which involves the production of low-cost clothing that imitate luxury fashion trends with a quick turnover rate. While providing clothes at accessible prices, the true cost of fast fashion is quite high, especially for Asian countries like Bangladesh, where the production part of the fast fashion industry is quite prominent. It includes negative environmental externalities; gendered labour issues and exploitation; and the intellectual property (IP) rights concerns that raise questions over the sustainability of the fast fashion trend. To be sure, this industry creates a variety of impediments to the UN Sustainable Development Goals (SDGs) and makes the achievement of these targets by 2030 even more difficult in the post-pandemic world. This paper explores the origin of the fast fashion trend and the various issues that arise and suggests possible paths for sustainable transformation in the industry.

## Perils of Fast Fashion

In the past decade, the world has undergone a tremendous shift and moved towards a fast-paced economy. This is reflected best in the technological advancements and policy decisions made, which indicate an underlying goal of improving the mechanisms by making it faster and more efficient. This trend has percolated to the functioning and sustainability of most industries, with the fashion industry being no different. The fashion industry broadly consists of four categories, namely textile, clothing, footwear and leather, which is characterised by fast market-driven changes and production that is dispersed across the world.

The fast fashion market is a USD 91.23 billion-dollar industry, as of 2021, and by the end of 2028 is expected to become a USD 197.05 billion-dollar industry with a CAGR of 8.5 percent.[1] The concept of fast fashion is to consume the product in the market and soon get rid of it, and this is a never-ending cycle. Garments move quickly from runways to the store, so the consumer can keep up with trends at an affordable price. Clothes are essentially treated as a disposable commodity, used, and discarded. This issue has been brought to light because of the globalisation of fashion supply chains and the scant attention that is being given to life-cycle sustainability issues in the industry.[2] The increasing growth in the supply and demand of clothing and footwear is driven by the rising wealth and consumption in developing countries. By expediting the rate at which new collections are designed and produced, fast fashion makes the repairing of clothes unnecessary, uneconomical and impossible.[3] Garments that have barely been used are either accumulated or thrown away. It is estimated that the average person currently buys 60 percent more clothing as compared to the year 2000, but the clothes are kept for only half the duration.[4]

The concept of fast fashion can trace its history to the early 1980s when globally famous fashion company Zara opened its first United States of America (US) store in 1989 and pioneered the fast fashion model to increase its business.[5] Several European and American countries leapt at the opportunity to outsource production at low costs to countries in Asia, empowering the fast fashion model. This led to the separation of the consumer and producer countries and helped conceal actors in the workforce, since they were nested in subcontractor relationships. Thus, sustainable, environmental and social impacts were not made prominent to the retailer. Total fibre production too increased, doubling from what it was in 2000. In 1995, 7.6 kg fibre/person was produced, which is expected to reach 17.5kg/person by 2030.[6] The garment trade and the fast fashion industry has played a vital role in the developing countries of Asia. Around 80 percent of Bangladesh's foreign earnings are generated from this industry.[7] However, while this is helping in the economic progress of Indo-Pacific countries, the negative impacts of the industry are massive. The volume of the products demanded are colossal which puts pressure on the manufacturers, which in turn impacts the workers as well as their families. The rising competition to source the cheapest products possible increases the pressure on the workers, making working conditions even harsher.

On the contrary, it is also worth noting that it is neither the American consumers nor the producers that are facing the direct consequences and risks associated with an industry dominated by the culture of fast fashion.[9] The primary risks of the fast fashion culture are borne out of the profit-driven agenda of the brands, which has led to manifold issues. Textile manufacturing has been shifting from China to South Asian and Southeast Asian countries like Bangladesh and Vietnam due to a combination of factors such as low wages, availability of land and availability of raw materials in the form of cotton, jute and silk.[10] Bangladesh has become the largest supplier for fashion brands. Child labour in countries such as Uzbekistan, El Salvador and Bangladesh are rampant, with increasing pressure to produce massive quantities of products.

There have been multiple labour law and human rights violations by these mega-conglomerates in underdeveloped and developing countries, especially in South Asia (India, Bangladesh) and Southeast Asia (Cambodia, Vietnam),

**Table 1: Major Global Apparel Manufacturers and Retailers**

| Sr. No | Name of Company | Country | Fiscal Year | Sales (in USD billion) |
|---|---|---|---|---|
| 1 | Inditex (Zara) | Spain | January 2022 | 31.10 |
| 2 | Hennes& Mauritz (H&M) | Sweden | November 2021 | 20.83 |
| 3 | Gap | USA | January 2022 | 16.67 |
| 4 | PVH (Calvin Klein, Tommy Hilfiger) | USA | January 2022 | 9.15 |
| 5 | NEXT | UK | January 2022 | 6.19 |
| 6 | American Eagle Outfitters | USA | January 2022 | 5.01 |
| 7 | Ralph Lauren | USA | March 2021 | 4.4 |
| 8 | Abercrombie & Fitch | USA | January 2022 | 3.71 |
| 9 | Esprit | Hong Kong | June 2021 | 1.06 |
| 10 | Uniqlo | Japan | August 2021 | 18.45 |

*Source: Authors own, data from Fast Retailing*[8]

where factories have been set up to meet increasing demand by way of cheap labour. The labour is gendered, and women are forced to work in harsh conditions for long hours, endangering their life. They experience verbal abuse, physical abuse and sexual harassment from which they have little or no protection legally. For instance, a report by Human Rights Watch highlights various cases of female workers experiencing physical and verbal abuse at workplaces, with minimal recourse to legal protection. Several female sewing operators often report intense pressure to complete orders, failure of which leads to significant reductions in salaries and unwarranted attendance than what is true.[11] Similarly, the India Committee of Netherlands (ICN) report highlights that the Sumangali scheme in Tamil Nadu, India, has been a subject of criticism for employing women in deplorable conditions, often under strict supervision and without safety measures for long hours.[12] Second, there have also been concerns about the IP rights and creative freedom of the designers working in the industry, with an emerging trend of products being plagiarised noted recently.[13] Third, the methodology adopted to produce these products has also raised alarming concerns regarding the environmental impact associated with it. Fourth, all these concerns along with the cost-benefit analysis also highlights issues regarding the sustainability of the industry from a financial standpoint, especially after the Covid-19 pandemic.

The concerns related to the fast fashion industry have dire implications on the UN SDG framework. The labour law and human rights issues are linked to SDG 1 (No Poverty), SDG 3 (Good Health and Well-Being), SDG 5 (Gender Equality) and SDG 8 (Decent Work and Economic Growth). The environmental impact is linked to SDG 12 (Responsible Consumption and Production), SDG 13 (Climate Action), SDG 14 (Life Below Water) and SDG 15 (Life on Land). The IP issues are linked to SDG 9 (Industry, Innovation, and Infrastructure). Thus, there is an overarching problem of sustainability that is associated with the fast fashion industry.

The sustainability aspect assumes greater importance in the context of the Covid-19 pandemic that has disrupted the industry. The falling demand, build-up of inventory with retailers and factories and the inability of most buyers to shop due to lockdown-related restrictions created severe cash flow problems for the industry. Although the low demand and subsequent reduction in industrial activity reduced the environmental footprint associated with the industry, it was short-lived and not a sustainable outcome. While the concept of sustainable fashion has become an emerging concept in contemporary times, the fast fashion industry has not been negatively impacted and continues to operate on a large scale. Initially, fast fashion brands faced numerous challenges, including store closures, supply-chain disruptions and changing consumer behaviour. However, these brands responded adeptly to the change by effectively leveraging digital technologies to extend their online presence. This resulted in alterations, leading to higher penetration in the market. For instance, Shein recorded a growth in its market share in the US due to booming digital adoption rates, leading to higher online sales during the pandemic. Presently, it is the second-most popular website among the Gen Zs in the US.[14]

## Sustainability in the Fashion Industry

The underlying effect of globalisation in the past decade has been the integration of global markets and trends which has hugely impacted the production process. This can be attributed to the continuous changes in the market brought forth by a shift towards liberalisation, privatisation, flexibility in policies and global competitiveness. Ever since the 1980s, when globalisation started to have an overarching effect on economies, consumers were introduced to transnational corporations, cyber technology and social media, thereby opening a new clothing market with a massive demand for fashionable and trendy clothes.[15] These changes have affected the way fashion is produced, marketed, perceived and worn. Fast fashion, thus, invariably places an emphasis on inexpensive manufacturing and allowing retailers to sell current fashion trends at a low price in an efficient manner.[16] This, however, has several negative implications, acting as a major obstacle in achieving the SDG Agenda 2030.

## *Labour Issues*

There are certain essential consequences of the revolution in the industry which are ignored often, with luxury brands unable to keep up with fast fashion retailers. Economically speaking, fast fashion has majorly impacted the production process, exports and manufacturing in the fashion industry. To keep up with the changing times, fashion houses have moved production to factories with lower wages and cheap, plentiful labour.[17] The introduction of fast fashion has been successful in satiating consumers' constantly changing desires in the industrialised world of luxury fashion. Yet, it comes at a terrible cost of unpaid, maltreated workers who are exploited in these factories. Systemic discrimination also plays a huge role in making it easier for fast fashion retailers to manufacture clothes.[18] Fast fashion retailers depend on the cheap labour provided by developing countries such as Bangladesh, Indonesia and India to manufacture fast and simultaneously keep costs low. This makes underdeveloped and developing countries the target due to their growing informal sector, lack of regulation and cheap labour provided mostly by women. For instance, there have been several cases of exploitation, particularly among female migrant workers. The age of globalisation has led to international brands like H&M, Levis, Benetton, and Gap Inc. benefitting from cheap labour and oppressive worker conditions in China, Myanmar and Bangladesh.[19] Moreover, the International Labour Organisation has identified several indicators of forced labour in the Indian fast fashion industry dominated by a few multinational corporations that often dictate the terms of trade, leading to oppressive worker conditions and unfair wage practices.[20]

It is also estimated that more than 70 percent of garment workers in China, 85 percent workers in Bangladesh and 90 percent of the garment workers in Cambodia are women.[21] The consequences of the same can be seen with the increasing demand brought on by fast fashion, which has led to sweatshops having grown immensely in size and number.[22] The soaring number of individuals employed by the industry is supporting the SDG 1 goal, eradicating poverty. However, clothes are being oversupplied, directly impacting the achievement of SDG 12, responsible consumption and production and SDG 13, climate action. SDG 12 commits to ensuring sustainable consumption and production patterns, which can be met by the mindfulness of not only the producers, but also the consumers of fast fashion. Overproduction in the industry subsequently leads to 85 percent of the waste being disposed in the US, and it is globally estimated that 92 million tonnes of waste is created every year.[23] Additionally, due to globalisation, manufacturing can now be outsourced more easily to these terrible sweatshops and to informal sectors in developing countries.[24] Moreover, all these factories are extremely unsafe; the workers are subjected to harmful chemicals, poor working conditions and abuse from managers. The unregulated informal economy and subcontracting allows for employers to trap workers into working longer hours for lower wages on top of not having insurance and other forms of social securities.[25] It is estimated that many workers are working between 60 to 140 hours of overtime per week and often cheated out of overtime pay.[26] Women workers are more susceptible to exploitation of this manner due to systemic discrimination bolstered through social norms entangled in patriarchal structures, and the fashion industry takes advantage of this daily.

## *Intellectual Property Rights*

The practices of the global chains had underlying repercussions in form of pre-made designs stitched from cheap and hazardous material. While countries like France provide extremely strong copyright protections, the situation in the US is completely the opposite, with lax copyright laws that offer minimal protections.[27] Most of the clothes in these fast fashion stores are therefore copies of runway designs from around the world. Forever 21 and H&M, for example, have been described as prototypes of retailers using a major designer's works while tweaking the finer details.[28] This practice is not even illegal, as the scope of copyright claim is limited to logos and specific prints and does not extend to designs. Popular retail chains like Forever 21 have been sued and have settled over fifty claims for stealing prints and designs from renowned designers.[29] The practice is still prevalent due to the realisation by the company that it can gain more from the production and sale of copied designs than it loses in court as compensation.[30] There was a time fashion was looked upon an as an art, but the stealing of designs and the bulk production at the cost of quality has changed the very character of this industry in recent times. Today, the fashion industry runs on revenue, and economics is the main reason the industry relies on trends like fast fashion to persist despite the horrible social deterioration.

## *Environmental Problems*

The costs of fast fashion are sometimes not just limited to such oppression and discrimination but are impacting the environment as well. Most factories and practices therein set up by brands are considered environmentally hazardous, which makes it one of the most polluting industries in the world. Traditionally, the fashion industry is a business involving long supply chains of production, raw material, textiles manufacture, shipping, retail and use and ultimately disposal of garments.[31] There are a variety of pollutants involved in each stage of production, such as pesticides used in cotton farming, toxic dyes and the gross amounts of environmental waste generated by the disposal of clothing. It is estimated that nearly half a million tonnes of microfibre are dumped into the ocean every year which is equivalent to 3 million tonnes of oil barrels.[32] Toxic chemicals are used in the entire process of manufacturing. In China, river pollution due to the manufacturing of textiles has become so normal, that it led to the saying, 'If you want to know what colour is fashionable this season, just look at the river'.[33]

Additionally, natural resources are being exploited in large numbers by the industry, such as water used in the harvesting, manufacturing and shipping processes. The fashion industry is the second largest consumer of the world's water supply.[34] An estimated 93 billion $m^3$ water is consumed by the industry every year, which can meet the needs of 5 million people.[35] Moreover, due to globalisation, clothes travel halfway across the world in container ships fuelled by the dirtiest of fossil fuels. China and India, the largest producers of cotton, which is vastly used in the fast fashion industry, are facing high levels of water stress.[36] Thus, SDG 6 (clean water and sanitation) is being severely impaired. It is estimated that the fashion industry produces about 1.2 billion tonnes of carbon emissions every year.[37] Textile production in massive quantities is leading to greenhouse emissions, compromising the climate action goal, SDG 13.[38] It can be concluded that the ever-changing trend of fast fashion and the exorbitant demands for quick and cheap clothes have an unimaginable impact on the environment.

## *Covid-19 Pandemic-induced Factors*

When the Covid-19 pandemic disrupted the world, a ray of hope towards a more sustainable production path was seen. With the fashion industry being impacted severely due to the plummet in demand for garments worldwide, there was speculation about the industry becoming more sustainable in nature. The lockdown led to individuals decluttering their wardrobes and getting rid of non-essentials. Thrifting and donating became a prominent practice during this time. This led to a massive build-up of inventory in stores and warehouses. Spending on apparel and the frequency of shopping decreased in the pandemic years. This was due to the reduction of disposable income as well as factors such as physical stores being shut.[39] Research suggests that the pandemic contributed to a change in the meanings that consumers would attribute to fashion consumption. What was earlier viewed as essential soon became 'non-essential' for many consumers. Consumers became more mindful of the adverse social and environmental impacts of fast fashion. Furthermore, the pandemic resulted in worsening labour conditions as factories shut with decreased demand. The slowdown and shift in the fashion industry also temporarily reduced IP rights violations but posed new challenges—such as digital transformation—as brands shifted to new forms of design dissemination and virtual platforms.[40] However, these changes are likely to be short-lived and are not the answer to a sustainable fashion industry.

## Case Study: RMG Sector in Bangladesh

The exploitative practices in the fashion industry can also be pinned down to the chasm created between the global North and South. The global North's hegemony over soft power politics and resources in the international sphere allows it to exploit these communities based on its whims and fancies. Predominantly, the consumers in the global North indulge in rapid consumption of clothing, which has a multi-fold knock-on effect linked to it. First, a large amount of investment is necessary for the growth of these countries, which can only happen on implementing relaxed regulations to allure brands to invest. Second, the global South has a large amount of human capital which is suffering from poverty and unemployment that can get tackled by these investments.[41] Countries in the global South are thus often left to make the difficult decision of either accepting lower environmental standards as compared to the global North or facing the prospect of flight of multinational corporations.

In April 2013, a garment factory complex in Bangladesh called the Rana Plaza collapsed, killing more than 1100 workers, mostly young women, and injuring 2500 individuals.[42] The tragic incident was one of the most horrific accidents in the history of the apparel industry. The collapse brought attention to the responsibility of multinational clothing brands to protect the rights of their workers in supply chains. The compensation envisaged as per the labour code was low and in the form of lump sum pay-outs which do not protect the beneficiaries from medium- and long-term shocks. However, no compensation was paid to the victims considering the labour code provisions on employer liability. A few global and local buyers made payments to the victims; however, this was on a voluntary basis.[43] The incident at the Rana Plaza brought to light the failures and oppression rampant in the garment sector that have boosted Bangladesh's economic growth over the past few decades.

The readymade garment sector (RMG) in Bangladesh achieved exports worth USD 42.6 billion in 2022, targeting USD 50 billion by 2025, and USD 100 billion by 2030.[44] It is important to note that the young women workers have contributed majorly to this sector's success. Nearly 85 percent of garment workers in Bangladesh are women. However, despite the horrors of the Rana Plaza incident, nearly 109 accidents have taken place since then, which have injured 491 workers and cost the lives of 27 workers.[45] This indicates that the lessons from the disaster have not been learnt. The country ranked 132$^{nd}$ out of 180 countries in the

2019 Global Sustainable Competitiveness Index, highlighting that sustainability remains an unaddressed concern in the country.[46]

The recent Covid-19 pandemic has led to severe disruptions in the Bangladeshi garment industry. Orders worth USD 3.18 billion have been cancelled and nearly 179 factories have shut down since March 2020, with several others on the verge of shutdown.[47] It is interesting to highlight that a large portion of the supply chain in Bangladesh consists of factories, that despite not maintaining any direct links with foreign brands, produce garments for such companies. This is done through a system of outsourcing, which is basically subcontracting without any transparency.[48] This sort of subcontracting and informal employment has allowed Bangladesh to become the second largest garment-producing country in the world and a high in-demand destination for the low-cost production of clothing.

**Figure 1: RMG Employment Trends in Bangladesh (in million)**

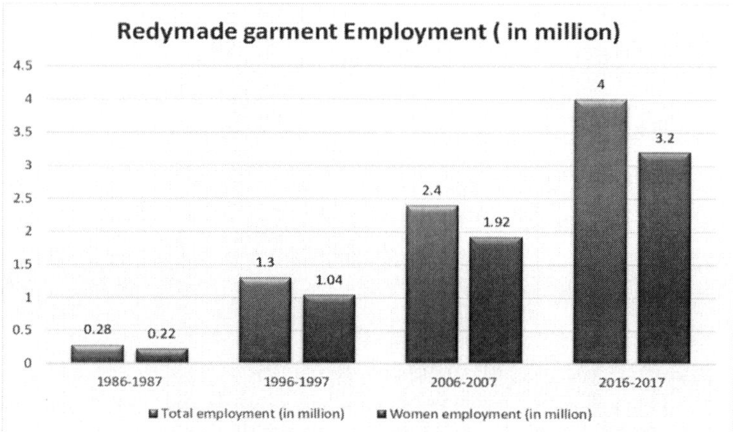


*Source: Mamun (2018), data from Bangladesh Garment*

*Manufacturers and Exporters Association (BGMEA)*[49]

The unfortunate reality of this industry, however, is that Western brands are attracted to Bangladesh because of the country's exceptionally low prices which make the business all the riskier for the workers. Despite Bangladesh's poor infrastructure and capital, the developing country became the go-to destination for the big foreign fashion industries. This is because when Bangladesh gained independence after the Bangladesh Liberation War in 1971, the country's new government encouraged private enterprise and foreign investment. The global export-quota system exempted Bangladesh from restrictions on sales to Europe and US and this, therefore, made it an ideal location for opening factories. It was Bangladesh's low-wage and low-price approach to manufacturing that attracted global apparel industries who in turn were looking for cheap and plentiful labour. Bangladesh has one of the lowest wages after Myanmar in the region.

In the 1990s, Bangladesh joined in on the consumer trend of fast fashion, thereby, adding massive pressures on the suppliers of big Western brands in Bangladesh. The situation in Bangladesh has worsened considerably due to the absence of a well-functioning labour inspection system and adequate enforcement mechanisms, and the conditions of the workers are even more deplorable. Despite securing a 77 percent wage increase in 2013, the monthly salary of a garment worker (5,800 taka) is far below the income (8,900 taka) needed to meet basic needs.[50] Moreover, the amount of environmental waste generated by the garment industry has increased immensely. However, Bangladesh is only part of a larger problem in the global fashion network. The tonnes of textile waste, non-recyclable clothes as well as plastic waste generated in developed countries are sent to developing countries like Bangladesh. The case in Bangladesh then highlights the hegemonic structures that maintain the gendered and economic discrimination of women and developing countries by men and dominant states. Therefore, the catastrophic collapse of the Rana Plaza and the loss of so many lives make visible the terrible systemic impacts of fast fashion and the new fashion industry.

## Legal Recourse and the Way Forward

The primary reason for exploitation and discrimination in underdeveloped and developing countries, mostly in South and Southeast Asia, is due to relaxed regulations and enforcement of law. This course of action is taken by governments to attract investments as well as revenue in the country. On the contrary, with the current global pandemic highlighting the gaping hole in dealing with concerns regarding environmental, labour and health law, it is imperative for states to enforce a strong mechanism to ensure compliance with practice sustainable for the industry. The issue lies in the fact that if brands aim to eradicate labour exploitation, they must take more control of their supply chains, which opens them up to risk in terms of legal liability. Currently, consumer and labour laws are implemented in certain countries, yet brands are rarely liable when a supplier or subsidiary in their chain commits an error. To implement any form of real change in the global fashion industry, the host countries where the companies are set up need to reconsider their legal policies. The existing liability rules need to be amended to incentivise the companies to have an approach which entails direct involvement in labour issues in their chains.[51]

In the international legal framework, recently there has been a shift by World Trade Organisation (WTO) to treat environmental and labour concerns in parity with the ones relating to trade. There is a need to bring in enforcement mechanisms by way of trade policies and regulations which can be applied unilaterally. Even the Investor State Dispute Settlement (ISDS) prioritised the health concerns of citizens while ruling against multi-billion-dollar corporations like

Philip Morris in a dispute.[52] Under the International Labour Organisation (ILO), gender-based violence is categorised as violence directed towards women because they are women, violent acts that disproportionately impact women, violent acts that disproportionately impact women or both. Most of the workers in the fashion industry are woman who are under the supervision of male dominant management, which results in a hierarchical power structure.[53] The inherent characteristic of fast fashion to create new trends to consume and set ambitious production targets puts women workers at risk of severe physical, emotional and sexual abuse. One of the biggest issues is the weak enforcement of international obligations that allow brands to violate the norms rather than abiding by them. In spite of the concerns, organisations like the WTO and ILO have already committed towards implementing a sustainable growth by following the SDGs, which may have a positive impact on society if enforced at large.

The difficulties in addressing IP rights issues arise due to the inconsistences in the IP rights laws of various jurisdictions. While some jurisdictions have become desirable arenas to enforce rights, others are lagging, thereby creating a gap that can be exploited. Design patents are being used by several countries to tackle issues related to copying. Jurisdictions like the European Union (EU) and Japan have laws that protect designs. While the EU law protects registered and unregistered designs, the Japanese law protects only registered designs.[54] Such ideas can be explored by countries at various trade and IP right law forums to ensure that effective legal recourse exists to prosecute firms guilty of copying.

The environmental impact of the highly polluting fast fashion industry can be limited by strengthening domestic environmental laws. Laws can also enforce ideas such as taxing new clothes. The British Environmental Audit Committee comprising Members of Parliament proposed a 1-penny charge on every new clothing to fund better collection and recycling of clothes.[55] Laws can also help reduce the imprint of non-biodegradable fibres like polyester by mandating companies slowly phase out the use of the material.

The tragic Rana Plaza collapse in Bangladesh created awareness about the dangers of the fast fashion industry, especially for the manufacturing nations in Asia, and led to the birth of the fashion revolution. This non-profit global movement, with teams in over one hundred countries around the world, campaigns for systemic reform of the fashion industry with a focus on the need for greater transparency in the fashion supply chain.[56] The fashion revolution started the #whomademyclothes campaign, posing this question to big brands and demanding transparency in the fashion supply chains. This campaign is urging masses to think about the people behind their clothes, how much they're paid and what their lives are like. At the same time, there are quite a few examples where women do voluntarily choose employment opportunities under the umbrella of subcontracted labour due to the flexibility of this work, relaxed eligibility criteria and, in some cases, better wages over their current state. In this sense, informal work and subcontracted labour have led to the formation of a vicious cycle, only making it more complex to tap into the root of the problem. Globalisation today is a double-edged sword for women, who see it as liberating and exploitative at the same time.

## Conclusion

The fashion revolution has thus created awareness about unsustainable fast fashion and paved the way for more transparency in the fashion industry. One of the major dilemmas here is that, given all the dangers of fast fashion, it is difficult to shift consumer trends to more sustainable forms of fashion unless such sustainable clothing is offered and sold at lower prices in a clean and just way. The Covid-19 pandemic has aggravated the challenges by disrupting global supply chains, reducing demand, contributing to factories being shut and workers being laid off who are forced to migrate. The overall unemployment reduces the purchasing power of the people, thus self- perpetuating the gloom in the industry by reducing the demand for clothes. There is, thus, a demand–supply challenge. A lot is at stake here from intellectual rights that can clean the environment to human rights. The concept of sustainable fashion is not yet normalised in the production systems, and so the cost of production is very high, making such commodities expensive. For policies, we need subsidies and most importantly, institutional changes in the market for sustainable fashion, which make the prices viable and regards the purchasing power of the global population.

Additionally, fast fashion has widened the consumer market for fashion and has created a sort of equality in the sense that it has made luxury fashion and popular trends more accessible to the masses. To add to that, even though environmental pollution and concerns have created a slight shift towards more sustainable commodities, companies that are promoting such commodities are capitalising on sustainability itself and making it yet another fashion trend. Often, environmentally friendly/conscious clothes have begun costing more than their regular, not environmentally friendly, counterpart. This toxic way of monetising the eco-friendly products only pushes people away from making sustainable choices. IP rights have a key role to play.

If given a strong rights framework, companies and designers can innovate without fear of their designs being cheaply imitated and can thus help develop sustainable fabrics. The patent designs can then be licenced to other companies, allowing for greater sustainability in prices. Therefore, it is difficult to tackle this issue of fast fashion unless fashion companies can not only produce sustainable clothing, but also do so at sustainable prices. To bring about sustainability in the industry, the SDGs can serve as the framework that can be used to build upon by the industry. The fast fashion industry must actively seek to partner with governments and civil society organisations to achieve the SDGs, which can provide the roadmap towards a sustainable industry.

## Endnotes

1 "Fast Fashion Global Market Report," *Research and Markets*. https://www.researchandmarkets.com/reports/5939667/fast-fashion-global-market-report.

2 Greg Peters, Mengyu Li and Manfred Lenzen, "The Need to Decelerate Fast Fashion in a Hot Climate - A Global Sustainability Perspective on the Garment Industry," *Journal of Cleaner Production*, 2021. https://www.sciencedirect.com/science/article/pii/S0959652621006107

3 Peters, Li and Lenzen, "The Need to Decelerate Fast Fashion in a Hot Climate - A Global Sustainability Perspective on the Garment Industry".

4 Natalie Huet, "Could the Coronavirus Crisis Spell the End of Fast Fashion?" 2022, https://www.euronews.com/2020/04/22/could-the-coronavirus-crisis-spell-the-end-of-fast-fashion

5 Victoria Ledezma, "Globalisation and Fashion: Too Fast, Too Furious," *Laurier Undergraduate Journal of the Arts,* 2017. https://scholars.wlu.ca/cgi/viewcontent.cgi?referer=https://www.google.com/&httpsredir=1&article=1052&context=luja

6 "Worldwide Production Volume of Textile Fibers Since 1975," *Statista.* https://www.statista.com/statistics/263154/worldwide-production-volume-of-textile-fibers-since-1975/#:~:text=Global%20fiber%20production%20is%20expected%20to%20reach%20149,to%2014%20kilograms%20per%20person%20a%20decade%20earlier.

7 Kyla Ryan, "Cheap and Trendy Fashion Comes at a Price," *The Diplomat*, 2015, https://thediplomat.com/2015/05/cheap-and-trendy-fashion-comes-at-a-price/

8 "Industry Ranking: Major Global Apparel and Retailer," *Fast Retailing*, 2022, https://www.fastretailing.com/eng/ir/

direction/position.html

9 Terry Nguyen, "Fast Fashion, Explained," *Vox*, 2020, https://www.vox.com/the-goods/2020/2/3/21080364/fast-fashion-h-and-m-zara

10 "Battle for the Textile and Apparel Industry in Southeast Asia," *Televisory*, 2017, https://www.televisory.com/blogs/-/blogs/battle-for-the-textile-and-apparel-industry-in-southeast-asia

11 Human Rights Watch, "Whoever Raises Their Head Suffers Most: Workers' Rights in Bangladesh's Garment," 2015. https://www.hrw.org/report/2015/04/22/whoever-raises-their-head-suffers-most/workers-rights-bangladeshs-garment.

12 India Committee of the Netherlands, "Captured by Cotton". https://www.indianet.nl/pdf/CapturedByCotton.pdf.

13 Justine Pila, "Challenges of Fast Fashion in the Garment Industry,"*Journal of Intellectual Property Law & Practice*,2023. https://academic.oup.com/jiplp/article/18/1/42/6974661.

14 McKinsey & Company, "What is Fast Fashion?" https://www.mckinsey.com/featured-insights/mckinsey-explainers/what-is-fast-fashion.

15 Victoria Ledezma. "Globalisation and Fashion: Too Fast, Too Furious," *Laurier Undergraduate Journal of the Art,* October, 2017, https://scholars.wlu.ca/cgi/viewcontent.cgi?referer=https://www.google.com/&httpsredir=1&article=1052&context=luja

16 Ledezma, "Globalisation and Fashion: Too Fast, Too Furious". https://scholars.wlu.ca/cgi/viewcontent.cgi?referer=https://www.google.com/&httpsredir=1&article=1052&context=luja

17 Ledezma, "Globalisation and Fashion: Too Fast, Too Furious". https://scholars.wlu.ca/cgi/viewcontent.cgi?referer=https://www.google.com/&httpsredir=1&article=1052&context=luja

18 "The Impact of Fast Fashion on Garment Workers," *Good On You.* https://goodonyou.eco/impact-fast-fashion-garment-workers.

19 "Modern Slavery in Fast Fashion Brands," *Fashion Law*

*Journal.* https://fashionlawjournal.com/modern-slavery-in-fast-fashion-brands.

20 "Fast Fashion in India," *Unsustainable Magazine.* https://www.unsustainablemagazine.com/fast-fashion-in-india.

21 Emile Schultze, "Exploitation or Emancipation? Women Workers in the Garment Industry," *Fashion Revolution* 2015. https://www.fashionrevolution.org/exploitation-or-emancipation-women-workers-in-the-garment-industry/

22 Ledezma, "Globalisation and Fashion: Too Fast, Too Furious". https://scholars.wlu.ca/cgi/viewcontent.cgi?referer=https://www.google.com/&httpsredir=1&article=1052&context=luja

23 Alex Kim, "The Dangerous Beauty of Fast Fashion," *100 K Deeds Challenge,* 2021. https://100kdeeds.org/the-dangerous-beauty-of-fast-fashion/

24 Robert J. S. Ross, "Slaves to Fashion: Poverty and Abuse in the New Sweatshops," University of Michigan Press, 2004, https://www.jstor.org/stable/10.3998/mpub.15439

25 GWU International Law and Policy Brief, "Fast Fashion Getting Faster: A Look at the Unethical Labor Practices Sustaining a Growing Industry," 2021, https://studentbriefs.law.gwu.edu/ilpb/2021/10/28/fast-fashion-getting-faster-a-look-at-the-unethical-labor-practices-sustaining-a-growing-industry.

26 Schultze, "Exploitation or Emancipation? Women Workers in the Garment Industry".

27 J. Donoian and M. Wallach, "Fast Fashion and IP Regulation: Will Fast Fashion Kill the Golden Goose?" *McCarter & English LLP*, 2018, https://www.lexology.com/library/detail.aspx?g=2b1efd99-6f50-486f-aec2-fa9569bc9102

28 "The Rise and Fall of Fast Fashion Purveyor Forever 21," *Business of Business.* https://www.businessofbusiness.com/articles/the-rise-and-fall-of-fast-fashion-purveyor-forever-21.

29 Cally Russell, "What Went Wrong with Forever 21?" *Forbes*, 2019. https://www.forbes.com/sites/callyrussell/2019/08/30/what-went1-wrong-with-forever-21.

30 Donoian and Wallach, "Fast Fashion and IP Regulation: Will Fast Fashion Kill the Golden Goose?"

31 Lydia Noyes, "Fast Fashion 101: Everything You Need to Know," *EcoWatch*, 2022. https://www.ecowatch.com/fast-fashion-guide-2655084121.html

32 "Sustainable Fashion Blueprint 2018," University of Cambridge Judge Business School, 2018. http://www.technofashionworld.com/files/2018/07/Mamoq-Sustainable-Fashion-Blueprint-2018.pdf

33 Sophie Bauer, "Fast Fashion: A Passing Trend?" *Eco Business,* 2019. https://www.eco-business.com/news/fast-fashion-a-passing-trend/

34 Yasaman Yousefi, "Environmental and Social Impacts of Fast Fashion," *SDW Watch,* 2020. https://sdwatch.eu/2020/02/environmental-and-social-impacts-of-fast-fashion/

35 United Nations, "UN Warns of Environmental Impact of Fast Fashion," 2019. https://news.un.org/en/story/2019/03/1035161#:~:text=According%20to%20UNCTAD%2C%20some%2093%20billion%20cubic%20metres,now%20being%20dumped%20into%20the%20ocean%20every%20year.

36 Yousefi, "Environmental and Social Impacts of Fast Fashion".

37 "Sustainable Fashion Blueprint 2018," University of Cambridge Judge Business School.

38 "Fashion and the SDGs: What Role for the UN?" *UNECE*, 2018. https://unece.org/DAM/RCM_Website/RFSD_2018_Side_event_sustainable_fashion.pdf

39 Katia Vladimirova, Claudia E. Henninger, et al. "Fashion Consumption during COVID-19: Comparative Analysis of Changing Acquisition Practices Across Nine Countries and Implications for Sustainability," *Cleaner and Responsible Consumption,* 2022. https://www.sciencedirect.com/science/article/pii/S2666784322000109

40 IMD Business School, "The Future of the Fashion Industry in a Post-COVID-19 World". https://www.imd.org/research-

knowledge/strategy/case-studies/the-future-of-the-fashion-industry-in-a-post-covid-19-world.

41 D. Wells, "Local Worker Struggles in the Global South: Reconsidering Northern Impacts on International Labor Standards," *Third World Quarterly* 30 no. 3(2009), 567–79. https://journals.sagepub.com/doi/abs/10.1177/1056492619846408

42 P. Barrett, D. Baumann-Pauly, A. GU, "Five years after Rana Plaza: The Way Forward," *NYU Center for Business and Human Rights*, 2018. https://static1.squarespace.com/static/547df270e4b0ba184dfc490e/t/5ac9514eaa4a998f3f30ae13/1523143088805/NYU+Bangladesh+Rana+Plaza+Report.pdf

43 "UN Partnership on the Sustainable Fashion and the SDGs," *International Labour Organization,* 2018. https://www.ilo.org/newyork/news/WCMS_634927/lang--en/index.htm

44 PwC, "What Next for the RMG Sector?" 2023. https://www.pwc.com/bd/en/assets/pdfs/research-insights/2023/27504_WhatNextForRMGSector_WCAG-Final.pdf.

45 "UN Partnership on the Sustainable Fashion and the SDGs".

46 Mohammad Ali, "Bangladesh up 21 Notches in Global Sustainable Competitiveness Index," *The Business Standard*, 2019. https://www.tbsnews.net/economy/bangladesh-21-notches-global-sustainable-competitiveness-index

47 Andreas Becker, "Coronavirus Disruptions Deal Severe Blow to Bangladesh's Garment Industry," *Deustsche Welle*, 2020. https://www.dw.com/en/coronavirus-disruptions-deal-severe-blow-to-bangladeshs-garment-industry/a-53895339

48 S. Labowitz and D. Baumann-Pauly, "Beyond the Tip of the Iceberg: Bangladesh's Forgotten Apparel Workers," *NYU Center for Business and Human Rights*, 2015. http://people.stern.nyu.edu/twadhwa/bangladesh/downloads/beyond_the_tip_of_the_iceberg_report.pdf

49 Al-Amin Mamun, "Empowering Women For The Textile And Fashion Business," *BGMEA*, 2018. https://www.researchgate.

net/figure/Total-employee-in-RMG-sector-in-Bangladesh-Data-BGMEA_fig8_328487510

50 Libcom.org, "Striking Bangladeshi Garment Workers Win 77% Pay Rise". https://libcom.org/article/striking-bangladeshi-garment-workers-win-77-pay-rise.

51 R. Bick, E. Halsey, and C. Ekenga, "The Global Environmental Injustice of Fast Fashion," *Environmental Health,* 2018. https://ehjournal.biomedcentral.com/articles/10.1186/s12940-018-0433-7.

52 T. Voon, A. Mitchell, "Time to Quit? Assessing International Investment Claims against Plain Tobacco Packaging in Australia," *Journal of International Economic Law* 14 no. 3(2011), 515–52. https://doi.org/10.1093/jiel/jgr030

53 "UN Partnership on the Sustainable Fashion and the SDGs".

54 Donoian and Wallach, "Fast Fashion and IP Regulation: Will Fast Fashion Kill the Golden Goose?"

55 N. Davis, "Fast Fashion Speeding Toward Environmental Disaster, Report Warns," *The Guardian,* 2020. https://www.theguardian.com/fashion/2020/apr/07/fast-fashion-speeding-toward-environmental-disaster-report-warns

56 L. Dearden, "Fashion Revolution Day: #WhoMadeMyClothesCampaign Remembers Rana Plaza Disaster," *The Independent,* 2015. https://www.independent.co.uk/life-style/fashion/news/fashion-revolution-day-whomademyclothes-campaign-remembers-rana-plaza-disaster-10201871.html

*Section II*

# Gender Spectrum: Beyond Binary

# Violence Against Widows in Colonial Bengal

*Aparna Bandyopadhyay*

## Introduction

The Act for the Abolition of Sati passed in 1829, and subsequently, it and the Hindu Widows' Remarriage Act of 1856 were together hailed as emancipatory legislations that rescued widows from death, ameliorated their sufferings and enabled a legitimate fulfilment of their desires. The legislations, by abolishing the heinous practice of 'burning alive' of widows, and providing Hindu widows the opportunity to remarry if they wished to, supposedly enabled them to lead a more humane, fulfilling and emancipated existence. While the legislation for the abolition of Sati had successfully minimised the incidence of sati, redefined by Rammohan Roy as a gruesome act of homicide, the legalisation of widow remarriage, as Iswarchandra Vidyasagar himself admitted, was a failure, and only a handful of widows remarried according to the provisions of this Act in the colonial era. Hindu society continued to resist the idea of remarriage despite its legalisation. Widows suffered daily humiliation, verbal abuse, deprivation and denial in their marital or natal household.

Kailashbasini Devi, in her *Hindu Mahilaganer Heenabastha*, wrote:

> ...No one cares for widow, just as a hallowed flower pot, when broken, is tuned into ashes, what shame that a widowed woman too faces the same predicament.

> Engaged in lowly housework, having one meal a day, they eke out their lives in a thoroughly piteous state.

More! On occasion, some wretches even have to crave for the day-end meal and a rag of clothing…[1]

Pandita Ramabai, in *The High Caste Hindu Woman*, poignantly depicted the plight of high-caste Hindu widows and the daily abuse they suffered within the inner precincts of the household.

A widow is called an "inauspicious" thing. The name "rand," by which she is generally known, is the same that is borne by a Nautch girl or a harlot. The relatives and neighbors of the young widow's husband are always ready to call her bad names, and to address her in abusive language at every opportunity. There is scarcely a day of her life on which she is not cursed by these people as the cause of their beloved friend's death. The mother-in-law gives vent to her grief by using such language as, when once heard, burns into a human heart. In short, the young widow's life is rendered intolerable in every possible way. There may be exceptions to this rule, but, unhappily, they are not many. In addition to all this, the young widow is always looked upon with suspicion, and closely guarded as if she were a prisoner, for fear she may at any time bring disgrace upon the family by committing some improper act…[2]

Ramabai's heart-wrenching depiction of the woes of Hindu widows in Maharashtrian society was also applicable to their counterparts in Bengal. Deprivation and denial, and grossly inhuman and cruel behaviour were integral to their everyday existence. A widow, moreover, was denied the right to love a man other than her deceased husband. She was denied the right to legitimately unite with the person she loved. She was punished for being in love by gruesome acts of violence despite the official 'legalisation' of her desires. According to

Tanika Sarkar, one of the positive outcomes of the legislation was the gradual absorption of love and widowhood within the framework of licit romance, their distancing from the register of salacious scandal and pulp satire.[3] However, evidence reveals that a widow in love was far removed from the framework of 'licit romance' even after 1856. The widow was subjected to sexual violence, forced abortions and killings for alleged transgressions that violated family honour. The body of the widow was subjected to continuous surveillance by the state and the different stakeholders of society. Thus, while she was spared mandatory death on her husband's funeral pyre and officially given the right to remarry, she continued to be an object of severe violence, torture, surveillance, neglect and control.

The present paper will unmask, on the basis of newspaper reports and personal narratives, the violence perpetrated against Hindu widows in the post-1856 era. It will bring to light the punitive violence inflicted on a widow for being in love and seeking to unite with her love either through marriage or through non-marital cohabitation. It will reveal the sexual violence that was endemic within the Hindu household, the forced abortions that often caused death, the surveillance exercised by people in power and a colonial bureaucracy that attempted to prevent abortions by widows, violating their right over their bodies and their reproductive choice. It will proceed to examine how women themselves perceived and addressed the widows' question and the solutions they proposed for alleviating the sufferings of widows.

## Violence against Widows in Love

Records available from the late 19$^{th}$ and early decades of the 20$^{th}$ century indicate that the non-marital romantic/sexual relationships of widows were a fairly endemic feature of the entire period. Contemporary sources indicate that while the elopement of upper-caste widows was fairly common, widows of high-caste status in the late $19^{th}$ and early $20^{th}$ centuries also engaged in clandestine relationships without forsaking the custody of their guardians. These widows, once discovered, were punished with severe violence.

A twenty-two-year-old widow named Pratima Dasi, for instance, was allegedly burnt to death by her elder brother-in-law and her husband's nephew. Pratima was suspected to be in love with one Haradhon Bhattacharjee, a zamindar and resident of Tribeni. She corresponded regularly with Haradhon and the latter would duly reply. In one of her letters she stated, 'I will not forget you, you will not forget me, when we die, we will die together'. In another letter, she wrote, 'If you keep me with you, I will live, otherwise not'. In yet another letter addressed to Haradhon, she asked him to come and take her away. It is not known whether Haradhon intended to take her away, but one of his letters carrying his name and address on the envelope fell into the hands of the accused men, who punished the girl by burning her to death. In the testimony he provided in the court, Haradhon pled that he had never been alone with Pratima and never had the opportunity to talk to her privately. The accused relatives tried to prove to the court that the girl had committed suicide, but they were incriminated on the basis of the girl's dying statement to the doctor. In this statement, she revealed how her elder brother-in-law and her husband's nephew had soaked her clothes with spirit and kerosene oil and then set them on fire.[4]

In another instance of violent reaction by members of a widow's family, one Haripada Naskar, a resident of Jyotbhusan village within Bhangar police station, it was reported in the *ABP*, 16 May 1927, was murdered for his alleged involvement with a widow. Haripada Naskar alias Nani doctor was reportedly having an *ashnai* (pejorative for romance) with the widowed sister of Kunjabihari Ghosh for quite some time. The widow's relatives had long suspected the liaison and had repeatedly warned him, but the day they discovered him in the widow's house, they killed him.[5]

Another widow who had eloped unsuccessfully could not bear the brutality of punishment and committed suicide. Sushma, a young wife of one Gopal Banerjee, money order clerk of Budge Budge, was in 'illicit' love with Gopal's nephew, Nirmal Chatterjee. They eloped but were caught red-handed at Budge Budge station. Gopal took her back home, cut her hair, tied up her limbs and locked her up in a room. His widowed daughter released her at night, but the next morning, she was once again tied up. Somehow unwinding herself, Sushma poured methylated spirit on her sari and committed suicide. In the court case that ensued, the widowed daughter, Lakshmimani, testified that when her father had asked Sushma to come back home, she had replied, 'You are an old man. How long will you live?' As for the lover, his moustache was shaved off on one side, his face was smeared with lime, he was paraded through the marketplace and finally driven out of town.[6]

The Brahmo leader, Sasipada Banerjee, recounted an incident in his paternal household in Baranagar. A widow, a member of the vast joint family to which Sasipada himself belonged, was found missing one day. The men in the family captured her that very night. She was locked up in a room and mercilessly beaten by the men of the family for several consecutive nights till finally she died. The next morning, word was spread that she had committed suicide. Sasipada later realised that this was no exceptional incident. Widows were brutally killed in many families of his time. This incident deeply affected Sasipada, and he devoted his life to the amelioration of the sufferings of widows.[7]

## The Pregnant Widow and Her Right To/Not To Abort

The pregnant widow was at times forced to abort; at other times, she was denied the right to abort. Contemporary plays and farces allude to abortions of widows as a regular feature of village life with certain lower-caste women such as the *malini,* (gardener woman) the *mechuni* (fisherwoman) and the *napitani* (the barberwoman) doing brisk business by selling abortion-inducing drugs to pregnant widows and *kulina* women. Some widows must have entered these relationships by choice, or given their consent on a promise of marriage. It is possible that many were raped by close members of their families. Some of these plays and farces also suggest that parents at times chose to deliberately overlook the '*byabhichar*' of their widowed daughters as they considered it less harmful than remarriage and actually arranged for secret abortions. Foeticide was, however, considered a sin in the ethical yardstick of traditional Hindu society. Parents who cooperated with their widowed daughters in this respect did so grudgingly to save family honour. Zamindars of villages were often found appealing to the widows of their villages not to commit foeticide. In fact, giving birth to a child was considered a better option, even though a widow's child born out of wedlock had no legitimacy. On 15 April 1866, the *Dacca Prakash* published a lecture by the zamindar of Bhawal, Kalinarayanbabu, on precisely this matter. Kalinarayanbabu admonished widows for killing their foetuses or their newborns to hide their shame and protect their honour. It was a sin to destroy human life, he argued. He proceeded to point out that foeticide was unbecoming of a mother and also the defiance of the will of God. He implored the residents of Bhowal to restrain their sexual instincts and thus prevent the grave sin of foeticide from polluting the region. If a widow became pregnant, he urged, the foetus ought to be preserved and duly given birth.[8]

Pregnancies of widows and the practice of abortion also invited unwarranted administrative surveillance, especially by the lower echelons of colonial administration. On 25 January 1861, J. H. Young, Commissioner of the Burdwan division, wrote to the Officiating Secretary to the Government of Bengal, drawing his attention to the practice of district-level officials of subjecting widows to enquiries and medical tests on suspicions of pregnancy. While the Commissioner declared the practice illegal and issued orders to stop the practice, his reports reveal a harrowing account of harassment and intimidation of widows by the local officialdom in their attempt to prevent abortion. Young's report reveals that in Bankura, when a petition was made to the police praying for enquiry on suspicion that a pregnant widow was about to procure an abortion, the Darogahs entered the particulars of the case in the Thannah diary and made enquiries to verify the truth. In Burdwan, the village authorities were expected to keep an eye on widows and report any attempt at abortion. In Budbud Sub-division, Young reported, widows were kept in charge of the Munduls, from whom a declaration was taken to the effect that they would be careful to see that no abortion took place in their village and to report to the police if it took place notwithstanding their surveillance. In cases where pregnancy was denied, the woman was examined by the Sub-Assistant Surgeon. A similar practice was reported to have more or less prevailed in other districts, pointing to an extraordinary level of administrative interference in a woman's reproductive sexuality, of the deployment of the coercive mechanisms of the state against a woman's body. While Young, with the approval of the Lt. Governor, issued orders to magistrates and sub-divisional officers to immediately stop the practice, he believed that this illegal practice was more likely to cause rather than prevent the crime of abortion, skirting questions of the legitimacy of a child born of a widow.[9]

Notwithstanding such bureaucratic surveillance, widows continued to abort their foetuses. An attempt at abortion at times cost the widow her life. In 1865, the *Bamabodhini Patrika* reported the death of a widow in Hadiapara on account of failed abortion.[10] Again, at the Alipore Criminal Session Court, one Rajendranath Bhandari of Diamond Harbour was charged under Section 314 of IPC for causing the death of one Soorobala Dasi, aged about 18 years for administering a drug in his attempt to cause miscarriage. After her husband's death, the girl lived in her marital home at Sorisa with a child and the accused looked after her property. The girl and the accused reportedly fell in love and as a result she conceived. The accused in order to hide her 'shame', gave her some drug and consequently she died.[11]

The Calcutta Coroner reported on 14 December 1885 the death of a young widow who had been married at ten and widowed at thirteen. She had been thrown out of her natal and matrimonial homes and had eventually become pregnant. She found no one to give her shelter. Eventually, she came to her old and abandoned ancestral home to die alone of miscarriage or self-induced abortion in a pitiable condition, while her wealthy relatives who lived in a new house nearby looked on.[12]

On many occasions, public exposure and scandal or the prospect of it drove many pregnant widows to commit suicide. For instance, the *Bamabodhini Patrika* of *Bhadra* 1271 B.S. [1864] reported that in Kashyap Palli, Shantipur, a beautiful widowed daughter of a Shiromani had committed suicide because of public outcry against her alleged loss of *satitva*.[13] The *Bamabodhini Patrika* reported in *Ashar* 1870 that in Khatura and the adjoining villages, many cases of suicide had come to light. Of these, a majority were cases of widows, the reason being *baidhabya jantranahetu adharmacharaner lokapabad*—scandals emanating from immoral behaviour on account of the agonies of widowhood. For instance, a young widow of a respectable family committed suicide because she was unable to abort her foetus.[14]

Ranajit Guha, in his essay, 'Chandra's Death', discusses the death of a Bagdi widow named Chandra in a remote village in Birbhum in 1849. She died on account of a drug administered by her relatives to terminate her pregnancy. She was reportedly involved in a sexual liaison with the husband of her sister-in-law, Magaram Chasha. Once she got pregnant, her paramour, Magaram Chasha, did admit his responsibility in the pregnancy but dictated two alternative courses of action, not to Chandra, but to her mother, Bhagabati. He directed her to arrange for Chandra's abortion, failing which he threatened to put her into *bhek*, that is, the attire of a Vaishnava woman. By doing this, he transformed himself, as Guha rightly pointed out, from the lover to that of a custodian of patriarchal ethics. Bhagabati decided in favour of Chandra's abortion, with the full support of various members of her immediate and extended family. The procedure of abortion cost Chandra her life, but Guha sees in her family's decision to arrange for her abortion an assertion of choice. They preferred Chandra's abortion to the prospect of a life of a *boshtomi* that is, a Vaishnava woman. The man responsible for the pregnancy wanted to destroy the evidence of his guilt, argues Guha, and this could be achieved as well by the physical destruction of the incriminating embryo as by the social destruction of the person who carried it. However, for the women who had rallied in support of Chandra, the alternatives were by no means of equal value. In their judgment, abortion with all its risks was preferable to *bhek.* According to Guha, this was a choice made by women entirely on their own to 'stop the engine of male authority from uprooting a woman from her place in the local society'. In choosing as an alternative to *bhek,* they not only defied the sentence of living death that had been already pronounced on Chandra, but took recourse to an alternative solidarity—the solidarity of women, a solidarity premised on the realisation of man's bad faith.[15]

Without questioning the validity of Guha's interpretation, it may be pointed out that Chandra's mother, Bhagabati, and other members of her extended family, which included male as well as female members, preferred abortion to *bhek* to save the honour and respectability of the family and their caste and to evade punishment by the disciplinary institutions operating at the village level. They conformed to the dominant ideology, evidently shared by both the high and the low castes, that considered a widow's desire incompatible with such honour and respectability and therefore punishable. In this respect, there is no evidence that the female members thought differently. No one knows whether Chandra herself chose abortion. It is possible that she desired remarriage and legitimacy and would have preferred to give birth to the child. Hence one should not overemphasise the assertion of agency and choice in Chandra's fatal abortion. Denied the chances of remarriage and, therefore, of legitimate childbirth, the widow was painfully aware that a child born of an illicit sexual liaison had no acceptance within the parameters of respectable society and she would be inevitably punished by ostracism on account of her illegitimate motherhood. Displaced from respectable society, she would either have to embrace prostitution or adopt *bhek*—that is, enrol in communities that accommodated outcastes like the Vaishnavas. Alternatively, she could decide to terminate her life, as the multiple instances of suicide of pregnant women cited earlier testify. If she wished to survive within respectable society, abortion was a necessary and unavoidable course of action.

Some widows proceeded with their pregnancies even after being abandoned by their lovers. They had to find a means of livelihood under these circumstances. In a report titled 'Kshiroda Namni Eekti Coolir Bibaran' (An Account of a Coolie named Kshiroda') in *Sanjivani,* 21 Agrahayan 1885, a gentleman described his encounter with a coolie named Kshiroda on his way to Assam aboard a steamer during the Puja holidays. Kshiroda got down at Tejpur. Her appearance betrayed that she was a widow of a respectable background but was pregnant. She revealed how her lover had dumped her in a coolie depot and fled.[16]

Haimabati Sen, in her memoirs, recalls meeting Tara, a pregnant widow, on one of her journeys to east Bengal.[17] Tara tearfully revealed how she had been ditched by Satya, the eldest son of the founder of the Baranagore Rescue Home, how Satya had pretended to be in love and made her pregnant but on the question of marriage wavered on grounds that his mother was unwilling to get them married. Incidentally, his mother too had been a widow before she married his father. She was probably referring to Satyaprakash, the eldest son of Sasipada Banerjee. The latter had married a widow, Girijakumari, after the death of his first wife, Rajkumari. It was indeed a grave charge against this reformist family, known for their concern for the welfare of widows. The charge, however, is not corroborated by any other source.

Contemporary journals reveal that a few widows proceeded with their pregnancies only to abandon their children after childbirth. On 8 January 1926, it was reported in the *Ananda Bazar Patrika* that a Hindu widow named Janaki Dasi had deserted her newborn baby in an earthen pot within a bathroom. The baby was discovered and taken to the hospital but it died. The widow was traced and a complaint lodged against her. In self-defence, she said that she had done this to conceal her sin. She was punished with imprisonment for six weeks and a fine of Rs. 50.[18] A similar incident occurring in Olpad, a remote village near Surat in south Gujarat that took the country by storm in 1881. Vijaylakshmi was a 24-year-old Brahman widow who killed her newborn child and threw it away in a rubbish heap. The local police had earlier come to know of her pregnancy and had reported to the district magistrate. Months later, when a newborn's body was discovered, the widow was arrested and tried. Initially awarded a death sentence, she was later punished with transportation for life. This incident deeply troubled Tarabai Shinde, who considered this incident symptomatic of a deeper malaise afflicting upper-caste Hindu women of India and she put forth her point of view in her book *A Comparison between Women and Men.*[19]

The plight of a widow punished for seeing her lover clandestinely and suffering its pitfalls can be better understood from an example from fiction. In Saratchandra's *Srikanta,* Nirudidi, a child widow, was a popular figure in her village. She 'slipped', was affected by *sutika*—a pregnancy-related health issue, and was thrown out of the village. She began to stay alone in a small hut outside the village, living and suffering all by herself, boycotted by the people of the village, with Srikanta the lone visitor to her house. She died quietly after a period of terrible suffering, Srikanta, the sole witness to her last moments. Srikanta lamented how 'the untainted and chaste Hindu society closed its doors and windows on the face of this hapless woman'.[20]

In *Bamuner Meye*, another novel by Saratchandra Chattopadhyay, Gyanada, a widow was made pregnant by her elder brother-in law, Golok Chatujje, who had recently lost his wife. Initially, it was probably a consensual relationship with the man having promised marriage or a committed relationship. Golok forced Gyanada to abort, accused her of having a relationship with the doctor who had executed her abortion, forcing her in a devastated state of mind and body to migrate to Brindaban.[21]

## Women and Widow Remarriage

What did women have to say about widow remarriage in colonial Bengal? Did they remain marginal to the debate on widow remarriage? Is it possible to retrieve their voices on the issue of widow remarriage? As early as 1835, a few elderly kulin maidens of Shantipur appealed to the rulers of the country to frame laws to redress the double standards of Hindu society. They asked whether the shastras were formulated only to deny women the pleasures of life.[22] A week later, a few women of Chinsurah presented a charter of demands, which included the right of women to choose their own husbands and the right of remarriage of widows.[23] On the eve of the passing of the Act of 1856, an anonymous widow who described herself as an advocate of widow remarriage showered blessings on Vidyasagar for his initiative and wished him success.[24]

Not all women of this time considered remarriage a panacea for the woes of widows. They were distressed by the torture, violence, abuse and financial hardship the widow suffered within the natal/marital space, and considered self-reliance and a life dedicated to social upliftment to be more important than remarriage. The poet Mankumari Basu, who became a widow at the age of nineteen, was deeply perturbed by the pitiable and hapless condition of widows and their duties and responsibilities. She did not remarry herself, and though she had a profound respect for Vidyasagar, did not recommend remarriage for other widows. She believed that acquisition of wisdom, surrendering herself to God, inscribing her husband's image in her heart, working for the progress of her sisters, imparting proper education to children and serving orphans, the destitute and the ill were the duties of a widow. To this end, she wrote a novel named *Banabasini* in *Bamabodhini Patrika.*[25]

Nirmala Das founded a widows' home in Dhaka in June 1911. She wrote in *Bharat Mahila* that many widows lived in a pitiable condition in our country. They not only suffered emotional loss on account of the death of their husbands but also suffered financial hardship. If these widows were educated and trained to teach in girls' schools they could help in the spread of women's education and lead a life of honour and dignity themselves (Das 1912).

Swarnakumari Devi, daughter of Devendranath Tagore, established the Sakhi *Samiti* in 1896. In 'Arekti Prastab', she wrote, 'If a widow receives education and is equipped to teach other women and young boys within the *antahpur* and engages in other socially useful activities, then she will be earn her own meals and lead a life freed from insult and oppression…A widow who desires to remarry may do so, but if a widow wants to lead a pious life of celibacy, she is welcome to do so'.[26]

Swarnakumari Devi's elder daughter, Hiranmoyee Devi, eventually took over the responsibility of the *Sakhi Samiti*, then in a moribund condition, and renamed it *Mahila Bidhaba Asram*, modelling it closely on the lines of the Brahmo leader, Sasipada Banerjee's *Bidhaba Shilpasram* established in 1887 in Baranagore. Hiranmoyee's ashram concentrated on industrial education. By 1909, the ashram had 30 members and 50 day scholars, and a larger building was needed to take in the many widows who had applied for admission. Classes were held in spinning and weaving, making stockings and vests, lace making, tailoring, painting, modelling, music and other subjects.27

After Hiranmoyee's death in 1925, the organisation was renamed Hiranmoyee *Bidhaba Shilpashram.*[28] Sarala Devi Chaudhurani, Hiranmoyee's younger sister, founded the *Bhrarat Stree Mahamandal* in 1910. This organisation similarly provided shelter and education to widows. The latter were especially trained to serve as teachers in the *antahpur.* Sarala envisaged a network of provincial organisations of the Mahamandal which would spread education among women, especially widows, throughout the country.[29] Krishnabhabini Das was the secretary of this body for quite some time.[30] Krishnabhabini had lost her husband and daughter within a year of the family's return from England. She put on a homespun sari and walked barefoot from door to door to convince the *purdanashins* (veiled and secluded women) of the value of zenana education.[31]

Abala Basu, wife of Jagadish Chandra Basu, founded the *Nari Shiksha Samiti* in 1919 for spreading primary education among rural women. But who would teach these women? Widows, answered Abala Basu. In 1925, she founded the *Vidyasagar Bani Bhavan* to train widows to become *antahpur shikshayitris* or zenana governesses. In a speech delivered at Rotary Club on 5 September 1934, Abala Basu stated that the *Vidyasagar Bani Bhavan* had been working tirelessly in order to make helpless widows self-reliant and boost their confidence. The Bhavan had begun with only two widows. In 1934, there were 60 widows residing in this Bhavan, among whom 40 were teachers and the rest were engaged in other occupations.[32]

Saroj Nalini Dutt established women's organisations dedicated to the upliftment of women, and widows in particular, in Bankura, Birbhum, Darjeeling and other districts of Bengal. Her husband, Gurusaday Dutt, was an ICS officer; Sarojnalini accompanied him to the districts where he was posted and immediately set to devote herself to the well-being of the women in these regions. After her death in 1925, Gurusaday Dutt established a central *Saroj-Nalini Nari Mangal Samiti*, which had branches in the districts. Abala Basu, Lady Sinha, Maharani Suniti Devi, Sarala Ray, Prabhabati Devi Saraswati and other leading women of the time became associated with this organisation and took charge of its various district-level branches.[33] Hemlata Thakur, wife of Dipendranath Tagore, was in charge of the *Saroj Nalini Asram* and *Basanta Bidhaba Asram* located in Puri.[34] Sasipada Banerjee's daughter, Banalata Devi, established *Sumati Samiti* in 1895. She was barely fifteen then. Her elder sister Sukhatara Dutta took over the responsibility of this *Samiti* after her untimely death at the age of twenty.[35]

Thus for many women of this period, self-dependence and a life of dignity were prerequisites for a widow's existence rather than remarriage. Through institution-building endeavours, they posited an alternative resolution to the widows' question and sought to emancipate widows from a daily saga of violence, from a deprived and tortured existence by providing them the necessary institutional support for their intellectual and economic empowerment.

In conclusion, it may be re-emphasised that the reformist endeavours by the Bengali bhadralok, and the consequent legislations by the colonial state did not significantly change the plight of Hindu widows in colonial Bengal. The patriarchal control over the minds and bodies of widows persisted, and even aggravated, manifesting in a worsening saga of deprivation, violence and surveillance. The widow continued to be denied a legitimate fulfilment of her affective and sexual desires, and control over her body, especially her reproductive choice. The educated women reformers of the time were deeply troubled by the predicament of widows and considered their self-reliance a more pressing necessity than their remarriage, and they engaged in institution-building endeavours to solve the problems of widows. Hence a re-evaluation of male-pioneered reformist initiatives is necessary and the lived experiences of widows, along with the initiatives of women themselves, need to be foregrounded in order to achieve a more nuanced understanding of the widow question in colonial Bengal.

## Endnotes

1 Kailashbasini Devi, "The Woeful Plight of Hindu Women," in *Talking of Power: Early Writings of Bengali Women from the Mid-Nineteenth Century to the Beginning of the Twentieth Century,* eds. Malini Bhattacharya and Abhijit Sen (Kolkata: Stree, 2003).

2 Pandita Ramabai, *The High Caste Hindu Woman* (Bombay: Maharashtra State Board of Literature and Culture, [1887] 1981).

3 Tanika Sarkar, *Rebels, Wives, Saints* (Ranikhet: Permanent Black, 2009), 142.

4 *Amrita Bazar Patrika*, 7 July 1929.

5 *Anandabazar Patrika*, 16 May 1927.

6 *Anandabazar Patrika* 1 April 1926.

7 Anonymous, "Brahmosamaje Sasipada," cited by Sunita Bandyopadhyay in *Brahmarshi Sasipada: Samay, Samaj, Sadhana* (Kolkata: Dolphin, 2007), 40–1.

8 "Bahoaler Zamindar Kalinarayanbabu Pradatta Bhrunhatya Sambandhe Baktrita, Dacca Prakash," in *Unish Shataker Bangladesher Sambad-Samayikpatra*, ed. Muntasir Mamun, 9 (DaccaL Bangla Academy, 1985).

9 Judicial file, February 1861, no.76. From J.H. Young, Esq., Commissioner of the Burdwan Division, to the Officiating Secretary to the Government of Bengal, no.19, dated the 25 January 1861. Judicial File, no.77, Circular from J.H. Young, Esq., Commissioner of the Burdwan Division to the Magistrates of the Division, (no. 78, dated the 16th November, 1860). Also No.78: From W.S. Seton-Karr, Esq., Officiating Secretary to the Government of Bengal to the Commissioner of the Burdwan Division (no. 298 A, dated 6 February 1861).

10 *Bamabodhini Patrika, Sraban* 1865.

11 Anonymous, "Sequel to Secret Love," *Amrita Bazar Patrika*, 27 January 1911.

12 Sarkar, *Rebels, Wives, Saints*, 143.

13 *Bamabodhini Patrika*, *Bhadra* 1864.

14 *Bamabodhini Patrika*, *Ashar* 1870.

15 Ranajit Guha, "Chandra's Death," in *Subaltern Studies* V, ed. Ranajit Guha (Delhi: OUP, 1987).

16 Anonymous, "Kshiroda Namni Ekti Coolir Bibaran," in *Sanjivani,* ed. Kanailal Chattopadhyay (21 Agrahayan 1885 [1989]).

17 Tapan Raychaudhuri and Geraldine Forbes, eds., *Memoirs of Haimabati Sen: from Child Widow to Lady Doctor* (Hyderabad: Roli Books), 164–7.

18 *Anandabazar Patrika,* 8 January 1926.

19 Rosalind o' Hanlon, *A Comparison Between Women and Men: Tarabai Shinde and the Critique of Gender Relations in Colonial India* (Madras: OUP, 1994).

20 Saratchandra Chattopadhyay, "Srikanta," in *Saratsahityasamagra* 1, ed. Sukumar Sen, 1 (Kolkata: Ananda Publishers, 2009 [1915–1932]), 268–523.

21 Saratchandra Chattopadhyay, "Bamuner Meye," in *Saratsahityasamagra* 1, ed. Sukumar Sen (Kolkata: Ananda Publishers, 2009 [1920]), 979–1013.

22 Brajnedranath Bandyopadhyay ed., *Sambadpatre Sekaler Katha* 2 (Calcutta: Bangiya Sahitya Parishad, 1977 [14 March 1835]), 35.

23 Bandyopadhyay, *Sambadpatre Sekaler Katha*, 21 March 1835, 45.

24 Benoy Ghose, *Selections from English Periodicals of 19th Century Bengal*, 3 (Calcutta: Papyrus, 1980), 209–10.

25 Jogendranath Gupta, *Banger Mahila Kabi* (Kolkata: Dey's Publishing, 2004 [1930]), 109–11.

26 Swarnakumari Devi, *Swarnakumari Devir Rachana Sankalan,* (Calcutta: Dey's Publishing and School of Women's Studies, 2000), 267–9.

27 Dagmar Engels, *Beyond Purdah?* (Delhi: OUP, 1996), 171.

28 Chitra Deb, *Thakurbarir Andarmahal* (Calcutta: Ananda Publishers, 1980), 106.

29 Dagmar Engels, *Beyond Purdah?* 172.

30 Engels, *Beyond Purdah?*, 172; Gopa Datta, "Achievement and Agony of Krishnabhabiini Das: A Social Activist of the

Nineteenth Century (1864–1919)". In *The Other Universe: An Anthology of Women's Studies*, eds., Aparna Bandyopadhyay and Krishna Dasgupta (Kolkata: Setu Prakashani, 2015), 284.

31 Engels, *Beyond Purdah?* 172.

32 Anonymous, "Girls' Education in Bengal Villages: Lady Bose's Address at Rotary Club," *Forward*, 5 September 1934.

33 Rajib Kundu, "Saroj-Nalini o Narimangal Samiti: Dhulat Smritir Abalokan," in *Nahi Samanya Nari: Itihase, Samaje Chintay*, eds., Mahasweta Mukhopadhyay and Aparna Bandyopadhyay (Kolkata: Setu Prakshani, 2018), 121–2.

34 Chitra Deb, *Thakurbarir Andarmahal* (Calcutta: Ananda Publishers, 1980), 138–9.

35 Sanghamitra Chowdhury, *Banalata Devir Nirbachito Rachana Sankalan* (Kolkata: Pratikshan, 2005), 25–6.

# Space and Variation in Dalit Women's Lived Experience

***Sayatri Dutta***

## Introduction

This paper is divided into three parts. The first part will give a background of caste and what I mean by space. The second part will deal with interviews given by Dalit women from across India to understand the spatiality of caste and gender. Finally, I will talk about how solidarity can be build built across spaces.

Before going into further detail, I will provide an overview of what the caste system is and how it functions in South Asia. In *Homo Hierarchicus,* Louis Dumont defined caste as a system based on the triple principle of hierarchy, separation and division of labour. Additionally, he stated that the three principles rest on the fundamental conception of purity and pollution. However, Dr B.R Ambedkar, in his undelivered speech titled *The Annihilation of Caste* (1936),[1] mentioned that in reality, the caste system is a division of labourers. He justified his stand by emphasising the rigidity of the caste system. He explained that caste identity is assigned to people on the basis of their birth and paralyses all options of upward mobility.

Therefore, caste is an axis of oppression but it does not function singularly. As Dr. B.R. Ambedkar mentioned in 'Castes in India: Their Mechanism, Genesis and Development' (1979),[2] the caste system is intrinsically linked with patriarchy. Gender intersects with caste to doubly marginalise

Dalit women. However, here I would ask the question, can 'Dalit women' be seen as a homogeneous category? In this context, I introduce the idea of 'space'. The word 'space' in the title refers to perceived space (the measurable, observable and material) and conceived space (the mental construct or space as imagined) which affect and are in turn affected by 'experiential or lived space'. Postmodernist scholar Edward Soja calls the experiential space the Third Space and regards it as 'lived time'. He talks about breaking down the dualism between the historical and the social to include the spatial and claims everything is simultaneously historical, social and spatial. So, in this sense, even gender and caste are not aspatial.

In my paper, I am not going to read 'space' as a pre-existing, unchanging container that people fill up but as something that also produces the social. Here, I refer to Edward Soja who observed in an interviews in 2011[3] that he began with the critique of the inherent practice of privileging of the social over the spatial. He argued instead that there was a socio-spatial dialectic in which the spatial and social forms, relations and processes were mutually constitutive; geography shaped class as much as class shaped geography. This brought in a much more balanced 'triple dialectic' or 'trialectic' which Soja calls the Third Space Perspective. However, following Michel Foucault and Henri Lefebvre, Soja comments that the two dominant ways of thinking about space –configuration of material forms and mental or ideational representations of those material forms (a more subjective alternative that emphasises 'thoughts about space')—are insufficient to comprehend the simultaneously real and imagined 'other spaces' in which we live or in which our individual biographies play out, in which our social relations develop and change and in which history is formed. It is seeing space as fully lived.

In this paper, I refer to certain autobiographical interviews given by Dalit women in India after 2010 to decipher the spatial aspect of gender and caste and how space has influenced the political actions of these Dalit women activists. Now, different parts of India have different caste and gender politics. For this paper, I broadly divide them into urban and rural spaces and talk about the regional specificities as and when required.

## Voices

I begin with an interview of Dr. Meera Velayudhan, one of the most prominent Dalit activists in India and Fellow Council for Social Development (CSD), Hyderabad. In her interview, she mentions that she has multiple identities depending on her history and location. She was born in Delhi, studied in Nainital but she has traces of Mulavukad and Uzhavoor (where her mother and father, respectively, grew up) in her. This hints to how spatial dynamics affect personalities and identities. Identifying herself as a second-generation learner, Dr. Velayudhan expresses that her parents' generation was first-generation learners, and this had a profound impact on the history of their communities in the regions. She mentions that, according to the economic condition of the space they inhabited, they could not be called poor. Despite witnessing her brothers being bullied for cutting their hair and second-generation Dalit women feeling embarrassed for being called to a conference that involved the participation of Dalit women, Dr. Velayudhan was assertive of her identity. This probably stems from the history she was a part of. Her parents were activists and worked for anti-caste causes. This shows how only considering the two dominant ways in which space is seen can be limiting. Lived time is much more than perceived and conceived space. It is this consciousness of hers that allowed her to appreciate the space that was created by the coming together of more than 200 Dalit women in a conference. She appreciated the emancipatory and revolutionary potential of this space. In this context, it could be concluded that this urge of middle class educated urban Dalit women to deny their Dalit identity is also a product of the consciousness that urban spaces develop. The capitalist urban society inherently commodifies subjects. Better jobs, social and economic stability increases the object value of individuals. Dr. Velayudhan mentions during the anti-Mandal Commission protests in Delhi women from upper castes gave slogans that said, 'Are we not deserving of IAS husbands?' This depicts the ways in which endogamy intersects with capitalist motives to create a consciousness of anti-Dalit politics. This politics also gives rise to the politics of the 'merit capital'. By merit capital, I mean the ideology which interprets that only the upper castes are the owner of merit. This in turn reduces Dalits to mere 'advantage seeking communities.' The blame comes on the Dalits for lowering the object value of savarnas in the marriage market. To avoid this shame, many Dalits feel compelled to hide their castes.

Another such activist is Pradnya Pawar. She is the daughter of Daya Pawar and grew up in the milieu of the Dalit Panther Movement in Maharashtra. In her interview (2018),[4] she talks about the spatiality of caste and how capitalism affects caste. She mentions,

At the macro level, the caste system that my father wrote about does not exist 100 percent as it did during his time. But if you are living in a village or small town, then caste is a reality like it was. Also, there is another way by which caste has staged a comeback. The economic concerns born out of globalisation and ascendance of capitalism are accentuating caste and communal identities, and people are coming together along caste lines to either hold on to their economic benefits or demand economic benefits. For instance, the Maratha caste mobilisation for quota. Caste continues to operate at multiple levels. In the India of 2018, there are 564 villages where lower castes are not allowed to take water from public taps and public places, and they must not be seen in public wearing new clothes.

In this context, she also talks about the solidarity needed between the urban and rural spaces in order to build a countrywide movement.

Abirami Jotheeswaran, in her interview to *Feminism in India* (2019),[5] explains how she being an urban woman came to know how caste functions in the rural space. While working with the *National Campaign on Dalit Human Rights* (NCDHR), she came to know how mobs attacked Dalits in the Hisar district of Haryana and how the judicial system does almost nothing in such cases, as most of the rural Dalit people are illiterate. Hence, the NCDHR has built a scope for solidarity between urban and rural spaces to be built.

Next, I am going to discuss an interview given by Manisha Mashaal to *Feminism in India* in 2016.[6] Manisha Mashaal is an activist, orator and singer. She grew up in a small village in Haryana. In her interview, she mentions that with time she understood why small community settlements are outside the village and excluded from the rest. So, here we can see, unlike the urban space, the rural space produces a fertile ground for practising untouchability through creation of separate spheres for the savarnas and the Dalits. She explains hiding one's caste is also difficult in a rural setup, as everyone knows each other. Therefore, even within the space of a school classroom where students come from different backgrounds, Mashaal was frowned upon when she did not stand up as the teacher asked all the Dalits to identify themselves by their caste names. Coming from the Valmiki community, Mashaal affirms that Dalit women are doubly marginalised and hardly find a space to voice their protests. Dalit women are seen as bodies that could be easily invaded by the upper castes as well as Dalit men. Mashaal points out that their fight is to reclaim their bodies with dignity. The rural setup and its embedded discrimination added fuel to her urge to protest. This is exactly from where her activism stems. She worked to build space for the Dalit women in the rural areas to voice their opinions. In 2012, when atrocities against Dalit women were at their peak, she started the Swabhimaan Yatra in Haryana. This yatra spread across Haryana, Bihar and Uttar Pradesh. Rural women from various villages started joining the march. Mashaal remembers that she was stopped from giving a speech in Gujarat, as she was from Haryana. This is where she recognises the importance of solidarity. To make the protest stronger, one needs to assemble more people and that will only happen when the boundaries between spaces are overcome despite differences. It is a question of strategic solidarity in activism. However, this was an activism that stemmed from the rural space where exposure to technology is limited. A march was a form of protest that the village space could accommodate. Hence, it was only through solidarity that the movement could have been made an international affair, by including the urban and rural spaces. Thenmozhi Soundaranjan, who was an artist in residence in the campaign, exposed Mashaal to the advantages of activism on social media. This led to the creation of a new space. A virtual space where Dalit women could come in contact with each other despite physical boundaries, voice their opinions and share their experiences. The dynamics of this space had the potential to create new opportunities and agencies. However, was this space really open for all Dalit women? Could all Dalit women really become 'citizens' of this space? Dr. M.M. Vinodini, a writer, scholar and activist from coastal Andhra Pradesh, talks about this in her interview to the *Journal for International Women's Studies*[7] in 2021. The space economy of the rural areas is such that many families cannot afford mobile phones. However, even if they can, the patriarchal belief inherited from the Brahminical structure hardly allows women to access them as mobile phones can expose them to the larger world, thereby making them less 'homely', which is a necessary trait for the 'feminine'. So, to understand the value of subaltern movements, social capital is required which comes to exposure, education and others. This is limited especially for the rural Dalit women. Therefore, entry to the space of social media is also restricted. This could only be overcome through activism that spreads across the borders that separate the urban from the rural spaces.

Being from Andhra Pradesh, Dr. Vinodini also talks about the jogini system that is prevalent in the Telangana area. Dr. Vinodini says, 'The jogini ritual is that a young girl is selected to serve the goddess Yellama as per superstition that such a sacrifice is needed'. However, she is forced to work as a prostitute for the rest of the year near the temple. The scholar observes it is easier in the village setup because people know each other. Being the most oppressed within the system of caste and gender, Dalit girls are usually chosen for this ritual. This is how Dalit girls are sexually exploited. Dr. Vinodini remembers that Ambedkar specifically asked the Dalits to move from the villages to the towns or cities. In towns and cities, because of the dynamics of the space, casteism exists but at least is less visible. However, Dr. Samrat Sengupta[8] differs slightly here. He writes,

> The apparent non-existence of caste or an erasure of the caste question could be one such appropriation by absorption of the negation, or a negation of the negation, suggesting, as if caste does not exist anymore in the modern governmental apparatus. This negation instead of being suggestive of a gradual erosion of the caste system shows its rendering as unspeakable…The alienation of the proletariat in capitalism resulting in the destitution of those who get alienated in the process of formation of private property follows the local historical trajectory of existing caste hierarchies in [the] Indian subcontinent. The outcaste has been the one who structurally could not have the right to space and is associated with exclusion and expendability. The deep association of waste with the outcaste from antiquity to modernity vouchsafe for that.

We can refer to Dr. Vinodini in this context, who points out how this discrimination became overt in urban spaces during the historical juncture of the Covid-19 pandemic. Many of the frontline workers who worked in Covid wards as cleaners and sweepers belonged to the Dalit castes. The upper-class urban people (who were mostly from the upper castes) had the luxury to work from home during the lockdown. During this time, the Dalits working in the Covid wards of hospitals started being treated as untouchables, as they were seen as a potential threat of infection. Now, before delving deeper into how caste and gender functions in the urban spaces, I refer to Surkirtharani, whose experience highlights the spatial dynamics of the rural space.

Sukirtharani's[9] activism develops from the rural space. She lived in a village in Tamil Nadu. The village was divided into two regions—the proper village and the cheri (where the Dalit families lived). These two areas existed in mutual exclusion. She mentions that people still call Dalits by offensive caste names. This discrimination provided grounds for Sukirtharani's urge to unite these two spaces in order to form an egalitarian society. Her father, who was considered the head of the family, was a liberal man. However, he had strict rules and Sukirtharani, being a woman, was not permitted to be outside the house beyond a certain time. In this case, we can trace how the politics of resistance against gender hierarchy is also spatial. In the rural space, women are expected to maintain a certain decorum and fulfil certain duties, like household chores. The rural space could not accommodate further liberty exercised by women. So educating herself and playing with the boys were the only ways in which Sukirtharani could challenge the existing patriarchal structure. This was doubly difficult for her given her caste and economic status. This is different from the experience of Christina Thomas Dhanaraj,[10] who is a Dalit activist from Bangalore. Dhanaraj talks about how, through the question of sexual liberty, one could trace caste and gender hierarchy operative in the urban spaces. She says that there is an inherent sense of promiscuousness attached to the figure of the Dalit woman. When savarna women practise liberating sexual acts like polyamory, it is seen as an exercise of female agency. When Dalit women practise the same, they are viewed as inherently 'easy to achieve'. This leads to various layers of exploitation. Dhanaraj supports this claim with her personal experience. She mentions, 'A year ago, a friend shared one of her conversations with a savarna man, who had spoken at length about his sexual experiences. She recalled him saying that if he knew the woman he was having sex with was Dalit, he would be extra rough and do *whatever he wanted*, as against a savarna woman with whom he would be '*gentle*'. This is because Dalit women are often seen as less 'feminine' than their savarna counterparts. In order to avoid these stereotypes and exploitation, Dalit families tend to develop a double consciousness where they become stricter about the sexual practices of Dalit women. Here, we can see how Dalit women face oppression both from outside as well as inside the community. Dhanaraj adds, 'No value is attached to the Dalit woman; she is regarded as one of the lowest of life forms—polluting and dirty, and on par with wild animals. I had begun investigating the intersection of caste and desire in my twenties, and I dug further into the roots of what is believed to legitimise violence and discrimination within Indian dating'. The activist concludes that love and desire are not apolitical. They are heavily influenced by social systems like gender and caste. I would argue over here that gender and caste themselves are also spatial. Hence, Dhanaraj, unlike Sukirtharani, expresses her Dalit feminist agency by claiming that practising liberating sexual practices should be the right of every woman without the fear of getting stereotyped.

Jyotsna Siddharth[11] also talks about how relationships are affected by caste in the urban spaces. Her first relationship was such an instance. When her partner explained to her that her caste would not be a problem only if she did not show it, she understood how influenced he was by caste hegemony. Siddharth also talks about how caste functions in elite urban institutes like IIMs, IITs and AIIMS. She explains that from not getting scholarships to not getting the chance to speak, discrimination is rampant in these spaces. Under such conditions, the position of the Dalit women is even more precarious. Even Kalyani Thakur talks about such discrimination in her interview to *The Scroll.*[12] She explains that the battle for recognition is tougher for Dalit women because of their doubly marginalised status. Thakur also exhibits how this sword of double marginalisation is denied by upper-caste feminists by recounting an incident that happened when she was invited to give a lecture on Dalit Sahitya at Jogesh Chandra Chowdhuri College. At the very beginning of the seminar, the dean of the department claimed that she was a feminist, hence did not believe in the caste system.

Kalyani Thakur also says that even in a government office she faced discrimination when an upper-caste man snidely asked her about her caste identity. She exclaims that someone also felt entitled to give her the advice to not wear an orange sari, as it did not suit her dark complexion. This entitlement came from the sense of accessibility and ownership upper-caste men (as well as Dalit men) feel over Dalit women's bodies. The Hathras Rape case of 2020 is one such instance. Rekha Raj in her interview to *Huffpost* in 2020[13] states that though many media outlets were enraged by the incident, a lot of them refused to see this as a caste crime. She explains that a Dalit woman's body is seen as a site of violence, hence it was so easy to rape and kill her and then burn her corpse. Raj mentions that though Dalit feminist discourses are now trying to find space in the urban academic circles, it is difficult for this activism to reach the rural areas. Here, we can refer back to Sukirtharani who mentions that at a seminar (attended by people from different places) she used her poetry to create a space where everyone could understand her ideas. She mentions, 'That poem transported people at that event, at that specific time and place'. Here, it is the power of words that created a common space for the rural and urban from different regions to come together.

If this is the condition in India, Nepal is also not far behind.

## South Asia in Perspective

The founder, the president of Feminist Dalit Organization (FEDO), Durga Sob describes the scenario in Nepal. Being brought up in a remote village in Nepal, Sob saw the cruel face of untouchability. Even her peers who belonged to the upper caste did not accept her. Under such circumstances, the condition of Dalit women is worse. Starting from domestic violence to child marriage, exploitation is rampant. Durga Sob explains though the conditions in Kathmandu are better, caste still does not cease to exist. However, Sob mentions that at global forums it is the urban that gets represented the most. She claims that the rural should appear in discussions. As it is not possible to relate the conditions of African women in rural Africa to Dalits in South Asian villages, she concludes that generalisations cannot be made. However, we should keep in mind that strategic solidarity is different from generalisations. It is about acknowledging the differences, but building a plan of action despite them. Otherwise, countries like Bangladesh would have to face the consequences. In this context, I will talk about an interview by Moni Rani Das who belongs to the 'cleaners' caste' in rural Bangladesh. Unlike Nepal and India, Bangladesh has no official recognition of caste. Zakir Hossain from Nagorik Uddyog, a local organisation working with Dalit women in Bangladesh, says crimes against Dalit women are rampant in the form of sexual and physical violence. 'There is an idea [that] she is a Dalit woman, therefore anything that is done to her is okay,' elaborated Zakir Hossain. Das herself was married off at the age of 15; however, now she is the first Dalit person to be part of the National Human Rights Commission of Bangladesh. The article "Dalit Rights Activists Break New Grounds in South Asia", mentions,

> Across the South Asia region, there are some 120 million Dalit women, facing a lifetime of discrimination, violence and poverty. A 2016 study, led by Asia Dalit Rights Forum and supported by UN Women, highlights that Dalit women labourers earn far less than the minimum wage; Dalit girls are more likely to drop out of secondary school than girls from upper castes; and less than one per cent of Dalit women own any land or property. They also experience high levels of gender-based violence…With the support of UN Women's Fund for Gender Equality (FGE), the Feminist Dalit Organization (FEDO) based in Nepal, is striving to address the challenges that Dalit women face in South Asia, in partnership with local organisations such as Nagorik Uddyog in Bangladesh, Swadhikar and Asia Dalit Rights Forum in India, and the Human Development Organization (HDO) in Sri Lanka.

## Conclusion

In this context, that solidarity becomes important. Creation of common spaces is necessary for solidarity to be formed. However, one question can arise—why should Dalit women always bear the responsibility of practising Dalit feminism? Anindita Pan, in her book *Mapping Dalit Feminism: Towards an Intersectional Standpoint* (2021),[14] considers Dalit feminism a methodological praxis. I believe this can be practised by anyone, including upper-caste people. This is how despite differences of caste, space and gender, solidarity can be built. It is this solidarity that was practised in the Bangkok Declaration and Call Seminar, as a Dalit Samaritan woman expressed, 'As Dalits and friends of Dalits we came from caste-affected countries, mostly India, but also Nepal, Pakistan, Sri Lanka and Nigeria, as well as from other countries in Africa, Asia, the Caribbean, Europe, Latin America, the Middle East, North America and the Pacific. We were called together by the World Council of Churches (WCC), the Lutheran World Federation (LWF), and the Christian Conference of Asia (CCA)'. This is the solidarity we need to make the cause of caste, gender and space an international issue. As we know, several countries do not have anti-caste laws, such solidarity would increase the strength of the movement and pressurise the governments to take the necessary steps.

## Endnotes

1 BR Ambedkar, *The Annihilation of Caste* (2004), 16. http://ccnmtl.columbia.edu/projects/mmt/ambedkar/web/readings/aoc_print_2004.pdf.

2 BR Ambedkar, "Castes in India: Genesis, Mechanism and Development," in *Dr. Babasaheb Ambedkar: Writings and Speeches Vol. 1* (p. 3). (Dr. Ambedkar Foundation, 1979).

3 C Borch, "Interview with Edward W. Soja: Thirdspace, Postmetropolis, and Social Theory," *Distinktion: Journal of Social Theory* 3, no.1(2011), 113. https://doi.org/10.1080/1600910x.2002.9672816.

4 A Ghadyalpatil, "A Dalit Woman Faces Layers of Victimization: Pradnya Daya Pawar," *Mint*, 2018, https://www.livemint.com/Politics/uf9yry68CRnw2YJ0ERWqFN/A-Dalit-woman-faces-layers-of-victimization-Pradnya-Daya-Pa.html.

5 A Smrithi, "In Conversation With Abirami Jotheeswaran: Dalit Human Rights Activist," *Feminism in India*, 2019, https://feminisminindia.com/2019/07/01/abirami-jotheeswaran-dalit-human-rights-interview/?fbclid=IwAR1qKqdcMhprJB4UCXymCYnGNA8Y-oGq3KphpwMCn1OIYDhg2bYiW7bnvg8.

6 N Alok P, "'I'm Going To Live A Leader's Life And Die A Leader Too': Manisha Mashaal," *Feminism in India*, 2016, https://feminisminindia.com/2016/09/21/interview-dalit-woman-manisha-mashaal/?fbclid=IwAR1jDF9B6hpxiNWBgRS_Znord2artYB1S-VdRgseYGc27sHHENf79Zwr1Q4.

7 B Zare, "'We are Working for a Caste-free India': An Interview with M. M. Vinodini," *Journal of International Women's Studies* 22 no. 10(2021), 8–16.

8 Samrat Sengupta, "Undecidable Spaces: Rethinking Caste and the Technologies of Abandonment in Manoranjan Byapari," *Sanglap: Journal for Literary and Cultural Inquiry* 6 no.1(2019), 64–77.

9 KS Sukirtharani and S Rangarajan, "The Moment I Set Foot Outside My House, Caste Chases After Me Like A Dog," *Indian Cultural Forum*, 2021, https://indianculturalforum.in/2021/09/11/sukirtharani-interview-from-lifescapes/?fbclid=IwAR0S8Gn5yqQai93qny1qZF9Wf_uUiDfMuOQ2C2UaUjpyocNZEbpbozECXBQ.

10 C Dhanaraj, "Notes on Dissonance," *Verve Magazine*, 2022, https://www.vervemagazine.in/people/notes-on-dissonance?fbclid=IwAR0boTpee9tKgPjyM5Zx3Kf-GrjFcja_Y1cMswayARltRCYz_MG2CJZ6fxE.

11 Kavya, "'All Romantic Experiences Are Essentially Caste Experiences': In Conversation With Jyotsna Siddharth," *Feminism in India*, 2019, https://feminisminindia.com/2019/05/20/jyotsna-siddharth-anti-caste-love-interview/?fbclid=IwAR0Q1MWC3eKRmyjFsiTPuF2efk1HjdFpD71EXRRovrV2JzUW0hSJxFJy5sA.

12 A Ghose, "Why Bengali Dalit Feminist Poet and Writer Kalyani Thakur Added Charal (for Chandal) to Her Name," *Scroll.in*, 2018, https://scroll.in/article/872273/why-bengali-dalit-feminist-poet-and-writer-kalyani-thakur-added-charal-for-chandal-

13 N Henry, "Caste-Ignorant People Speak For Dalit Women In India: Academic Rekha Raj," *HuffPost*, 2020, https://www.huffpost.com/archive/in/entry/hathras-dalit-atrocities-privilege-rekha-raj-interview_in_5f7dd671c5b63de65f08b307?fbclid=IwAR0ysiviqfv9ODCpU-NLSk2fQK5GLcsxnmoWEe3ujHwWHDFyhg1k43xtM8s

14 A Pan, *Mapping Dalit Feminism* (Sage Publications Pvt. Limited, 2021).

# Fighting Against Macaulay's Legacy: LGBTQ People's Struggle for Removal of Section 377 in South and Southeast Asia

*Rajarshi Chakrabarty*

## Introduction

People with different genders and sexual orientations have been present in south and southeast Asia since time immemorial. Their presence is attested by ancient mythology, epics, law books, temple sculptures, historical texts, religious literature and a large number of other sources. A level of acceptance of diverse gender identities and sexual practices is also evident from various sources. The situation changed with the establishment of British colonial rule in parts of south and southeast Asia. The Judeo-Christian concept of sex for procreation, coupled with Victorian morality, led to the enactment of Section 377 of the Indian Penal Code (IPC) by the British in 1861. This section was inspired by the 1553 Buggery Act that outlawed homosexuality in England. It was reportedly imposed to protect soldiers and colonial administrators from 'corruption' out of a fear that these men sent far from home (and their wives) may turn to homosexuality. The IPC, along with the Queensland Criminal Code of 1899 (QCC), was used as a model for legal systems in other British colonies around the world. Thus, through its colonial administration, the British managed to impose and institutionalise a set of laws in south and southeast Asian colonies that criminalised homosexual conduct.[1] Following decades of activism, legal battles and protests, the Indian Supreme Court finally declared portions of the law unconstitutional on 6 September 2018. However, homosexuality is still a crime in post-colonial states like Pakistan, Bangladesh, Sri Lanka, Myanmar, Malaysia, Brunei and Singapore. In these post-colonial states, homosexuality is still punishable with a fine, imprisonment or both. Moreover, these laws help to propagate homophobia and transphobia in these respective post-colonial states. LGBTQ people in these countries are still suffering under the yoke of this draconian colonial legislation and struggling for its removal. This paper wishes to document and analyse all these struggles.

British colonialism was particularly detrimental towards LGBTQ rights in colonial societies. From 1860 onwards, the British Empire spread a specific set of legal codes and common laws throughout its colonies, including prominent examples of the colonial criminal codes of India and Queensland, both of which specifically penalised male-to-male sexual relations with long-term imprisonment. For example, Section 377 of IPC reads as follows:

Unnatural offences - Whoever voluntarily has carnal intercourse against the order of nature with any man, woman or animal shall be punished with imprisonment for life, or with imprisonment for a term which may extend to 10 years, and shall be liable to fine.

Explanation: Penetration is sufficient to constitute the carnal intercourse necessary for the offense described in this section.

The IPC was the first comprehensive codified criminal law produced anywhere in the British Empire. At that time, British colonial judicial officers were inexperienced lay magistrates without legal resources who relied upon importing extant examples of criminal regulations. Thus, the

IPC—together with the QCC and others—became the model for many British colonies' legal systems and was exported and imposed on various other British colonial acquisitions throughout Asia, Africa and beyond.[2]

In Britain, the Parliament repealed Buggery Laws for England and Wales in 1967 (as they related to consensual homosexual acts in private), ten years after the Report of the Departmental Committee on Homosexual Offences and Prostitution (better known as the Wolfenden Report, after Sir John Wolfenden, the Chairman of the Committee) was published on 4 September 1957.[3] Ironically, in the former British colonies in south and southeast Asia, laws prohibiting 'crimes against the order of nature' persist as relics of the colonial past.

## India

In India, the history of public debate on the repeal of Section 377 of IPC began soon after the release of the AIDS Bhedbhav Virodhi Andolan's (ABVA) report titled 'Less Than Gay: A Citizens' Report on the Status of Homosexuality in India', which was the first document to publicly demand queer rights in India. A petition was moved by the ABVA in the Petitions Committee of Parliament. The repeal of Section 377 was demanded on the grounds that it violated Articles 14, 15, 19 and 21 of the Indian Constitution. This parliamentary petition, however, remained dormant for want of a Member of Parliament to argue it in Parliament.

Meanwhile, in 1994, media attention focused on Tihar Jail, where Inspector General of Prisons Kiran Bedi refused to allow distribution of condoms to male prisoners on the grounds that there was no homosexual activity in prisons. She argued that even if there was, the prison authorities would be encouraging a crime. The ABVA used this incident to initiate a public interest litigation in the Delhi High Court for the reading down of Section 377. This petition used the immediate reasons of the sexual health of prison inmates as one ground for the reading down.[4]

In 2001, the non-governmental organisation NAZ Foundation (India) Trust, filed a lawsuit in the Delhi High Court seeking legalisation of homosexual intercourse among consenting adults. In 2003, the Delhi High Court refused to consider a petition regarding the legality of the law, saying that the petitioners had no *locus standi* in the matter. The NAZ Foundation appealed to the Supreme Court of India against the decision of the High Court to dismiss the petition on technical grounds. The Supreme Court decided that the NAZ Foundation had the standing to file a public interest lawsuit in the case and sent the case back to the Delhi High Court for reconsideration.

The case came up for hearing before a bench comprising Chief Justice Ajit Prakash Shah and Justice S Muralidhar, and the judgment was delivered on 2 July 2009. The court located the rights to dignity and privacy within the right to life and liberty guaranteed by Article 21 (under the fundamental Right to Freedom charter) of the Constitution, because it creates an unreasonable classification and targets homosexuals as a class. Public *animus* and disgust towards a particular social group or vulnerable minority, it held, is not a valid ground for classification under Article 14. Article 15 of the Constitution forbids discrimination based on certain characteristics, including sex. The court held that the word 'sex' includes not only biological sex but also sexual orientation. The court also noted that the right to life under Article 21 includes the right to health and concluded that Section 377 is an impediment to public health, because it hinders HIV prevention efforts. The court did not strike down Section 377 of the IPC as a whole. The section was declared unconstitutional as it criminalised consensual sexual acts of adults in private.

Some special leave petitions were filed in the Supreme Court requesting an interim stay of the judgment, pending an appeal. However, the Supreme Court rejected those requests. A batch of appeals was filed with the Supreme Court, challenging the Delhi High Court judgement. On 27 March 2012, the Supreme Court reserved verdict on these. After initially opposing the judgement, the Attorney General G.E. Vahanvati decided not to file any appeal against the Delhi High Court's verdict.

On 11 December 2013, the Supreme Court's two-member bench of Justices GS Singhvi and SJ Mukhopadhyay overturned the decision of the Delhi High Court. It said that the 2009 order of the High Court is 'constitutionally unsustainable as only Parliament can change a law, not courts'.[5] In 2015, Congress MP Shashi Tharoor prepared a Private Member's Bill to amend Section 377. However, it was defeated in the Lok Sabha without having a discussion on it.

On 27 April 2016, five people filed a new writ petition in the Supreme Court challenging the constitutionality of Section 377. The petitioners claimed that the issue which they raised in their petition was varied and diverse from those raised in the pending curative petition in the 2013 *Koushal v. NAZ* case, in which the Supreme Court had upheld the constitutionality of Section 377. The NAZ case had been earlier referred to a five-judge bench in order to decide whether the curative petition could be accepted for consideration. The petitioners were dancer Navtej Singh Johar, journalist Sunil Mehra, chef Ritu Dalmia, hoteliers Aman Nath and Keshav Suri and businesswoman Ayesha Kapur. This case was the first instance wherein the petitioners argued that they had all been directly aggrieved because of Section 377, alleging it to be a direct violation of fundamental rights. The opposition to decriminalisation petitions was led by the Apostolic Alliance of Churches, Utkal Christian Council and Trust God Ministries. Advocate Manoj George represented the first two and Senior Advocate KS Radhakrishnan the third. The NDA government took a neutral stance, leaving the decision to the 'wisdom of the court' as long as it applies to 'consensual acts of adults in private'.

The petition was first placed before former Chief Justice of India Justice SA Bobde and Justice AK Bhushan on 29 June 2016. An order was passed to post the matter before Justice Dipak Misra for appropriate orders, since a curative petition was already pending before the constitution bench. On 8 January 2018, the case (*Navtej Singh Johar and others v. Union of India*) was listed to be heard by the Chief Justice's bench, which passed an order stating that the case would be heard by a constitution bench.

The matter was heard from 17 January 2018 by a five-judge constitution bench of the Supreme Court. On 10 July 2018, the Supreme Court commenced hearing of the pleas challenging the constitutionality of Section 377. The bench ended its hearing on 17 July and reserved its verdict, asking for both sides to submit written submissions for their claims by 20 July. On 6 September 2018, the court delivered its unanimous verdict, declaring portions of the law relating to consensual sexual acts between adults unconstitutional. This decision overturned the 2013 ruling in *Suresh Kumar Koushal v. NAZ Foundation*, in which the court upheld the law. However, other portions of Section 377 relating to sex with minors, non-consensual sexual acts and bestiality remain in force.[6]

This marked the end of an era, and this law will no longer be available for use or abuse, to foster, facilitate or perpetuate an atmosphere conducive to human rights violations of a certain kind and will put an end to the discrimination that many millions have faced because of sexual orientation or gender identity and sexual expression.[7]

## South Asia

In other South Asian post-colonial states like Pakistan, Bangladesh, Sri Lanka and Myanmar, Section 377 is still in force. After Pakistan's independence in 1947, the Parliament retained the penal code, merely changing the title to Pakistan Penal Code, which includes Article 377. No civil rights legislation exists to prohibit discrimination on the basis of sexual orientation. Rather same-sex behaviour is still a crime punishable with imprisonment between two and ten years, if not for life and a fine. The Pakistani government has always shown resistance towards the issue of LGBT rights and never hid its intolerance.

On 4 July 2011, the US embassy in Islamabad hosted an LGBT event in support of gay rights in Pakistan. The embassy described the event as its first gay, lesbian, bisexual and transgender pride celebration. Jamaat-e-Islami and other groups of religious conservatives in Pakistan condemned the event and went on a protest. Many Pakistanis were greatly offended by this and called this event an act of 'social and cultural terrorism against the country'. Pakistani society is the least accepting of homosexuality.[8]

In 2018, however, Pakistan's parliament passed the Transgender Persons (Protection of Rights) Act, which legally provides equality to transgender people and safeguards their rights. The law aims to legally recognise transgender people in the country. It also allows them to legally have the same rights as cisgender people.[9]

In Bangladesh, LGBT rights are heavily suppressed. Section 377 carried over into the Pakistan Penal Code and has continued to be part of Bangladesh's legal code since its independence from Pakistan in 1971. Homosexuality is punishable in Bangladesh with a life sentence and fine. In 2009 and 2013, the Bangladesh Parliament refused to overturn Section 377.

The first attempt to create an LGBT organisation in Bangladesh came in 1999, when a man called Rengyu opened the first online group for Bangladeshi gay people, called

Gay Bangladesh, which was moderated by a man named Abrar. In 2002, two other online groups appeared on the Yahoo! Portal—Teen Gay Bangladesh operated by Abrar and Boys Only Bangladesh, which were deleted in 2022. In January 2014, Bangladesh's first LGBT magazine named *Roopbaan* was published. In 2014, Bangladesh held its first *hijra* parade. On 25 April 2016, Xulhaz Mannan, founder of *Roopbaan* magazine and organiser of the Rainbow Rally, was assassinated in his apartment together with a friend, Mahbub Rabbi Tonoy. Ansar-al-Islam, a group linked to Al Qaeda, claimed responsibility for the murders, stating that as he had himself confirmed his sexuality, he needed to be killed according to Shariah law.[10]

LGBT people in Sri Lanka face legal and social challenges. Article 365 of the Sri Lankan Penal Code, which dates from the time of colonial British Ceylon, criminalises sexual acts deemed 'against the order of nature'. For much of the law's history, the prohibition applied only to males; in 1995, Article 365 was amended to replace the word 'males' with 'persons' so that sexual activity between consenting adult females was also outlawed in addition to that between consenting adult males. Other laws that marginalise LGBT individuals are enforced against purported gender impersonation (Article 399, used against transgender people) and public indecency (Section 7, 1841 Vagrants Ordinance, used against sex workers and anyone whose public behaviours are deemed to indicate same-sex sexual activity).

Sri Lankan society generally takes a modestly unobtrusive and traditionalist view of homosexuality; certain traditions exist for the promotion and, consequently, these laws have mostly been applied loosely (if ever). In 1994, Sherman de Rose set up Companions on a Journey (CoJ), the first LGBT support group in Sri Lanka. The Women's Support Group split off from CoJ in 1999, forming a separate organisation for lesbian, bisexual and transgender women. Equal Ground was then set up as a LGBTI group.

In March 2021, in order to commemorate Zero Discrimination Day, the President of Sri Lanka Gotabaya Rajapaksa tweeted, 'As the president of Sri Lanka, I am determined to secure everybody's right to live life with dignity regardless of age, gender, sexuality, race, physical appearance and beliefs.' Both the socialist government of Rajapaksa and the conservative government of Sirisena have stated that 'discrimination against LGBT people was unconstitutional and that the application of sections 365 and 365A in a manner that was discriminatory against LGBT persons was unconstitutional'.[11]

In Myanmar, LGBT people are subjected to official persecution and discrimination, with LGBT people facing legal and social challenges not experienced by others. Same-sex sexual activity is illegal, and section 377 of Myanmar's Penal Code subjects same-sex sexual acts (regardless of whether they are consensual or done in private) to a term of imprisonment of up to 20 years. Heterosexual anal intercourse and oral sex are also illegal. Transgender people are subject to police harassment and sexual assault, and their gender identity is not recognised by the state. Following the 2011–2015 Myanmar political reforms, improvements in media and civil freedoms have allowed LGBT people to gain more visibility and support in the country. Nevertheless, LGBT activists have noted a growing climate of societal acceptance and tolerance toward LGBT people, in line with worldwide trends.

In 2001, an exile group, the All Burma Students' Democratic Front, voted to have the law repealed. This was seen as a victory by the Committee for Lesbigay Rights in Burma, although such a change was considered unlikely to occur given the prevailing political climate against change. In 2013, then-Opposition leader Aung San Suu Kyi called on the country to decriminalise homosexuality, which later she didn't after she attained political majority.[12]

## Southeast Asia

In Malaysia, LGBT people face significant challenges not experienced by non-LGBT residents. Sodomy is a crime in the country, with strictly enforced laws, and social attitudes towards the LGBT community are shaped by Islam, the official state religion of Malaysia. Breaking the law is punishable by up to 20 years in prison and authorities will also bring the person to several corporal punishments.

In 1994, the government banned anyone who is homosexual, bisexual or transsexual from appearing in state-controlled media. In 1995, the Religious Affairs Minister of the state of Selangor praised the Islamic Badar vigilante groups, who had organised in 1994, for assisting in the arrest of 7000 individuals for engaging in 'unIslamic' activities such as homosexuality. In 2005, the Royal Malaysian Navy (RMN) chief Mohd Anwar Mohd Nor stated that the Navy would never accept homosexuals.

There is no legal protection for LGBTQ individuals in Malaysia. A few MPs from the previous ruling coalition such as Pakatan Harapan have voiced support for LGBTQ rights, as has Marina Mahathir, the daughter of former prime minister Mahathir Mohamad, who called for an end to discrimination based on sexual orientation in 1998 and 1999. Parti Sosialis Malaysia is the only political party to openly support and defend the rights of LGBT people alongside other minority rights.[13]

Homosexuality is illegal in Brunei. Sexual relations between men are punishable by death or whipping; sex between women is punishable by caning or imprisonment. The sultanate applied a moratorium on the death penalty in 2019, which could be revoked at any time. Out Right Action International has described Brunei as 'the country that has the most worrisome state of rights for LGBT people in Southeast Asia'. Before the 2019 implementation of the Syariah Penal

Code Order (SPCO), homosexual acts were illegal and punishable by up to 10 years' imprisonment, even if they were private and consensual. From 2014, Brunei began a staged implementation of Shariah law. Provisions of the SPCO dealing with adultery and sodomy and prescribing death by stoning and corporal punishments came into force on 3 April 2019.

Following widespread international condemnation and media attention, which included an open letter from American actor George Clooney calling for the boycott of the Sultan of Brunei›s luxury hotels—The Beverly Hills Hotel and Hotel Bel-Air among them—the Brunei government extended its moratorium on the death penalty to encompass the SPCO in May 2019. Under the moratorium, the code›s death by stoning penalty provisions are not enacted for as long as the moratorium continues. As the Sultan is an absolute monarch with full executive power, removing the moratorium and reinstating capital punishment would require minimal process and could occur without warning. The LGBT community in Brunei is very hidden and secret. Bruneian society tends to associate homosexuality with 'effeminate men'.[14]

Singapore law inherited from the British Empire prohibited sodomy regardless of sex. As such, heterosexual and homosexual anal or oral sex was illegal. In 2007, such sexual activity was legalised for heterosexuals and lesbians, but not between men. The punishment is two years' imprisonment.

On 21 August 2022, Prime Minister Lee Hsien Loong announced at the National Day Rally that the government intended to repeal section 377A, noting that there would be significant risk of the law being struck down in future legal challenges 'on the grounds that it breaches Article 12 of the Constitution—the Equal Protection provision'. Lee added that the repeal would be deliberated through Parliament.

In 2019, the Maintenance of Religious Harmony Act was amended to protect the LGBTQ community from religiously motivated violence. Legal action can be taken against a religious group or its members for urging violence against certain 'target groups'. The Explanatory Statement states, 'The target group need not be confined to persons who practise a certain religion. The target group may be made up of atheists, individuals from a specific racial community, who share a similar sexual orientation, or have a certain nationality or descent like foreign workers or new citizens'. In 2022, Home Affairs and Law Minister K Shanmugam confirmed that now LGBTQ people were protected against threats or acts of violence.[15]

From the inception to the present day, we can thereby conclude that societal and living conditions of LGBTQ people living in these countries, which were former colonies of Great Britain, were adverse, and they faced several attempts of hostility and discrimination. In most of these countries, LGBTQ people are treated as criminals and often forced to live an exceedingly clandestine lifestyle, camouflaging their innate identity from the society that they were born and grew up in. Furthermore, pre-colonial times LGBTQ+ people in these nations had more tolerance and societal acceptance from their own people than they have today. Thus, the British colonial rule exceedingly made the lives of their colonial subjects difficult and less tolerable, filled with banality and vast inequality. Modern-day Great Britain has repealed its own Buggery Act. The Supreme Court of India has also read down Section 377 in an apposite historic judgement in 2018. We can only hope and envision that this will be a leading example for other Commonwealth nations to follow suit to bring forth true egalitarianism.

## Endnotes

1 Enze Han and Joseph O' Mahoney, *British Colonialism and the Criminalization of Homosexuality: Queens, Crime and Empire* (Routledge Focus, 2018).

2 Han and O'Mahoney, *British Colonialism and the Criminalization of Homosexuality.*

3 https://en.wikipedia.org/wiki/Wolfenden_report

4 Shobha Aggarwal, "ABVA Writ Petition for the Repeal of Section 377," in *Humjinsi: A Resource Book on Lesbian, Gay, Bisexual Rights in India*, ed. Bina Fernandez (India Centre for Human Rights and Law, 1999), 34.

5 https://en.wikipedia.org/wiki/NAZ_Foundation_V.Govt._of_NCT_of_Delhi

6 https://en.wikipedia.org/wiki/Navtej_Singh _Johar_v._Union_of_India

7 http://timesofindia.indiatimes.com/articleshow/65712471.cms?utm_source=contentofinterest&utm_medium=text&utm_campaign=cppst

8 LGBT rights in Pakistan—Wikipedia.

9 https://en.wikipedia.org/wiki/Transgender_Persons_(Protection_of_Rights)_Act,_2018

10 https://en.wikipedia.org/wiki/LGBT_rights_in_Bangladesh

11 https://en.wikipedia.org/wiki/LGBT_rights_in_Sri _Lanka

12 LGBT rights in Myanmar—Wikipedia.

13 LGBT rights in Malaysia—Wikipedia.

14 LGBT rights in Brunei—Wikipedia.

15 LGBT rights in Singapore—Wikipedia.

# Gender Issues in Asia through the Prism of Counselling—Adolescent Counselling

*Sumana Bagchi*

## Introduction

The World Health Organization (WHO) defines adolescence as the period of life between 10–19 years. It is the transient period from dependent childhood to self-sufficient adulthood. It is a time of psychological maturation, becoming adult-like in behaviour. It is a period of rapid physical and biological changes, which may lead to confusion, tension, frustration and insecurity. Adolescence is said to be a period of stress and strain. Adolescents are a special group because of their developmental stage and special problems. Because adolescence is a stage of human development during which a young person must move from dependence to independence and develop autonomy and maturity, young people in particular are faced with many challenges. Some young people are more successful than others when confronting and dealing with the stress associated with the challenges of adolescent life; they are more resilient and have better coping strategies. However, some adolescents are unable to confront and deal with these challenges successfully.

## Nature of Child Abuse

We all know about domestic violence against women, children and the elderly. Abuse and violence are obnoxious forms of power equations, a complicated relationship between strong and weak or powerful and powerless. Here, child abuse is any behaviour that harms a child, anyone under 18. It can take many forms including physical, sexual, emotional and psychological abuse. It is also a form of neglect and exploitation.

Child abuse is against the law. It may also include any act or failure to act by a parent or caregiver that results in actual or potential harm to a child in any place, such as the child's home, school or communities where they interact with acquaintances and strangers. The terms 'child abuse' and 'child maltreatment' are explained differently by experts. Some researchers explained that child maltreatment is an umbrella term to cover neglect, exploitation and trafficking. Child abuse is harmful, irrespective of the reason. Abusive behaviour involves treating someone with cruelty and violence. It often happens regularly or repeatedly.[1]

## Types of Child Abuse

### 1. *Physical Abuse*

Physical injury or any kind of physical harassment against a child is the actual form of physical abuse. Hitting, beating, smacking, scratching and choking a child are all brutal example of child abuse.

### 2. *Sexual Abuse*

There are two types of sexual abuse: contact and non-contact abuse. Contact abuse can include sexual touching of any part of a child's body. Non-contact abuse is to harass the child with many signs, such as wrong indications. Sexual abuse can have both long- and short-term effects. The main effects are shame and guilt, fear, anxiety, aggression and self-harm. When a child gets sexually abused by their own family members or any unknown person, they might not understand what sexual abuse is and whether it is wrong or right. So, their nascent psychological development gets totally shattered. When they want to share their pain and trauma with any family member or confidant, they get muted by the concern of social stigma.

## 3. *Emotional Abuse*

All children are different. Some are aggressive, some shy and some are very emotional. These are all signs of how they have grown up in the abode of their family. Bullying, yelling, isolating, criticising and comparison are all types of emotional abuse. Gender discrimination also plays a major role in a child's emotional abuse.

## 4. *Neglect*

Negligence also takes a major role in child abuse. Failing to provide a child with the things they need to grow, such as shelter, food, hygiene, supervision, medical attention and safety purposely is a form of child abuse.

## Psychological Impact of Child Abuse

Exposing a child to domestic violence with the mentioned four forms of abuse is unhealthy and inappropriate for the child's physiological development. Psychological abuse of a child is a pattern of physical, behavioural and mental actions against the child's normal psychological development. When the child feels that they are worthless, unloved and unwanted, they can't express their sorrow and pain to their close ones. There are some important symptoms of psychological abuse of a child, as mentioned below:

1. Difficulties in school
2. Eating disorders
3. Low self-esteem
4. Depression

5. Anxiety
6. Aggressive Behaviour
7. Sleep disorders
8. Relationship problems with relatives, friends and partners
9. Denial[2,3]

Any of the forms of psychological abuse is responsible for future development. Due to emotional and psychological abuse, they become aggressive and suspicious. Negative thoughts and negative behaviours trigger their mind to act like negative-minded people. They seldom show hope or positivity. Also, jealousy, narcissism and other pathologies are the most negative impacts of low self-esteem. Forceful physical enjoyment with others and painful sexual acts with partners are all negative impacts of child sexual abuse. These all are synonymous with crime. The findings of a recent study from the American Psychological Association are right on target: 'Given the prevalence of childhood psychological abuse and the severity of harm to young victims, it should be at the forefront of mental health'. The study confirms that childhood psychological abuse has lasting significant damage, equal to exceeding the long-term consequences of physical abuse.

Justice Ramana, in the *Indian Express* on 5 June 2020, said that ensuring effective legal services in collaboration with the NGO Commonwealth Human Rights Initiative was imperative. The focus right now—including that of essential service providers such as the police—is on the pandemic, so abuse cases remained unresolved, with no immediate healing available, claims Yogita Bhayana, a women and child's right activist and the founder of NGO PARI. Psychologist Sachita Sethi feels that abusers lack power and control in other aspects of life. In this time, the victim is in front of their eyes, so it becomes even more acceptable to them to commit such acts. A Press Trust of India (PTI) report stated that during 31 March 2020, the first week of the lockdown, the Child Line India Helpline received over 92,000 SOS calls across the country, asking for protection from abuse and violence. According to another PTI report, the National Commission for Women (NCW) received 315 complaints of domestic violence in April 2020.[4]

Gender discrimination in our society is also a huge issue; women face many problems from a ripe age, and the family also has a hand in these issues. For example, the dowry system, low-income housing, divorce, abortion, etc.

## Importance of Adolescent Counselling

Seeking professional help in the form of counselling can be useful but is limited to a prescribed relationship, often with a one-way focus on personal disclosure, problem-solving and challenging self-destructive thought processes. However, seeking professional help is not generally a preferred option for young people. It is well-documented that young people generally prefer to seek help from their peers, suggesting that it is unlikely that they will seek adult counselling help in the first instance. Up to 19 percent of adolescents tell their peers rather than a professional of their distress. However, research has identified a number of factors that influence help-seeking behaviour, including gender, availability of social support, expectations about outcomes, type of psychological problem and emotional competence. Additionally, Boldero and Fallon identified that older adolescents asked peers for help frequently while greater numbers of younger respondents in their study asked family members. Considering all the facts, we have to lay more emphasis on the adolescent age group. Counselling is one of the important modalities of treatment for adolescent-related problems. It is defined as an interactive process conjoining the counselee who needs assistance and the counsellor who is trained and educated to give assistance.

Counselling is a process where clients are helped in dealing with their personal and interpersonal conflicts by a third-party therapist. The main objective is to help the client to bring about a voluntary change in the client. Various techniques like directive counselling, non-directive or client-centred counselling and elective counselling are used for the purpose. In directive counselling, the counsellor plays the major role. He tries to direct the thinking of the counselee by informing, explaining, interpreting and advising. In non-directive counselling, the client is more important. The client takes active part in the therapy. They gain insight into problems with the help of the counsellor. In elective counselling, we use the combination of directive and non-directive processes.[5]

## Case Studies

Here I will mention three cases of adolescent problems in their own words.

### *Person 1*

> 'Having lost my mother at the age of 6, my childhood was particularly difficult. Growing up by myself, I had always been extra cautious about being the best version of myself. Slowly this habit manifested as a people-pleasing attitude. I sought parental and academic validation in order to become the "best". However, little did I know that this self-imposed pressure would backfire. In the eighth grade, when my father decided to marry again, I retaliated with the most vindictive version of teenage rebel. I slipped back into episodic aggressive behaviours as well as refused to do daily tasks on my own. This was accompanied by performance anxiety and a deep sense of detachment from family and also my grandmother who raised me. This dissonance in identity pushed me to think but not create, until I found poetry. Although I was not particularly well-acquainted with the styles, I tried my

novice hand at poetry, sought validation on Facebook and enjoyed interacting with strangers online. Although that process gave me insight and helped me stay put, in retrospect, I was nothing but a vulnerable teenager with a strong online presence. My gender, specifically speaking, has factored in all of these incidents. Losing my mother affected my sensibility around a gendered identity. I have often assumed mother-like roles in friend circles, leading to consequences both good and bad. Furthermore, in dealing with the absence of absolute parental guidance, I have superimposed unreal standards of perfection on myself. Both within the home and outside, I have tried to outperform my abilities in an effort to prove my worth. However, with growing age and an increasing sense of cathartic acceptance, I have come to look for meaning in life. Despite my personal efforts, I often fall prey to bouts of immense anxiety, which I am currently trying to work on and improve'.

## *Person 2*

'My childhood was full of solitude. I am a single child. I didn't even have a cousin or someone of my age around me to play with. And as my mother was a teacher in the school where I studied, most of my friends also kept a distance from me. So, I created a utopian world of mine.

Eventually, I became habituated to being excluded. But it was not entirely their fault. I was not allowed to go anywhere, neither at a picnic nor at any birthday party. So, if some of them invited me over, I used to avoid the topic because I knew what the possible answer of my family members would be if I sought permission to go out with my friends. So, I refused to go with them without even asking for my parents' permission. So, most of them thought that I am snobbish and haughty.

Some of them even started judging me, like discussing having a crush is cool for them but is prohibited for me as I am a 'teacher's daughter'.

There I created my own world of comfort, my imaginary world. I pretended to have a large group of friends. I told people about their habits, what conversation we had the previous day, as if they really existed. I felt so comfortable in my utopian world, that I started finding it difficult to relate to the real world around me. It was like a show-off for me that, "Look, even I can have a friend group of mine", and I even started getting attention because I created those characters according to my imagination, so interesting and attractive. I even started mumbling when no one was around as if I was talking to those imaginary friends. Even when something bad happened to me, some sort of harassment, I complained to them and no one from the real world knew anything. I was so introverted that I almost stopped communicating with everyone. Eventually, I also started to feel that it was exceeding its limit, and I started finding it cumbersome to fit myself in the real world.

Then like a ray of hope, I met two friends from a new batch, who literally pulled me out of this situation. They were not from my school, so I had no fear of being judged by them as an alien, that is, a 'teacher's daughter'. I opened up for the first time and laughed with them. As I mentioned earlier, I was not allowed to go out and hang out with my friends. Instead of judging my situation, they understood it and started coming over. Though my habit of creating an imaginary world is not fully gone till date, from being an extremely introvert person, I am now an ambivert and can easily talk to like-minded people. Though I still find it difficult to open up in front of people'.

## *Person 3*

'I faced three specific problems in my adolescence, which despite perhaps being common to all teenagers, were significantly difficult to overcome. I don't believe I have overcome these problems completely in my adulthood, but I have formulated better coping mechanisms for them. Following are the problems and the coping mechanisms adopted:

1. Agency vs Support: I had some difficulty understanding the expectations of adulthood or maturity that were thrust upon me as a teenager. Suddenly I was expected to make serious decisions about my life (especially around the ages of 15–18), while also having to be obedient to the rules and discipline of the school environment. Where on the one hand I dearly desired the autonomy to make my own decisions, on the other hand, I felt very lost without my parents' guidance. It felt a little ridiculous to have to plan what to do with my life when I had to ask permission to go to the bathroom in school! This is in addition to having grown up very sheltered and protected, thus not knowing anything about how to manage in the world outside my home, school and tuition class. There was a constant conflict with my parents, because I could not understand why they would not stop pressuring me while emphasising that I be independent. They could not understand why I was finding it difficult to comprehend their actions. Eventually, the only way I coped was by becoming an adult. As I left school and adapted to the plethora of new changes in college and beyond, I learnt how to balance the desire of autonomy with that of parental support. Time was the only mitigating factor.[6]

2. Identity and Conflict: Another issue that caused a lot of anxiety in adolescence was that I was gradually forming an identity of my own, separate from my parents. This began to range from the choice of subjects in Class 11, to the choice of partner, to the choice of friends, to the choice of clothes and hairstyle. My parents also struggled to understand why I was suddenly so different from them, and I could not understand why they suddenly became like strangers to me. This is perhaps why I grew closer to my mother than my father in my adolescence, because my evolving personality aligned with her more than my father's. This period of my life also created a permanent rift with my father, as he slowly began to realise that he simply does not like or understand the person I was becoming, and I could not like or understand him either. It is difficult for parents to grow used to the fact that their children are no longer the moulds they were fashioned into. I coped with this simply by continuing to remain who I was, and doing exactly what I wanted to do. I would not have been able to forgive myself if I had yielded to my parents' efforts to make me more like them. Eventually, they too grew to understand who I was, and to appreciate how I was different, and love where I was similar to them.

3. Love vs Abuse: The aforementioned problems seem significant in hindsight, but the most pervasive issue I faced in adolescence was navigating the desire for love and intimacy. My parents' marriage was not a good ideal and neither were the marriages of my friends' parents. I had nowhere to turn to, to understand what to expect from a partner, what kind of behaviour was unacceptable and what boundaries should be maintained. Given that my father,

> especially, was extremely hostile to my choice of partner then, I felt extremely isolated from my family and felt that I could only depend on my partner. Of course, overdependence at any age is not good. However, because my family became estranged from me, it took me a long time to realise that my partner was physically and emotionally abusive. There came a time when I had nowhere else to turn and would only look to my partner, because I felt that only he understood me. Leaving him was the most difficult decision I made in my adolescence, because I felt completely alone, completely alienated from my friends and parents. I coped with this by going out into the world, meeting new people and trying to understand that my model of love and attachment was flawed'.[7,8]

## Conclusion

During adolescence, young people inevitably face physiological and biological changes. These changes influence the young person's emotional state. Additionally, the emergence of a sexual drive predisposes young people to explore new relationships that produce social and interpersonal challenges. During adolescence, young people also experience cognitive changes. They develop a capacity for abstract thinking, discern new ways of processing information and learn to think creatively and critically. Forming an identity, parental expectations, societal expectations and managing the influence of peers are also challenging for most young people. These adolescent challenges, combined with the stresses and demands of life, lead many young people to become disillusioned, overwhelmed and unable to cope. Other tension reduction strategies such as drug and alcohol use run the risk of developing into substance abuse behaviours. This is particularly so among the adolescent population, who typically take risks and experiment with new behaviours. All these things can be helped and proper guidance can be given with the help of adolescent counselling.[9,10]

## Endnotes

1 J Maybe and B Sorensen, *Counseling for Young People* (Buckingham: Open University Press, 1995).

2 FA White, "Parent, Adolescent Communication and Adolescent Decision-Making," *Journal of Family Studies* 2, (1996): 41–56.

3 AH Winefield and M Tiggeman, "Employment Status and Psychological Well-Being: A Longitudinal Study," *Journal of Applied Psychology* 75, no. 4(1990): 455–9.

4 D Baumrind, "Effective Parenting During the Early Adolescent Transition," in *Family Transitions*, eds. PA Cowan and EM Hetherington (Hillsdale: Lawrence Erilbaum, 1991), 219–44.

5 D Baumrind, "The Influence of Parenting Style on Adolescent Competence and Substance Use," *Journal of Early Adolescence* 11, no. 1(1991): 56–95.

6 ML Borrine et al., "Family Conflict and Adolescent Adjustment in Intact, Divorced and Blended Families," *Journal of Consulting and Clinical Psychology* 59, no. 5(1991): 753–5.

7 L Chassin and M Barrera, "Substance Use Escalation and Substance Use Restraint Among Adolescent Children of Alcoholics," *Society of Psychologists in Addictive Behaviors* 7(1993): 3–20.

8 E Frydenberg and R Lewis, "Adolescent Well-Being: Building Young People's Resources," in *Beyond Coping: Meeting Goals Visions and Challenges*, ed. E Frydenberg (London: Oxford University Press, 2002), 175–94.

9 Marimuthu Sivakumar, *Gender Discrimination and Women's Development in India* (Erode: Chikkaiah Naicker College).

10 Sumana Bagchi, Personal research and counselling (Adolescence Mental Health, Gender Studies), 2005–2020

# Law for Women and Advocate Cornelia Sorabji's Vision of Women's Rights in Colonial India

***Sumit Kumar Bar***

## Introduction

Advocate Cornelia Sorabji(1866–1954) was first woman advocate and first female graduate from the erstwhile Bombay University. She was the first Indian woman who took admission to Oxford University. She was born in a Parsi Christian family of Nasik within the jurisdiction of Bombay Presidency, British India. Her father was Reverend Sorabji Karshedji, who was originally Parsi but converted to Christianity. He was the key person who insisted on women's entry into the contemporary university education system. In 1892, Cornelia Sorabji appeared for the Bachelor of Civil Law in Somerville College, Oxford. In 1899, she presented herself for the LLB examination in Bombay University and, in the same year, the pleaders' examination in the Allahabad High Court.

Sorabji completed the first two years of her probation as a lawyer in 1905–1906. During this period, she had been assigned to find some disputes in Indian families regarding the position and status of women that the male members of the law court could not understand clearly. These families had to face internal conflicts regarding the inheritance of family property. Women in contemporary orthodox Indian families were pardanashins[1] among whom Sorabji felt the need for women's education to empower them enough to claim their legal rights. These legal rights included the rights of landed properties, but the absence of proper education restricted them from this inheritance process.

## Problems of the Pardanashins

Sorabji understood clearly that pardanashin women had their own ideas, which could equally be applied for social welfare if properly trimmed. But the major difference between their ideas and the real world as found by Sorabji was caused by the disequilibrium in legal rights. Sorabji wrote at a time when India was struggling with the last spell of the freedom struggle. After nearly three centuries of foreign rule, India was to achieve her freedom in spite of having various opinions on her procedures and achievements. It is historically true that India had a hard achievement to coalesce the holistic inclusion of representatives from different corners of social life so as to place it on the map of independent India in the true sense. In pre-independent Indian society, the native men had hardly any opportunity to argue for any corrective measure in legal affairs. The women, being a subjugated race under male dominance, were doubly marginalised. In that situation, the orthodoxy in Indian society compelled them to remain within the confinement of purdah, that is, the curtain. Advocate Sorabji from her early youth felt a strong consciousness for women's life behind the purdah. After returning from England, she tried to help the pardanashin women for their legal justice.

Protection of property rights is the basis of the legal help that Sorabji offered to the suffering Indian women. Sorabji's attempts gave an impetus to 20$^{th}$ century women's rights in India. Her attempts offered spaces or resistance within which women could secure at least basic rights against oppressive social relations.[2] Critics may debate how much Sorabji succeeded in addressing the problems of women of colonial India, but it is said that her pleading behind the purdah for the pardanashin women was a landmark in the history of feminine movements in the Indian subcontinent. The troublesome situation was that Sorabji herself had to keep a distance from the courtroom, especially to face the jury because she was a woman. A courtroom in her time was meant for male persons practising law and pleading before the honourable judges.

Lord Hobhouse (1819–1904) problematised legal provisions for pardanashin women in colonial India, especially upper-class Hindu women who faced disputes over their properties. This corresponds to Sorabji's solicitation as an advocate's appeal before the honourable court for justification in their favour, especially when it was related to the question of inheritance of property. Lord Hobhouse, in his letter to Advocate Sorabji[3] stated that adequate legal services for the women of a colonial country like India were seriously threatened by the term of impersonation to the pardanashin women.

Since no aristocratic lady could face a male lawyer for her legal claim of property rights, very often she had to rely on a male messenger, which might include a member of her own family. But due to the social side of the seclusion of women, the pardanashin women were very often victimised by this falsity, leading to a spell of deprivation. This social impediment was so harmful, as observed by Lord Hobhouse, that it even weakened the political structure of a country like India. Sorabji's attempt seriously questioned the conventionality of law in social parameters.

## Two Schools of Indian Law

The two prime subcategories of Indian inheritance law are the 'Dayabhaga' and the 'Mitakshara'. The Dayabhaga school of Indian law[4] ensures that with the non-availability of male descendants, the widow has the right to enforce partition and can inherit the husband's share. Sorabji seemed to advocate against the ambiguity regarding the issue of *stridhana*[5] because *stridhana* has been vaguely defined by the two schools of Indian law. Sorabji, being an Oxford graduate, tried to establish a scientific attitude towards the legal definition in this discipline, eradicating the mythical lineage of the origin of law. The establishment of law requires a practical approach of the human movement which serves as the root of a law that perpetuates over certain periods of history.

Sorabji in *Pardanashins* spoke in favour of the enactment or judicial establishment of succession rights of women for inheriting the property. In this connection one may consider the verdicts of Privy Council on the widows which have been recorded by Rishindranath Nath Sarkar:

> The privy council held the doctrine of the *Mitakshara*[6] on widow's right in the property inherited from her husband to be erroneous by reason of its being in conflict with the text of *Katyayana*—their Lordships of the Judicial Committee were misled into their position by assuming the interpretation put on her right to her husband's inheritance by Dayabhaga to be its only real meaning.

Rishindranath Sarkar gave an account of the Mitakshara school. According to him, in this school of Indian law as held by the courts of justice, the widow could inherit only the exceptional circumstances of the husband being separate, that is when he was neither joint nor re-united with any co-heir. The Mitakshara is actually a commentary based upon the Yajnavalka Smriti, which advocates the theory of 'inheritance by birth'. The British court of law adopted Mitakshara only on the ground that it was pre-existing in Indian society. Cornelia Sorabji understood the obligations that the British law system had to face in India, but in spite of this she strongly opined to eradicate such practices in the 20th century. The Mitakshara legal provision generally restricts women to being coparceners.

Even the widow of a deceased coparcener is restricted in this matter till the share of the partitioned property is enforced by her husband or sons. The uncertainty of being a woman always created a major hindrance to Sorabji for a successful practice in the court of law. Mr Gadgil insisted that Advocate Sorabji specialise as a criminal defence lawyer. She agreed to that, but she expressed her willingness to help the pardanashin women for which she said,

I wanted to be able to help *purdahnashins* in relation to their property and disabilities concerned with their status.[7]

Sorabji had a varied accession to the case of 'inheritance', 'succession', 'maintenance allowances' and 'stridhana' or the Hindu women's peculium. Sorabji understood clearly that the Hindu pardanashins had to face several obstacles due to the demand for an heir from their husbands. Polygamy in Hindu families was perhaps caused by this demand, because Hinduism is in theory monogamous. Evidently, their demand for the share of the property became complicated in case of a coparcener. Sorabji's concern grew with the fact that there was no law of divorce in contemporary Hinduism. In 1932, a group of progressives attempted to legislate it, which caused severe criticism in the orthodox Hindu community. Sorabji seems to problematise it in the sense that most of the clients being widows did not accept the advantages of the British-made law for India especially for the women. They seemed to be still in favour of the orthodox Hindu widow.

Sorabji also perceived clearly that the confinement of women inside the purdah was culturally deep-rooted and the women must be enlightened about the falsity of the myth associated with the purdah. In India, the subjugation of women has been perpetuated as a social system which a modern scholar like Reena Patel too has opined in this regard:

> To evaluate the role of law in establishing effective property rights for women, it is necessary to specify

> what one means by 'law' within the analysis. Law may be conceptualized and evaluated in various ways and at various levels, given its very nature and ability to operate as a social system in society as well as prescribe and enforce norms of behaviour.[8]

Patel, while defining law, mentioned to Cotterell that it is both a prescriptive norm and a descriptive fact. Patel seemed to term law as a social structure which should be studied within its own terms and in an individual conception. Law operates within a certain social structure; to some extent, in various cases, a certain group of people had to undergo a hegemonic power in the name of law. During the last spell of colonial India, the law had a provision for being discursive. It is true that Sorabji understood that the law for women set by the colonial rulers still sustained a dichotomy because of the succession of women's property rights. Indian women are located within the family and their identities are framed by some preordained religious ideologies. In this situation, their claim to the right of the landed property dwindles, and its determination thereof is negotiated. Several cases were found where women's rights were very often overpowered by the male heirs. The colonial process for the formation of law in this regard is another picture in the incorporation of the Hindu structure of women's rights within the traditional family structure, which evolved through a historical process. Sorabji understood clearly that legal empowerment in favour of women, in the contemporary situation, must be furthered towards modernity, even if they could not deny the traditional family structure. Sorabji's acts were exemplary in the case of interrogating about the infringement of human rights, and these were embedded in women's disadvantages, both physically and culturally.

It is pertinent to say that the disadvantages both physically and culturally are best understood by the interpretation of the two identities of women, the wife and the widow. *Manusmriti*, in antiquity, stated regarding women's rights of property that a wife is not entitled to any part of her husband's property during her husband's lifetime. She has only the right of maintenance against her husband and it is applicable too in the case of being complained about as unchaste or if she is an outcast or indulges in immorality. In this regard, it also means that if she earns something, it must belong to her husband. In another instance, the same legacy of *Manusmriti* derecognises the widow as the actual legal heir to her husband's property. This is further stressed when a widow is sonless. Accordingly, the property of a dead man without any male successor would devolve to the other male members of his family, like his father, brother or any other close male relative.[9] Therefore, the woman, in spite of being physically present and competent enough to own and maintain her deceased husband, is non-existing in the eyes of the law court.

## Conclusion

Sorabji attempted to bring the purdahnashin's property rights under the purview of right judicature and, therefore, a justified evaluation of their claims to the share of the property is regarded as a precursor to contemporary women's empowerment. Sorabji's lifelong endeavour for the upliftment of pardanashin women's condition in colonial India is an early major landmark for this empowerment, because she realised that the law must have an independent vision free from the clutches of religious and cultural frameworks. Women in colonial India were not exonerated from gender-based oppression within any single attempt. It has also been stated by Prof Janki Nayar that that stated that the effectiveness of legislative reform was an important tool for improving the status of women in pre-independent India, but to do that there had to be a justified power relation because 'the language of rights of women could only be legitimately deployed' as per the larger question of 'national independence'.[10] Advocate Sorabji's vision of the inclusion of women in the modern legal paradigm would embolden the contemporary demand of a modern and independent state formation.

## Endnotes

1 The word pardanashin is an Indian word which denotes the status of women who had to stay behind the curtain. It had been the custom of Indian society from several ages and practised by mostly the upper class of the society. It had been ordained to keep dignity of women and keep aloof from the gaze of male persons other than the male members of a woman's family.

2 In pardanashin, Sorabji included both secluded women and widows, because the widow too had to keep herself aloof, mostly behind the curtain if she resided in the family.

3 Arthur Hobhouse (1819–1904) was an English lawyer and judge who was sent to India and became a law member of the Council of the Governor General of India. Lord Hobhouse's extended letter to Sorabji, where he put his advisory to Miss Sorabji is regarded as a major source of inspiration that 'if pardanashin owners of property could be visited by ladies competent to understand their cases, to prepare them for advice, or perhaps to advice on them at first-hand; to take evidence direct from them for when required for judicial purpose, to explain documents—in short to do things face to face which are now done through a veil—they would own those properties more fully, in much nearer accordance with the provision of the law'.

4 The Dayabhaga School introduced a complete change in the law recognising the heritable right of the widow in default of male issue even when the husband was joint or re-united with the coparceners. The Dayabhaga School in this respect may confer higher rights on women but seriously curtail their rights in other respects by introducing restrictions on the widow's power of alienation. See Rishindranath Sarkar, Hindu Women's Rights to Property (Act No. XVIII of 197 As Amended by Act No. XI of 1938), 1938.

5 It is still debated whether *stridhana* is actually under a woman's independent ownership, but there is a prejudice

that the precious jewellery should be owned jointly with her husband.

6 The Mitakshara School of Indian Law is nearly similar to the Dayabhaga School of Indian law. The Mitakshara was among the customary laws in the subcontinent in the context of property inheritance. While the Dayabhaga School was mostly active in eastern India, the Mitakshara was mostly found in western India.

7 Cornelia Sorabji, *India Calling: The Memories of Cornelia Sorabji* (New Delhi: Oxford University Press, 2001), 64.

8 Reena Patel, *Hindu Women's Property Rights in Rural India: Law, Labour and Culture in Action* (Hampshire, England: Ashgate Publishing Limited, 2007), 14.

9 *c.f.* Jane Austen's novel *Pride and Prejudice*. This novel portrayed the equally sorry plight of English women during the 19$^{th}$ century, where British law did not allow unmarried women to inherit property. To inherit or to maintain any property, she had to be associated with any male person with a familial relation.

10 Janki Nair, *Women and Law in Colonial India: A Social History* (New Delhi: Kali for Women, 1996), 84.

*Section III*

# Foreign Policy Dynamics

# India and the ASEAN: The Logic of Partnership in the Indo-Pacific Region

*Sayantani Sen Mazumdar*

## Introduction

Significant transformation in the objectives and approaches of a state's foreign policy is primarily the outcome of the changes in the systemic variables, followed by modification in either state or individual-level variables. Indian foreign policy under the leadership of Prime Minister Modi has undertaken a proactive shape, which has redefined India's foreign policy priorities and has largely elevated external engagement. To reinvigorate India's foreign policy orientations, the government has taken several initiatives such as the Act East policy and Neighbourhood First policy, induced towards imparting relevant changes in India's external affairs. The geopolitical standpoint of India's foreign policy has focused on soft power dynamics, cultural rejuvenation and political connection with the diaspora. Regional institutions like the ASEAN (Association of Southeast Asian Nations) play a pivotal role in facilitating the development of regional identity in the world's most economically vibrant region. Though India is not a member of this institutional development, its involvement in the evolving strategic order of the Indo-Pacific region, where the spheres of influence of both China and India overlap, is crucial to its eminence as a global player.

India's inclination towards Southeast Asia initially was not enthusiastically perceived by the ASEAN leaders, as they apprehended that India would exploit this platform to address its challenging equations with Pakistan and China. It was categorically emphasised that only after strengthening of economic interaction would the wider political and security dynamics be taken into consideration. ASEAN's reservations about India can be outlined as:

India remains effectively contained geopolitically in South Asia by Pakistan and China. As long as this is so, its geopolitical impact on Southeast Asia will continue to be limited. To break out of this geopolitical impasse, the emergence of an open, outward-looking and dynamic economy is an essential condition but not a sufficient one. Other important requirements may include diplomatic ingenuity and political will to resolve disputes with Pakistan at an appropriate time and the continued maintenance of domestic political stability under secular conditions.[1]

With the onset of the Look East Policy in the early nineties, India started expanding the geographic ambit and substance of its foreign policy dynamics to cover the Western Pacific as an important arena of strategic engagement. Manmohan Singh, who was present at the creation of India's Look East Policy as India's finance minister, and later as Prime Minister, elevated the essence of the foreign policy endeavour by stating in 2006,

I must pay tribute to our East and Southeast Asian neighbours for shaping our own thinking on globalisation and the means to deal with it...in 1992, our Government launched India's 'Look East' policy. This was not merely an external economic policy; it was also a strategic shift in India's vision of the world and India's place in the evolving global economy. Most of all it was about reaching out to our civilisational Asian neighbours.[2]

Emphasising the second phase of India's Look East Policy, Vajpayee's foreign minister, Yashwant Sinha, reiterated that,

> The first phase of India's Look East policy was ASEAN-centered and focused primarily on trade and investment linkages. The new phase of this policy is characterised by an expanded definition of 'East', extending from Australia to East Asia, with ASEAN at its core. The new phase also marks a shift from trade to wider economic and security issues, including joint efforts to protect the sea-lanes and coordinate counter-terrorism activities. The military contacts and joint exercises that India launched with ASEAN states on a low-key basis in the early 1990s are now expanding into full-fledged cooperation.[3]

While the rationale of rebalancing provided the base for India's engagement with Southeast Asia, it was primarily the Indian navy that emphasised the prospects for New Delhi in the Pacific. Even before India's joining the East Asia Summit and upholding of the impression that New Delhi could be part of the region's security politics, New Delhi was consolidating the Pacific into its perception of extended neighbourhood. The strategic and economic opportunities unleashed by the changing contours of global politics motivated India to highlight that the Look East Policy was not merely restricted to the Southeast Asian region. In his Singapore Lecture in 2002, Vajpayee declared that geography and politics make India a pertinent part of the Asia Pacific community and that 'it does not require formal membership of any regional organisation for its recognition or sustenance'.[4]

## Act East Policy in the Indo-Pacific Region

India's eminence as a manufacturing powerhouse and prime mover of strategic and economic progress in the Indo-Pacific region has been emphasised through its evolving cooperation with its Southeast Asian neighbours, redefined as the Act East Policy. The 12$^{th}$ ASEAN-India Summit held in Nay Pyi Taw in the year 2014 marked the official onset of India's Act East

Policy with the opening statement of Prime Minister Modi, wherein he underscored the pertinence of launching a new era of economic development, industrialisation and trade and commerce in India.[5] India's Look East Policy has been redefined as the Act East Policy, which is aimed at facilitating the strengthening of the functioning of crucial institutional mechanisms, thereby widening the ambit of communication and networking skills between government institutions, parliamentarians, business circles, scientists, academicians, media and research institutions and the young generation. The thrust is to stimulate the building of a peaceful, coordinated and balanced community in the region. The Act East Policy centres on fundamentals like the improved economic ties among the ASEAN member countries, adherence to ASEAN's conformity and centrality, solidarity in operational ventures and reinforcement of an open and comprehensive regional security architecture. the Prime Minister of India mentioned at the Shangri-La Dialogue that an Asia of rivalry will retard the pace of development and hold India back, whereas an Asia of cooperation will invariably lead to development, thereby shaping this century. The revision of India's Look East Policy to Act East Policy has considerably expanded the country's geographic focus and the orientation has been extended to emphasise the Indo-Pacific region without factually deviating from ASEAN-centric strategy. Prime Minister Modi unveiled and highlighted India's vision of the Indo-Pacific at the Shangri-La Dialogue, 2018 in Singapore. The preponderance of Indo-Pacific dynamics was intensified with India's renewed emphasis to highlight its equations with the ASEAN as the essence of India's Indo-Pacific policy.[6] The Act East Policy has indeed reinvigorated India's relations with the great powers in Asia—the United States, China and Japan. As a consequence, India gets significantly connected to the regional politics of East Asia and the great-power system that predominantly outlines the Asia Pacific theatre. The Act East Policy plays a pivotal role in adopting an outward approach and reintegrating India with the global economy and dividends like large size, congenial geographic location, productive population, increasing military and economic prospect, essentially making India an important factor in the structuring of the Asian economic and security order.[7]

The restructuring of India's foreign policy after the end of the Cold War highlights much of Asia and the Indian Ocean as its 'extended neighbourhood'.[8] With the revival of India's relations with Southeast Asia, Central Asia, the Persian Gulf and the Middle East, there was a resurgence of the old concept of developing a security and political role from Aden to Malacca.[9] India's Indo-Pacific dynamics call for the realisation of the Act East Policy in facilitating regional stability, where each country can pursue its legitimate interests without jeopardising another's security, thereby creating a more balanced Asia. New Delhi's striving towards a balanced and comprehensive Indo-Pacific region thus encompasses an all-embracing pursuit of peace and stability. A well-orchestrated and balanced approach synchronising India's Act East Policy in the country's bilateral equations with the countries of the Indo-Pacific region can uphold India's goals and interests. India attempts to devise a clear-cut framework of its foreign policy objectives focusing on a comprehensive, advanced and development-oriented strategy in the Indo-Pacific region. India's insightful perception of Security and Growth for All in the Region (SAGAR) has been valued by the ASEAN. Unanimity of viewpoints on the relevance of a rules-based order in the region was highlighted; emphasis was accorded to the upholding of international laws like the 1982 United Nations Conventions on the Laws of the Seas, the significance of the aspects of peace, security, safety and stability, and the freedom of navigation has been pronounced. While the ASEAN forms the epicentre of East Asian politics, India's concerns have expanded to include the western Pacific as a whole. ASEAN is quite optimistic about India's rising profile, and the 10-nation international organisation distinctly commends New Delhi's growing significance in the Indo-Pacific region on a number of occasions as the two sides, with a combined GDP of $5 trillion, pledge to advance their strategic ties and encounter major challenges such as terrorism collectively. In his address at the annual India-ASEAN summit, Prime Minister Narendra Modi talked about the mutual coordination between India's vision of the Indo-Pacific and ASEAN Outlook for the strategically key region, which has been noticing increasing Chinese assertiveness. Mentions about cross-border terrorism, spread of violent extremism and the situation in the South China Sea were also made and the need for greater cooperation between India and the ASEAN to unitedly confront major challenges impeding the region was underlined. It was reiterated that India's Act East Policy is an important pillar of its Indo-Pacific vision.

The ASEAN is and always will be the core of the Act East Policy. The integrated, organised and economically developing ASEAN is inevitably going to further India's basic interest. The greatest outcome of the 16th India-ASEAN summit was the acknowledgement of the ASEAN leaders about India's increasing role in the Indo-Pacific region for the first time after the bloc came out with a substantive outlook for the region. The endorsement of India's role acquires preponderance as it was highlighted in the context of geo-political power play in the Indo-Pacific region and escalating territorial confrontation between China and a number of ASEAN countries. All the ASEAN countries broadly endorsed that India's growing relevance is a primary determinant of peace and stability in the region. India has vowed its commitment towards strengthening of partnership and cooperation with the ASEAN through stronger surface, maritime, air connectivity and digital links. India is also enthusiastic to accelerate capacity building and partnerships in areas of agriculture, science, research, ICT and engineering.

It has been officially announced that India would be interested in creating an endowment of Rs 50 million for promoting exchanges between faculty as well as students under India-ASEAN network. Enhancement of bilateral cooperation in the defence industries sector and the possibility of boosting trade and investment facilities have also been explored.[10] India's prospect in the Pacific does not only connote to the matching of the military weight of China in the littoral; rather, it augurs the generating of strategic options that did not previously prevail for the littoral states of the western Pacific. India's influence in the Pacific stretch can only expand if it continues to maintain substantial economic growth ratio and creates the groundwork for security cooperation in the region. India's less ambitious maritime pursuits focus on realistic parameters rather than on ideological perceptions, and its collaborative maritime strategies make it virtually a potential security partner for a number of countries in the Indo-Pacific region. India's Act East policy has accorded added impetus to India's role as a regional action by institutionalising India's engagement with the Indo-Pacific countries. But India's scarce resources on the military and diplomatic fronts and the slow nature of its defence diplomacy has put it much behind China in establishing strategic footprint in the Pacific region.[11]

## ASEAN and the Indo-Pacific Regional Players

There is an increasing interdependence between maritime and continental resources and activities.[12] The advancement of the economic power of China and the subsequent growth of India are factors significantly impacting the Indian Ocean since their prerogatives and leverage coincide. The importance lies in the rejuvenation of linkages with countries in the Bay of Bengal and Western Indian Ocean region. The confluence of the Bay of Bengal and Western Pacific Ocean may be perceived as a large ocean space wherein mutual influence is inevitable. Strategic competition and suspicion are impeding the progress of the region. India possesses global advantages such as democracy, human resources, digital technologies and a global value chain and aspires to be a global leader commensurate with the capacities and the abilities. India's initiative SAGAR aims at security and growth for all countries in the region, and Sagarmala, a national programme, is oriented towards accelerating economic development by a port along the coastline, river networks and hinterland connectivity. Moreover, the Act East Policy has revived economic and political equations with the members of ASEAN and countries like Japan and Australia. China has, several times, declared its mission to be a major power with a modernised military system, though it has asserted that it does not have any hegemonic or expansionist intention. However, the USA, India and Japan are quite apprehensive about China's unilateral behaviour in the South China Sea and East China Sea as a threat to the freedom of maritime commerce in the Indo-Pacific Ocean region. Further, Chinese infrastructure and loan diplomacy are counted as China's attempt to strategically suppress India. The USA is also keen to make its moves with 'Quad', Australia, India, Japan and the USA. There is sheer probability for a 'Quad Plus' involving the UK and France as well. The USA endeavours to maintain predominance in all contested and interlinked global commons such as the maritime arena steers for the enhancement of its deterrence posture and annihilate the growing perception of America's decline. Japan is heavily dependent on the energy security aspects of the Indo-Pacific region. Japan has even made crucial political changes to enable its maritime forces to play a proactive role in the defence of its energy supplies and maritime trade. India and Japan have introduced a maritime initiative, the Asia Africa Growth Corridor (AAGC) to connect Asia with Africa by using Japanese technology and funding as well as to expand the Indian influence in the East African Region. PM Abe announced the 'Free and Open Indo-Pacific Strategy' in 2017, with the intent of developing an environment for international peace, stability and prosperity and sharing universal values as well as to rejuvenate connectivity between Asia and Africa to promote stability across the regions.[13] Japan is concerned about Chinese assertive advances in the western Pacific region, especially in the East China Sea, and aims to cooperate with India since India's Act East Policy tallies with Japanese strategy.

Building a multi-polar, open and inclusive security order across the Indo-Pacific region will not be an easy task due to multiple factors. These include varying parameters like the aims and objectives of the Great Powers, mutual suspicion, differences, existing inequalities and the vastness of the ocean. But securing a win-win situation is desirable. In order to achieve this condition, there is an imperative to eradicate a trust deficiency with confidence-building measures. As such, collaborative solutions across national boundaries, regions and sectors are ardently required, as there are also other issues such as environmental, energy, terrorism, radicalisation and cyber security concerns. Therefore, it is necessary to take into account the security sector in arriving at a regional solution. In this context, it is necessary to link up ASEAN and IORA. The need of the hour is to have a more energetic and vibrant Indian Ocean with respect for international law and expanded connectivity. The coordination of all states is necessary for vigorous cooperation in safeguarding the sanctity of the ocean space. The IOR needs to look intricately at the ASEAN and revitalise connectivity and collaboration with the ten-member countries of the ASEAN. It is important to frame a security architecture that strengthens the culture of cooperation and collective action. Growing self-awareness of its strategic location in the Indian Ocean as well as its vulnerability in the context of Great Power competition is pertinent to ponder over.

ASEAN's mode of functioning as a regional organisation is based on the rationale of balance of power. The principle of ASEAN's security policy is to maintain its autonomous and independent position as a regional bloc. In the meantime, ASEAN encourages all the other major powers to participate in regional security architecture, but does not allow any single power to dominate.[14] A cursory glance at the Sino-Indian interaction across the Asian littoral will uphold a number of significant issues. During the first decade of the 21st century, the maritime concerns and naval dynamics of China and India increased in the Arabian Sea, the Bay of Bengal, the South China Sea and the western Pacific. With the expansion of economic and naval capabilities, maritime advances of both neighbours intensified. Though China has made considerable headway, India is also proactively engaged. In the Arabian Sea, which is the repository of the energy resources that both nations need, Beijing and New Delhi are just beginning to undertake their respective overtures. Although India is aware of Sino-Pakistan strategic collaboration and has been concerned about the Gwadar port, the ramifications of extending this partnership to the maritime domain remain unexplored. These trends have not been confronted yet in any significant manner. India is more concerned about its maritime interests in the Bay of Bengal, wherein China is collaborating with Dhaka and establishing itself on the Burmese coast in order to address its presumed susceptibility to being choked off at the Strait of Malacca. Meanwhile, India's maritime activities have extended in the South China Sea and the Pacific, which is a matter of concern to Chinese interests in a fundamental way. As their initiatives began to impact the Indo-Pacific maritime domain, and their naval footprints started to intersect, there is plausibility of the emergence of increased mutual suspicions. China's advances into the Indian Ocean as well as India's approaches to the western Pacific have endorsed the aspects of mutual encirclement that have largely characterised the Sino-Indian rivalry. An exploration of possible resolutions that might wither the possibility of potential maritime conflicts between China and India is required.[15]

China's land-grabbing strides by means of aggression, artificial construction of islands and subsequent militarisation to alarm others have taken a terrible shape, turning the South China Sea into a critical zone that may go out of control any moment. The onus of restraining China and eulogising a strategy to manage conflict in South China Sea largely rests on the ASEAN. ASEAN has undertaken formidable measures on this account; in June 2019, in the ASEAN Foreign Ministers' Meeting in ASEAN Summit in Bangkok, the Chairman's statement projecting concerns about Beijing's assertive expanses in the South China Sea made significant mentions of the land reclamations and activities in the area that have shattered the essence of trust and confidence, thereby intensifying tensions and undermining peace, security and stability in the region. It is imperative for the organisation to focus on greater unity steered towards Chinese restraint. India must accord precedence to the South China Sea geo-economic realities in its foreign orientation. This is because the South China Sea is a pivotal channel through which approximately $5 trillion of trade passes every year. The Straits of Malacca, the choke point which connects the Indian Ocean with the South China Sea, deals with nearly five times the volume of oil than the Suez Canal. India's strategic ties with countries in the region, especially with Malaysia, Indonesia, Singapore, Vietnam and the Philippines have gained momentum with the Act East Policy. More importantly, the Indo-Pacific is virtually an arena of strategic credence to India. In fact, India has as much stake in peace and tranquillity in the South China Sea as any other regional power, such as ASEAN, China, Japan or the US. ASEAN also encourages India to play a decisive role in the emerging political, economic and security architecture of the Indo-Pacific, thereby inculcating the image of a global power. India, thus, is expected to emphasise crucial facets as the freedom of navigation, a rule-based maritime order and settlement of disputes through peaceful means in the Indo-Pacific region.[16]

## India's Forays in the Indo-Pacific Region

Underlining the essence of India's Act East Policy, PM Modi emphasised that its centrality in the regional security architecture of the Indo-Pacific region is evident. Therefore, it is required for the stakeholders to jointly address the limitations by increasing cooperation in the crucial areas. India needs to be more competent as a beneficial strategic partner of the ASEAN and must steer towards a deeper and more broad-based engagement by revitalising its domestic economic reforms agenda, expanding connectivity facilities within the region and maximising its role in regional institutions. [17]

In order to realise the objectives of the ASEAN-India partnership for peace, progress and shared prosperity, both ASEAN and India need to:

- Promote maritime security and safety, freedom of navigation and overflight, uninterrupted conduction of trade and commerce, the exercise of self-restraint, the non-application of threatening or forceful means and the resolution of disputes by peaceful methods in accordance with the universally recognised principles of international law, including the 1982 United Nations Convention on the Law of the Sea (UNCLOS) and the relevant code and recommended practices by the International Civil Aviation Organisation (ICAO).
- Rejuvenate maritime cooperation, including maritime security, counter piracy and search and rescue cooperation through proper ASEAN mechanisms and ASEAN-led platforms, such as the ASEAN-India framework, EAS, ARF, ADMM-Plus, ASEAN Maritime Forum and its expanded ASEAN Maritime Forum. India-ASEAN cooperation need to emphasise the promotion of technical cooperation, capacity-building measures, interchange of experiences and sharing of knowledge and expertise.

- Encourage coordination in preventing and combating transnational crimes such as terrorism and the financing of terrorism, arms smuggling and sea piracy.[18]

India's equations with the Pacific Island nations have strengthened the rationale of its Act East Policy, leading to the formation of the action-oriented Forum for India-Pacific Island Cooperation. The first and second summits were conducted in Fiji (2015) and Jaipur (2016) respectively, wherein the Prime Minister highlighted India's focus on the essence of cooperation with the Pacific island nations and its inclination towards the advancement of their developmental goals. To tackle the impact of climate change, the developmental policies need to be inclusive and sustainable and should be focussed on the reduction of inequalities and on the contribution to the empowerment and improvement of people's standard of living.[19] It is often argued that India's strategic ventures through the coasts by the Indian Ocean, the Pacific Ocean and the Bering Sea would enable it to expand its footprints in the Arctic Ocean. In lieu of this, India needs to take into consideration the significance of the Arctic not only from the perspective of strategic concerns but also from the prism of climate change. India needs to foster proactive collaboration with other countries to establish an enduring mark in the Arctic. Geographically, the Arctic may be far away from India, as it is at the northernmost tip of the world, but the impact of climate change across the coasts of India and its economic consequences should accord certain precedence to the Arctic region with respect to India's geo-political concerns. Therefore, politically as well as strategically, the Arctic can no longer be considered too distant. Prime Minister Modi's 2019 visit to Vladivostok for a bilateral summit highlighted the convergence of interests on the Arctic by both India and Russia, and the discussions between the two leaders provided a platform for India to pursue a substantive Arctic plan. The proposition of a Vladivostok-Chennai maritime route upholds the congruity of Russia's Far East in tune with India's Act East Policy thereby enabling India to facilitate a larger construct to realise its strategic interests. Linking the coastal city of Chennai to Vladivostok with a maritime route fundamentally projects the extension of Russia's Far East to India, thereby raising the prospect of the expansion of India's Act East approach into Russia and further into the Arctic. Adequate nurturing of these dynamics into the collaborative ventures between India and Russia could catalyse the eminence of India as a maritime power.[20]

## Conclusion

For any trade agreement to materialise, it is imperative to emphasise the underlying merits. Diplomatic endeavours between the concerned states play a pivotal role in the facilitation of the overall economic and strategic interests. Certain factors contribute to the realisation of trade and commercial benefits like the intricacies of the deal being negotiated among the partners, the strengthening of trade dynamics, the scope of new trade opportunities and the stimulating of competitiveness among the domestic producers. The outcome would yield to increased investment, policy certainties and regional security. For the fostering of the tangible offshoots of multilateral trading arrangements, efficient diplomacy needs to be nurtured. It is pertinent to note that trade and diplomatic initiatives complement each other, and compatibility between the two must be followed in the pursuit of economic transaction for the cause of greater prospects so that most of the economy's trade potential can be realised. The Act East Policy focuses on economic cooperation between Northeast India and its Southeast Asian neighbours, which has become the highlight in the context of the Indo-Pacific region. Now with $76 billion plus in 2019, India has become the fourth largest trade partner of ASEAN and ASEAN the seventh largest trading partner of India.[21]

The AEP as an economic initiative is oriented towards the development of Northeast India, and the ASEAN's Economic Community is liable to emerge as an integrated and cohesive region that will facilitate growth, progress and prosperity for all. Development, from an economic standpoint, accrues growth, modernisation, infrastructure development, increase in trade and investment. But development also implies people's participation and endorsement to meet their basic needs and concerns. ASEAN endeavours towards a more holistic, inclusive people-participatory type of development, which is underlined in the ASEAN Socio-Cultural Community, and inclusive sustainable capacity to acquire prosperity for all of ASEAN.[22] The relevance of India's northeastern region as a harbinger of improved economic connectivity with the countries of the Indo-Pacific region is crucial. In August 2007, while addressing the Indian Parliament, Prime Minister Abe referred to a 'confluence of the Indian and Pacific Oceans'. As strategic partners, India and Japan have acquired the role of the preserver, thereby ensuring the essence of protection and security of the Indo-Pacific region. Japan has emerged as the leading partner in India's attempts to direct soft loans to projects for the development of road, port and urban infrastructure, industrial nodes and corridors, skills training and sustainable forestry and agriculture in eastern India, as both the countries aim to emphasise the synergies between India's AEP and Japan's Free and Open Pacific Strategy, which upholds the bolstering of connectivity linkages to build supply chains connecting industrial networks to boost the economic prosperity of the region. The northeast region represents a culturally connected and viable economic region. The landlocked northeast region needs to have smooth connectivity and infrastructure facilities. The challenges of underdevelopment, lack of human resources development and constraints to access to investments and exports from the Indo-Pacific region have hindered the development of the region. India's Act East Policy aims to rejuvenate India's multi-faceted engagement with the ASEAN and the wider Asia Pacific region and deepen economic integration, politico-security cooperation and socio-cultural interaction with other countries in the region for consolidation of ties between India's northeast region and its Southeast Asian neighbours.[23] Transformational policies and cooperative governments in the northeastern states could enable the government at the centre to facilitate development schemes and infrastructure projects quickly. A collective focus on inter-state boundary disputes and other ethnic conflicts with the northeast states is required as well as a coordinated approach towards developing connectivity facilities and trade facilitation with ASEAN. At the same time, it is pertinent to build efficient institutional connectivity by harmonising trade, investment and financial policies between India and the ASEAN in particular and Southeast Asia in general.

## Endnotes

1 Daljit Singh, 'The Geopolitical Interconnection Between South and Southeast Asia,' in *India and ASEAN: The Politics of India's Look East Policy*, eds. Frederic Grare and Amitabh Mattoo (New Delhi: Manohar, 2001), 28.

2 Prime Minister Manmohan Singh's address to the Asia Society Corporate Conference, Mumbai, March 18, 2006, https://www.rediff.com › money › 2006 › mar › 18asoc.

3 Yashwant Sinha's speech at Harvard University, September 29, 2003, *http://meaindia.nic.in/ speech/2003/09/29ss09.htm.*

4 C. Raja Mohan, ed., *Samudra Manthan: Sino-Indian Rivalry in the Indo-Pacific* (New Delhi: Oxford University Press, 2013), 95.

5 Opening Statement by Prime Minister at the 12th India-ASEAN Summit, Nay Pyi Taw, Myanmar, November 12, 2014, http://mea.gov.in/aseanindia/SpeechStatementASEM.htm?dtl/22566/Opening+Statement+by+Prime+Minister+at+the+12th+IndiaASEAN+Summit+Nay+Pyi+Taw+Myanmar.

6 Rajiv Bhatia, 'Locating India-ASEAN in the Indo-Pacific,' https://www.gatewayhouse.in/india-asean-in-indo-pacific/

7 Mohan, ed., *Samudra Manthan: Sino-Indian Rivalry in the Indo-Pacific*, 89–90.

8 David Scott, 'India's 'Extended Neighbourhood' Concept: Power Projection for a Rising Power,' *India Review* 8, no. 2(2009): 107–43.

9 C. Raja Mohan, *Crossing the Rubicon: The Shaping of India's New Foreign Policy* (New Delhi: Viking, 2003), 204–36.

10 'ASEAN backs India's rising role in Indo-Pacific region,' *The Statesman*, Kolkata, November 4, 2019.

11 Mohan, ed., *Samudra Manthan: Sino-Indian Rivalry in the Indo-Pacific*, 108.

12 G Padmaja, 'IMOs View on Shipping and India's Sagarmala: Examining the Convergences,' in *Maritime Perspectives 2017*, eds. P. Chauhan and G. Khurana (New Delhi: National Maritime Foundation, 2018).

13 'Priority Policy for Development Cooperation for FY 2017,' Ministry of Foreign Affairs (MOFA) Japan, 2017, http://www.mofa.go.jp/files/000259285.pdf.

14 Zhao Gancheng, 'India: Look East Policy and Role in Asian Security Architecture,' *Indian Ocean Digest* 21, no. 2(2006): 38.

15 Mohan, ed., *Samudra Manthan: Sino-Indian Rivalry in the Indo-Pacific*, 186–7.

16 Baladas Ghoshal, 'Crossing A Red Line,' *The Times of India*, Kolkata, November 1, 2019.

17 Harsh V Pant, 'India and the Indo-Pacific: The Logic of Partnerships,' in *Purbasa East Meets East Synergising the North-East and Eastern India with the Indo-Pacific*, eds. Lalit Mansingh, Anup K Mudgal and Udai Bhanu Singh (New Delhi: Pentagon Press, 2019), 171–5.

18 Aruna Gopinath, 'India-ASEAN Maritime Security Cooperation,' in *Purbasa East Meets East Synergising the*

*North-East and Eastern India with the Indo-Pacific*, eds. Lalit Mansingh, Anup K Mudgal and Udai Bhanu Singh (New Delhi: Pentagon Press, 2019), 68–9.

19 '$150 Million Line of Credit for Pacific Island Nations,' https://www.asianage.com/india/all-india/260919/150-million-line-of-credit-for-pacific-island-nations.html.

20 Pradeep S Mehta, 'The Art of Deploying Diplomacy to Advance Our Trade Interests,' https://www.livemint.com/opinion/online-views/diplomacy-can-be-used-to-advance-our-trade-interests-1569237085567.html.

21 Lalit Mansingh, Anup K Mudgal and Udai Bhanu Singh, eds., *Purbasa East Meets East Synergising the North-East and Eastern India with the Indo-Pacific* (New Delhi: Pentagon Press, 2019), 2, 21.

22 Maria Teresita C. Daza, 'The Role of Women: A Perspective from the Philippines,' in *Purbasa East Meets East Synergising the North-East and Eastern India with the Indo-Pacific*, eds. Lalit Mansingh, Anup K Mudgal and Udai Bhanu Singh (New Delhi: Pentagon Press, 2019), 190.

23 Deepa G. Wadhwa, 'Japan's Role in the Development of India's Eastern States and Connectivity with ASEAN', in *Purbasa East Meets East Synergising the North-East and Eastern India with the Indo-Pacific*, eds. Lalit Mansingh, Anup K Mudgal and Udai Bhanu Singh (New Delhi: Pentagon Press, 2019), 290–2.

# Deliberating Disaster Diplomacy in the Bay of Bengal: India's Interests and Imperatives

*Sohini Bose*

## Introduction

The Bay of Bengal, located northeast of the Indian Ocean, has garnered significant strategic interest in recent years. Traversed by sea lanes of communication that are important for trade in energy and other resources and home to a wealth of hydrocarbons, the Bay has attracted many countries to its waters in a future riddled with energy insecurity. The arrival of extra-regional major powers in this maritime space coupled with the keenness of its littorals to engage in collaborations to secure their interests has transformed the Bay into a stage for geopolitical cooperation and competition. The assertive rise of China in the region through strategic policy initiatives such as the Belt and Road Initiative and the New Maritime Silk route, aggressive investments in littorals through developmental partnerships and efforts to evade its 'Malacca Dilemma', has raised uncertainty about the future stability of the Bay, particularly with regard to the continued autonomy of its shipping routes.[1] This apprehension over freedom of navigation is the reigning traditional security concern in the Bay of Bengal. Naturally, other powers with an interest in these waters have joined the Bay littorals in efforts to preserve the Bay's stability. Many such efforts include India's role as the largest regional power, framing the Bay entirely in the west.

China's growing presence in the region has served as a reawakening call to India about its opportunities and challenges as a peninsular country, especially in a maritime space that it identifies as a 'primary area of interest'. Not only is the Bay important for India's domestic trade, connectivity and security, but it also serves as a facilitator of India's foreign policy aspirations. Intent on emerging as a major power in the Indo-Pacific zone, India seeks to cultivate its regional prominence through strong ties with its eastern neighbourhood. As the common maritime space between India and Southeast Asia, the Bay is ideally situated to function as a theatre for collaborative endeavours through which the country can realise its 'Neighbourhood First' and 'Act East' policies. The Bay also has the potential to be a gateway for India into the wider waters of the Indo-Pacific, as it opens into the Malacca Strait via the Andaman Sea. Stability in the Bay and favourable engagements with its littorals is therefore of paramount importance to India.

The domain of traditional security however offers little scope for undertaking collaborative ventures, as most Bay littoral countries including India remain dependent on China for trade. Purely military partnerships, which may be interpreted as efforts to thwart the dragon's advances, have the potential to rouse its discontentment. Attention has thus turned to building security cooperation in the purview of non-traditional or non-state centric security threats, which are equally daunting for the Bay's stability. Interestingly, the rise in the Bay's strategic significance has highlighted the potential of collectively addressing many of these transnational threats as avenues for strengthening inter-country relations and better integrating this region.

Among the many non-traditional security concerns prevalent in the Bay, the overarching threat is of natural disasters, with the littoral countries suffering the impact of frequent cyclones and recurrent tsunamis. India itself ranks high in the vulnerability index with a perennial record of deaths and damage to property. Nonetheless, the country has been able to develop a sophisticated system of disaster management for this risk unlike other Bay littorals and, consequently, often receives requests for help from affected neighbouring countries in crisis situations. Lately, it has also begun nurturing disaster preparedness in the region through bilateral and multilateral means. In doing so, India is not only trying to manage a humanitarian concern but is also using the tool of disaster diplomacy to strengthen its ties with its eastern neighbourhood as its foreign policy mandates. Indeed, security cooperation to promote disaster management is an ingenious avenue for confidence building amongst nations as, being humanitarian in nature, it does not run the risk of rousing the political displeasure of China. It is therefore important to deliberate how India can further strengthen its disaster diplomacy to realise its strategic aspirations in the Bay. Endowed with this aim, the paper will be structured along the following objectives:

1. To comprehend the disaster risk emanating from the Bay and the birth of India's disaster diplomacy.
2. To analyse how India has fared so far by investigating factors contributing to its acceptability as an HADR provider and the reasons behind its rejection.
3. To estimate how India will navigate the course of disaster diplomacy in the future with the Bay of Bengal Multi-Sectoral Technical and Economic Cooperation (BIMSTEC) gaining prominence and the Quad prioritising HADR.

Accordingly, it is time to gauge the turbulence of the Bay, which earned it the name 'Kalapani'.

## The Dark and Stormy Sea

The Bay of Bengal, before it got its present name, was often referred to as 'Kalapani'[2] or 'dark waters', referring to its storminess. The Bay owes its tempestuousness to its triangular shape, low flat coastal terrain, shallow depth and 'easterly waves'.[3] Apart from the cyclones that originate in these waters, the Bay also attracts cyclonic winds from the Pacific Ocean as there is an absence of any large landmass at the intersection of these two seas. Tsunamis are also frequent here as the Andaman Sea zone of the Bay is home to the Andaman-Sumatra Subduction Zone, the seismic activity-intense area along the mutually jostling European and Indo-Australian tectonic plates. The resultant earthquakes frequently trigger tsunamis, the largest and most intense of which was witnessed in 2004.

Consequently, the entire shoreline of the Bay and the islands that are situated in its midst are exposed to frequent calamities. Sri Lanka, situated southwest of the Bay, is subject to intermittent cyclones and floods. Tsunamis, though infrequent, cause substantial damage.[4] North of Sri Lanka, the Indian east coast witnesses an average of three cyclones every year. The northern and southern parts of the country are also highly susceptible to tsunamigenic activity.[5] Moreover, as India's Andaman and Nicobar Islands lie parallel to the Andaman-Sumatra Subduction Zone, they experience frequent and high intensity tsunamis and cyclones.[6] Located at the triangular peak of the Bay, Bangladesh is frequently affected by severe tropical cyclones. The country is also a victim of regular floods and earthquakes.[7] Moving east, Myanmar is susceptible to destructive cyclones, earthquakes and floods.[8] Finally, the west coast of Thailand is relatively less vulnerable to disasters as the Andaman and Nicobar Islands act as a buffer to the parallel three Thai states of Ranong, Phang Nga and Phuket. Nonetheless, it experiences regular floods and was significantly affected by the 2004 tsunami. An account of the impact of cyclones on Bay littorals in the last five years is given below.

**Figure 1: Impact of cyclones and tsunamis on Bay littorals[9]**

| Year | Disasters | Impact |
|---|---|---|
| **2017** | Cyclone Ockhi | In India 350 died[10] and coastal fisheries suffered a loss of 821 crores.[11] In Sri Lanka 414 died and 32,000 houses were damaged.[12] |
| | Cyclone Mora | In Bangladesh 200,000 people were displaced and 6 were killed.[13] In Sri Lanka 150 people died.[14] Damage was inflicted on Rakhine, Myanmar.[15] |
| **2018** | Cyclone Titli | In India 8 lives were lost and almost 2000 electric poles were uprooted.[16] |
| | Cyclone Gaja | In India, 45 lives were lost.[17] Damage to houses was estimated at 3.4 lakh.[18] 1000 homes damaged in Sri Lanka.[19] |
| **2019** | Cyclone Fani | In Odisha, India 64 people died[20] and over 10 million people were affected.[21] In Bangladesh almost 12 people were killed.[22] |
| | Cyclone Bulbul | 12 people killed in India and another 12 in Bangladesh. The latter evacuated 2.1 million people to cyclone shelters.[23] |
| **2020** | Cyclone Amphan | In India almost 98 people were killed[24] and thousands of 'kutcha' houses were destroyed.[25] Economic damage stood at almost 13 billion USD. Bangladesh suffered a loss of 130 million USD.[26] |
| **2021** | Cyclone Yaas | In India, 4 lives were lost[27], 1 crore people were affected and 3 lakh houses damaged.[28] 2 deaths were reported in Bangladesh.[29] |

## The Onset of 'Disaster Diplomacy' in India

Over the past two centuries, 20 out of 23 major cyclonic disasters in the world have occurred bordering the Bay of Bengal and 'of the 35 deadliest tropical cyclones (lives lost in excess of 100, 000 people) in world history, 24 have occurred in the Bay of Bengal'.[30] However, the worst disaster was experienced by the Bay in December 2004, when the region was engulfed by the most devastating tsunami in recorded history. However, despite being severely affected itself, India deployed three simultaneous HADR operations to disaster-affected littorals at the behest of the navy and air force. Those affected appreciated India's spontaneous and effective assistance, and the country's HADR credibility gained prominence internationally. Since then, India has provided HADR to Bay littorals on several occasions.

However, it wasn't till the last decade that India realised the diplomatic benefits of this public service. Disaster diplomacy is popularly understood to be the practice of offering relief assistance in the event of disasters, which in the process 'has the potential to alter interstate rivalries in the direction of decreasing tensions'. In 2014, under a new government led by Prime Minister Narendra Modi,[31] as India embarked on its 'Act East' policy, it began exploring avenues for strengthening ties with Southeast Asia. Naturally, the disaster risk from the Bay emerged as a collective concern, to address which India could cooperate with its eastern neighbourhood.

Accordingly, the government stressed collaboration in disaster preparedness and response as a means of expanding India's outreach to its neighbours. Consequently, the 'five-fold framework for India's maritime engagement' that was outlined by Modi in 2015 established India's focus to deepen cooperation with its regional partners to cope with matters of maritime security like natural disasters through multilateral collaboration.[32] Subsequently, India's first National Disaster Management Plan was released in 2016, articulating India's enthusiasm to build disaster resilience in the region through sustained regional partnerships.[33] The vision of Security And Growth for All in the (Indian Ocean) Region (SAGAR), launched in 2016, also provided further impetus for collaboration in this domain.[34] India's recent Indo-Pacific Oceans Initiative (IPOI) has only strengthened it further with 'Disaster Risk Reduction and Management' recognised as one of its seven pillars of cooperation.[35] Naturally, disaster management has emerged as a primary means of India's outreach in the region. While India has certainly nurtured its HADR prowess, it is also important to analyse what makes India's assistance acceptable to other littorals and whether there are such factors which can inhibit the country's disaster diplomacy.

## India's Acceptability as an HADR Provider

Among all the Bay littorals, India has the most developed system of disaster management and is therefore ideally positioned to provide disaster assistance. Furthermore, India conceived the idea of aiding as 'extending sympathy' or a 'goodwill gesture' to the affected countries.[36] One of the main 'benign tasks' of the Indian navy and air force is to provide HADR and, as such, its assistance has often been sought by other Bay littorals. As a major provider of relief assistance, India thus ensures that 'responsibility to protect should not be a pretext for intervention'. Hence, it does not provide relief assistance unless requested to do so.[37] This is in accordance with the UN Oslo guidelines of 2007, which clearly state that, 'All disaster relief, ... should be provided at the request or with the consent of the Affected State and, in principle, on the basis of an appeal for international assistance'.[38] India's HADR conforms to the 'typically Asian view' being 'apolitical', 'decentralised', and mostly following a 'government-to-government approach'.[39] Unofficially, it has therefore become almost customary for affected Bay littorals to seek India's assistance on a bilateral basis.

However, although a prolific provider of disaster relief, India usually refrains from requesting any help from the other countries. Protecting this stance in the purview of accepting response assistance in the aftermath of the 2004 tsunami, India responded that rescue and relief were tasks that India was better equipped to execute on its own given its economic profile and advanced technological know-how. The country's gesture was thus to be viewed as an act of solidarity towards worse-affected countries like Indonesia and Thailand.[40] Analysts have, however, attributed this hesitation to a 'policy precedent' set in 2004, when then Indian Prime Minister Manmohan Singh stated, 'We feel that we can cope with the situation on our own and we will take their help if needed' in the context of the tsunami. Since then, it has been customary for India to refuse foreign help in the event of calamities.[41] This practice has now found reflection in India's National Disaster Management Plan of 2016 which states that 'as a matter of policy the Government of India does not issue any appeal for foreign assistance in the wake of a disaster'. But if a foreign government voluntarily offers relief aid as a 'goodwill gesture' India may accept the same.[42] This abstinence from requesting aid has also been explained in terms of India's 'national pride' and aspiration to cultivate a narrative of strength and dependability in the region.

Yet, despite India's efforts, the culture of 'sensitivity to sovereignty' characterising many Bay littorals, especially those with a colonial past has been a hindering factor. These countries, precautious as they are of their hard-earned independence, are selective about which external actors they accept HADR from. They are vigilant in ensuring that the external actor does not intervene in their domestic affairs. These countries are also mindful of the degree to which they allow another country to provide assistance. Consequently, despite India's recognition as a sensitive provider of relief assistance, there have been instances where the recipient country has restricted its engagements to certain parts of its territory, preventing it from entering other affected locales.[43] For example, when Cyclone Sidr struck Bangladesh in 2007, Bangladesh limited India's HADR involvement to the port of Chittagong and Dhaka airport. Offers to deploy helicopters to conduct rescue operations in more remote affected areas were declined. Also, while naval relief via fixed-wing aircraft was accepted, relief via rotary-wing aircraft in remote areas was declined.[44] It may thus be observed that collaboration in disaster response amongst India and the littorals in question in real crisis situations remains limited. The sector of disaster preparedness, however, shows more promise in building disaster diplomacy as efforts are underway to enhance bilateral and multilateral engagements in this domain.

## The Potential of Partnerships

India has begun engaging in bilateral agreements and naval exercises with the Bay littorals to improve disaster preparedness in the region. During PM Modi's visit to Bangladesh in 2019, the two governments agreed to enhance cooperation in the area of disaster management and accordingly emphasised the need for early completion of a Memorandum of Understanding.[45] In February 2020, the first joint military exercise between India and Bangladesh-Sampriti-IX was held as part of which the military personnel of both countries shared their experiences on aid to civil authorities for disaster management in jungles and semi-urban terrain amongst other issues.[46] It is hoped that such exercises will soon be extended to the maritime domain. Recently, in March 2021, India and Bangladesh signed an MoU on disaster management. As regards Myanmar, in February 2020, when President U Win Myint of Myanmar visited India at the invitation of the Indian President Ram Nath Kovind, India reiterated the significance of the Coalition of Disaster Resilient Infrastructure (CDRI) for disaster-prone countries like India and Myanmar and encouraged Myanmar to consider joining the CDRI.[47] As regards Thailand, the Indo-Thai HADR Table-Top Exercise began in 2016, aiming to lay down a procedure for joint disaster relief operations and establish a decision support system at various stages of relief operations. Its most recent edition, 'Ex Siam-Bharat: 17' was held in 2017. More recently, in 2018, both countries sought to enhance defence ties by promoting cooperation in several areas, including disaster management. The two countries also engage in Coordinated Patrol or CORPAT Exercises, the 26th cycle of which was held in 2018 and which include practices of search and rescue (SAR) operations.[48] India is yet to have constructive bilateral engagements on disaster management with Sri Lanka.

In the multilateral domain, India's efforts in disaster diplomacy are slightly more prominent. After a sluggish decade, since 2015, India has actively cultivated the BIMSTEC sector on 'Environment and Disaster Management', which it leads. The BIMSTEC is the only regional organisation devoted to the Bay of Bengal. With the onset of disaster diplomacy, India has taken the lead to organise a number of new initiatives in this platform ranging from meetings to disaster management exercises. Currently, BIMSTEC is emphasising cultivating disaster preparedness in the region although there continue to be hiccups in hosting its joint disaster management exercises, for which the term 'annual' was dropped after the first edition. The organisation is still too nascent to undertake disaster response in crisis situations and rehabilitation efforts lie outside its purview, requiring national jurisdiction.[49] Its inclusion under the gamut of 'security' at the 5$^{th}$ BIMSTEC Summit Meeting in March 2022 nonetheless makes sense, as it involves relief operations undertaken by the military. The adoption of the BIMSTEC charter is hoped to provide a further push towards active cultivation of disaster diplomacy on this platform.

The return of the Quad in the Indo-Pacific also has the potential to enhance India's aspiration of disaster diplomacy with its fellow Quad members United States, Australia and Japan. The Quad traces its origin to the ad hoc Tsunami Core Group, created to deliver a coordinated response after the Indian Ocean tsunami of 2004. Unfortunately, after its formation, the Quad's overtly conventional strategic-security image made it difficult for the grouping to function sustainably in the face of Chinese discontent. As a result, the Quad has begun exploring other areas of collaboration for its survival. The entire Indian Ocean region is referred to as the 'world hazard belt' due to frequent cyclones, tsunamis, earthquakes, floods and droughts. Natural disaster management is thus a prime area of cooperation for these like-minded Indo-Pacific countries. Validating this rationale at the Quad Leaders' Summit in Tokyo in May 2022, the partners have agreed to engage in disaster mitigation and HADR workshops. They will also work together to improve crisis preparedness and early warning systems. In the same manner, the Quad can host joint disaster management exercises, which would train the participating countries to deliver better disaster responses. While these initiatives certainly seem promising on paper, the future of India's disaster diplomacy appears to be a mixed bag of chances and challenges.

## The Way Forward

In its efforts to promote disaster diplomacy in the Bay of Bengal region, the primary challenge facing India is its inability to consistently nurture this domain. This problem is a conglomeration of several hindrances that characterise this region. At the very outset, there is the issue of ad hocism. Despite the Bay's tempestuous nature, its littoral countries maintain a reactive rather than proactive approach to the onslaught of natural disasters. Therefore, India's scope to cultivate disaster diplomacy is essentially limited to erratic instances when the country's assistance is sought to provide relief. The second factor is the culture of 'sensitivity to sovereignty' characterising many Bay littorals, which make them very selective about whom they accept assistance from and to what extent. It is due to these hindering factors that India finds it difficult to nurture disaster diplomacy with consistency, which is necessary if it is to become a vehicle for confidence building with the neighbourhood. The country has thus embarked on a path of promoting disaster preparedness in the region by initiating bilateral and multilateral disaster response exercises. While taking the lead to create a regional response force certainly seems the most convenient way to bypass the problem of sovereignty cautiousness by negating interventions from a single country, BIMSTEC with its structural and financial limitations is yet too nascent to undertake such measures. The Quad too certainly has the potential, but it is yet to take any concrete shape and can mostly be relied on for ad hoc disaster-preparedness initiatives, if not only for responses in crisis situations. Even then, it is likely that the Quad members will respond separately, unless a disaster of the magnitude of the 2004 tsunami occurs. India's best bet to promote disaster diplomacy is therefore in the bilateral realm. It will serve the country to build confidence and strong relations with each littoral country in the Bay through disaster-preparedness agreements, information sharing, capacity-building initiatives and joint exercises. In time, this has the potential to create a more integrated Bay of Bengal region, securing India's strategic interests of a more prominent position in its primary area of interest.

## Endnotes

1 Anasua Basu Ray Chaudhury et al., "India's Maritime Connectivity Importance of the Bay of Bengal," Special Report, Observer Research Foundation, 2018, 86. https://www.orfonline.org/wp-content/uploads/2018/03/ORF_Maritime_Connectivity.pdf

2 Sunil S. Amrith, *Crossing the Bay of Bengal: The Furies of Nature and the Fortunes of Migrants* (Cambridge and London: Harvard University Press), 24–26.

3 Easterly waves are small travelling circulations which have the potential to develop into larger tropical cyclones. For more details please see, "Frequently Asked Questions on Tropical Cyclones," Regional Specialized Meteorological Centre for Tropical Cyclones over North Indian Ocean, Indian Meteorological Department, Ministry of Earth Sciences, Government of India. http://www.rsmcnewdelhi.imd.gov.in/images/pdf/cyclone-awareness/terminology/faq.pdf

4 Lareef Zubair et al., "Natural Disaster Risks in Sri Lanka: Mapping Hazards and Risk Hotspots," 109. http://www.water.columbia.edu/files/2011/11/Zubair2006NaturalDisaster.pdf

5 Anasua Basu Ray Chaudhury and Sohini Bose, "In the Eye of Tempestuous Bay of Bengal: Measuring the Disaster Resilience of Major Ports on India's East Coast," *Issue Brief*, no. 289, Observer Research Foundation, 2019, 1. https://www.orfonline.org/wp-content/uploads/2019/04/ORF_Issue_Brief_289_DisastersPorts.pdf

6 Pratnashree Basu, Sohini Bose and Anasua Basu Ray Chaudhury, "The Andaman and Nicobar Islands: Facilitating India's Connectivity in the Bay of Bengal," *Journal of Indian Ocean Region*, (2019): 8. https://www.tandfonline.com/doi/full/10.1080/19480881.2019.1637553

7 Bangladesh Disaster Risk and Climate Resilience Program, Relief Web, 2018. https://reliefweb.int/report/bangladesh/bangladesh-disaster-risk-and-climate-resilience-program

8 *Myanmar Disaster Management Reference Handbook*, Centre for Excellence in Disaster Management and Humanitarian Assistance, 2017, 22. https://www.cfe-dmha.org/LinkClick.aspx?fileticket=zf5i3c7xwDA%3d&portalid=0

30 Vijay Sakhuja and Somen Banerjee, *Sea of Collective Destiny: Bay of Bengal and BIMSTEC* (New Delhi: Pentagon Press and Vivekananda India Foundation, 2020).

31 "Narendra Modi Sworn In as Indian PM in Spectacular Ceremony," *The Guardian*, May 26, 2014, https://www.theguardian.com/world/2014/may/26/narendra-modi-sworn-in-india-prime-minister

32 C. Raja Mohan, "Modi and the Indian Ocean: Restoring India's Sphere of Influence," *Institute of South Asian Studies*, no. 277(2015): 4. https://www.files.ethz.ch/isn/189804/ISAS_Insights_No._277_-_ Modi_and_the_Indian_Ocean_20032015163047.pdf

33 *National Disaster Management Plan 2016*, National Disaster Management Authority Government of India, New Delhi, 2016, 145. https://ndma.gov.in/images/policyplan/dmplan/National%20Disaster%20Management%20Plan%20May%202016.pdf.

34 G. Padmaja, "Revisiting 'SAGAR'—India's Template for Cooperation in the Indian Ocean Region," National Maritime Foundation, 2018, http://maritimeindia.org/View%20Profile/636602941847320911.pdf

35 "Indo-Pacific Division Briefs," Ministry of External Affairs, Government of India, February 7, 2020, https://mea.gov.in/Portal/ForeignRelation/Indo_Feb_07_2020.pdf

36 Anasua Basu Ray Chaudhury and Sohini Bose, "Disasters Without Borders: Strengthening BIMSTEC Cooperation in Humanitarian Assistance," Issue Brief, no. 207, Observer Research Foundation, 2017, 2, https://www.orfonline.org/wp-content/uploads/2017/11/ORF_Issue_Brief_207_BIMSTEC-HADR.pdf

37 Sarabjit Singh Parmar, "Humanitarian Assistance and Disaster Relief (HADR) in India's National Strategy," *Journal of Defence Studies* 6, no. 1(2012). https://www.researchgate.net/publication/260041843_Humanitarian_Assistance_and_Disaster_Relief_HADR_in_India%27s_National_Strategy_Focus 91

38 *Oslo Guidelines: Guidelines For the Use of Foreign Military and Civil Defence Assets in Disaster Relief*, Revised 1.1, United Nations Office for the Coordination of Humanitarian

Affairs, 2007, 13. https://www.unocha.org/sites/unocha/files/OSLO%20Guidelines%20Rev%201.1%20-%20Nov%2007.pdf

39 *Oslo Guidelines: Guidelines For the Use of Foreign Military and Civil Defence Assets in Disaster Relief.*

40 "Bridging the Ocean: India Leads Relief Measures in Tsunami-Hit Areas, December 2004–January 2005," Ministry of External Affairs, Government of India, 7. https://mea.gov.in/Uploads/PublicationDocs/185_bridging-the-ocean-tsunami.pdf

41 Happymon Jacob, "Pride and foreign aid," *The Hindu*, August 31, 2018, https://www.thehindu.com/opinion/lead/pride-and-foreign-aid/article24822860.ece

42 The draft National Disaster Management Plan of 2018 further specifies that all such offers must be routed though the Indian Ministry of External Affairs and will only be accepted in consultation with the Ministry of Home Affairs after evaluation on a case by case basis. For more details please see, *National Disaster Management Plan 2018 (draft)*, National Disaster Management Authority, Ministry of Home Affairs, Government of India, 2018, 287. https://ndma.gov.in/images/pdf/NDMP-2018-Revised-Draft-1-2018OCT16-A.pdf

43 Anasua Basu Ray Chaudhury, Pratnashree Basu and Sohini Bose, *Exploring Maritime Connectivity in the Extended Bay of Bengal* (New Delhi: Observer Research Foundation, 2019), 44. https://www.orfonline.org/wp-content/uploads/2019/11/ORF_Report_India-ExtendedBOB.pdf

44 "Statement by External Affairs Minister, Shri Pranab Mukherjee to the Bangladeshi media Followed by Question and Answer Session Prior to Departure from Dhaka," Media Center, Ministry of External Affairs, Government of India, 2007, https://www.mea.gov.in/media-briefings.htm?dtl/3879/Statement+by+External+Affairs+Minister+Shri+Pranab+Mukherjee+to+the+Bangladeshi+media+followed+by+Question+and+Answer+session+prior+to+departure+from+Dhaka

45 "India-Bangladesh Joint Statement during Official Visit of Prime Minister of Bangladesh to India", Media Center, Ministry of External Affairs, Government of India, 2019, https://mea.gov.in/bilateral-documents.htm?dtl/31911/IndiaBangladesh+Joint+Statement+during+Official+Visit+of+Prime+Minister+of+Bangladesh+to+India

46 "Joint India, Bangladesh Military Drill Concludes," *The Statesman*, May 5, 2020, https://www.thestatesman.com/bengal/joint-india-bangladesh-military-drill-concludes-1502856859.html

47 "India-Myanmar Joint Statement during the State Visit of the President of Myanmar to India," *Narendra Modi*, 2020, https://www.narendramodi.in/india-myanmar-joint-statement-during-the-state-visit-of-the-president-of-myanmar-to-india-548585

48 Chaudhury, Basu and Bose, *Exploring Maritime Connectivity in the Extended Bay of Bengal*, p. 45.

49 Sohini Bose, "BIMSTEC and Disaster Management: Future Prospects for Regional Cooperation," *Observer Research Foundation*, Issue Brief no. 383, 2020, https://www.orfonline.org/wp-content/uploads/2020/07/ORF_IssueBrief_383_BIMSTEC-Disasters.pdf

# India in the Indo-Pacific: Evaluating Maritime Strategies, Envisioning Strengthened Analogies

*Sohini Nayak*

## Introduction

### *Delineating the Indo-Pacific*

The ever-changing maritime strategy of India is a response to myriad geopolitical demands, to suit its ambition in the wider global order of substantial competition. Consequently, there is a perpetual renewal of maritime security propositions, aimed at widening the diplomatic pursuit for India. One such domain gaining salience in the recent past is the Indo-Pacific, where India has been trying to ensure and stabilise its presence.[1] As a single interspersed geostrategic segment, it holds within itself several geo-economic opportunities, multiplied with security challenges, thereby making this vast maritime domain attract the keen attention of the major global powers at large. For instance, the United States of America, Japan, India, Australia and European countries like France and United Kingdom, to mention a few, have been establishing and securing their interests in the region, hitherto necessitating the strike of the perfect chord for preserving a specific 'rules-based' global order herein. As aptly explored by Ash Rossiter and Brendon J. Cannon in *Conflict and Cooperation in the Indo-Pacific: New Geopolitical Realities* (eds.), the Indian and Pacific Oceans have unlocked 'a new spatially coherent zone', with the contemporary geopolitical reality being a major power rivalry with narratives and strategic constructs built as a response to Chinese predominance.[2] At this juncture, China's growing footprint has caused a deep sense of anxiety in the region.[3] China's navy has actively been making inroads into the Indian Ocean in the recent years. Apart from creating friendly relations with the littoral states using maritime diplomacy and other tools, the Chinese navy today is a frequent guest at the ports of Karachi, Colombo and many other Southeast Asian countries. In addition to this, the Chinese navy has conducted numerous exercises well beyond its traditional sphere of influence, indicating a clear intent on its part to become a major player in this region. In this is the aspect of developing prospective retaliatory capabilities to befit and correspond with the various definitions and identities of security that have come across in the present time within a multilateral structure, dissuading a state or non-state actor in the region from threatening peace and openness and violating customary international laws and regulations.[4]

## The Indian Stance

As elaborated by Gurpreet S. Khurana in India's *Maritime Strategy: Context and Subtext,*[5] India is preparing to assume an integral role in the domains of economy, security and geopolitics in the Indo-Pacific, moving beyond any sort of ambiguity. India has outlined an expansive maritime strategy, which is often considered a strategic reorientation from its traditional continental outlook.[6] With this aforesaid perspective, the ever-changing maritime strategy of India has been a response to myriad geopolitical demands, to suit its ambition in the wider global order of substantial competition. Consequently, there is a perpetual renewal of maritime security propositions, aimed at widening the diplomatic pursuit for India. One such domain of constant discourse has been the Indo-Pacific region, gaining salience in the recent past, where India has been trying to ensure and stabilise its presence. Juxtaposed with Japanese Prime Minister Shinzo Abe's 'Confluence of the Two Seas',[7] clearly denoting the amalgamation of the Indian and the Pacific Ocean realms into one geopolitical zone of convergence, India too demarcated its own thoroughfare. In this light came Indian Prime Minister Narendra Modi's speech at the Shangri La Dialogue on June 1, 2018,[8] distinguishing this space as a 'natural region', along with endowing within it the responsibility of its 'Act East' policy (2014) for better economic connectivity with the eastern neighbourhood.[9]

The latest Indian maritime blueprint entitled, 'Ensuring Secure Seas: Indian Maritime Security Strategy' (2015)[10] is a consequent instance of this expanding perspective which takes note of a maritime security arena wherein India was never formally engaged. Consequently, the Indo-Pacific region has now become an integral part of the document to address India's greater presence and its role as the probable 'net security provider' therein.

Even though this aspect of Indian maritime diplomacy has been ambiguous in recent years, the objective is clear from defining it as '.... the state of actual security available in an area, upon balancing prevailing threats, inherent risks, and rising challenges in the maritime environment, against the ability to monitor, contain and counter all of these' in the document, primarily to constrain a few impediments that have been clearly noted by Lieutenant Colonel Dhiraj Kumar in his article, 'Indian Ocean Region (IOR): India as a Net Security Provider—The Way Ahead'.[11] As compared to Strategy-2007, Strategy-2015 indicates a significant dilation of India's maritime strategic outlook. While the darker shade, in Figure 1, represents the new Primary Area, the lighter shade shows the new Secondary Area. In Strategy-2007, the areas marked 'X' were not included in areas of interest at all, whereas the areas marked 'S' were Secondary Areas, which are now Primary Areas. The expansion of areas is in tandem with its maritime and overseas interests, and strategic factors. Effectively, these are 'geo-strategic frontiers', though none of the strategy.

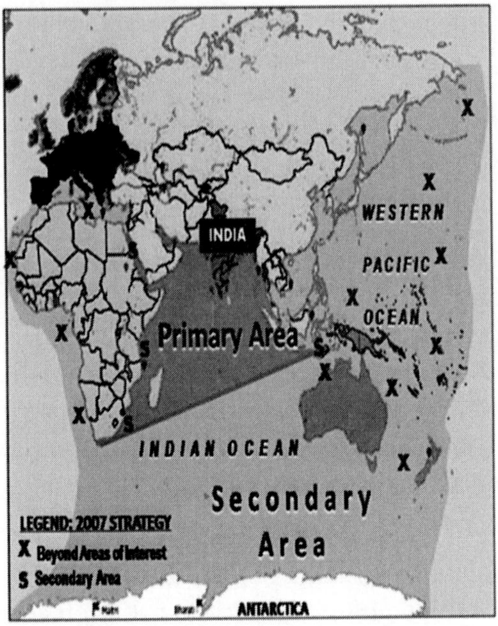


**Figure 1: India's metamorphosing interest in the Indo-Pacific region**

Thus, India witnessed a very crucial transformation in its maritime approach replacing the 2007 national maritime document, *Freedom to Use the Seas: India's Maritime Military Strategy,* as it did not want to compromise on its forward journey to becoming one of the powers associated with the Indo-Pacific great power game. In keeping with the 2008 'Pakistan-based proxy war', a terror attack through sea, India is now much more apprehensive and protective of its littoral periphery—specifically the coast, which is also its stepping stone to reach eastwards—often identified as an important key of the Narendra Modi government's Act East Policy. Thus, with the new doctrine of 2015 released by the navy, a more holistic security of the water came to be ensured and was also a natural reaction from the Indian authorities for the establishment of cooperative frameworks and associations with other major powers in the region of concern. India realised that, without moving a notch higher in its naval capability, it would not be able to sustain in a wider platform like the Indo-Pacific, where every country has been projecting its best capability developed. While comprehending so, the maritime military capability of countries was singled out as one of the most crucial 'enablers' that would in turn help to sustain law and order in this domain, along with being a thrust for India to come up with its most reliable framework.[12]

C. Raja Mohan, in *Samudra Manthan: Sino-Indian Rivalry in the Indo-Pacific*, specifically pointed out the country's predisposition to move ahead from the past unrealistic ambition of designating itself as a leader while maintaining a low-key role with pragmatic cooperation. India undoubtedly intends to repose itself as an ideal security partner, which can prove to be valuable for many big and small nations here. Even though the ASEAN countries have blamed India of episodic interest with the inability to quickly follow through with agreements, the country has become willing to progress in the recent past.[13] For this, what is needed is to make a cautious observation of the inadequate capabilities on the military and diplomatic fronts.[14] Circumstantially, this development leads to the prospects of multilateral collaborations and the rise of regional, neo-regional and sub-regional dimensions[15] in the space of maritime security and justifies the significance being attached to the concept of an imperative 'free and open Indo-Pacific Strategy'[16] in this ocean realm.

Coming to the vitality of the Indo-Pacific, almost all the powerful nations of the world have been trying to harness the untapped potential of the region. This area hosts the passage of around 32.2 million barrels of crude oil annually and approximately 40 percent of the total global exports.[17]

Maherbaanali Sheliya and Hitakshi Joshi in *India's Maritime Wall in the Indo-Pacific* (July 2019),[18] clearly mention that as a developing country with a decent economy, India is also a part of this race to bring about maximum utilisation of the trade routes in this area. Ninety percent of India's trade is heavily dependent upon merchant shipping. India also imports energy from this passage. It is very important for India to have a free and undisrupted flow for its sustained commercial development. If there is any disruption in the open sea lines of communication here, the country would have to bear a heavy brunt. Such a situation can occur only when there is obstruction in the important chokepoints here like the Strait of Malacca, the Cape of Good Hope, the Mozambique Channel or the Strait of Hormuz, to mention a few. Given the present security threats like organised crimes and terror attacks, the necessity of maintaining naval military bases have increased in significance. It has become important for India to protect its exclusive economic zone of around 2 million square kilometres and the adjoining 7,500 kilometres of coastline with more than 12,000 islands, covering around 30 percent of the Indo-Pacific (According to United Nations Convention on the Law of the Sea-UNCLOS).[19] Now the point is, this is the shared mental framework of all the major powers present here, who are trying to protect their own share of accessibility. This is creating a situation tense enough to re-think whether this protection is against any anti-social outcome or threat emanating from amongst themselves, which would mean the occupation of certain territories or zones or even encroachment in an unconstitutional manner. In this circumstance, emerging from the aforesaid necessity to protect its interests in the region, the strategic presence of China here and its increasing footsteps all around the Indo-Pacific has been often labelled the most crucial threat to India and its ambitions. As recently as 2019, China was noted directly as a 'Revisionist' power[20] by the United States of America in its Indo-Pacific Strategy

Report. This majorly holds true with the political and military developments of China in the South China Sea and China's 'firm strategic presence' and 'exploration rights in the south-west Indian Ocean'.[21] Rajesh Rajagopalan in *Evasive Balancing: India's Unviable Indo-Pacific Strategy*[22] talks about the concept of 'internal balancing' vis a vis India and China that has emanated from this assumption of Chinese threat to India. He claims that with the passage of time, balancing the presence of China has become the most predominant purpose and aspect of India's Indo-Pacific strategy. He also moves on to explaining two important apprehensions that are borne by India. First, there is reference to China's policy of strategic encirclement of India, specifically affecting the relationship with immediate neighbours like Nepal, Bhutan and Bangladesh, not to mention Myanmar. Secondly, India fears losing out on the powerplay in the South China Sea. In the garb of anti-piracy tools, China has been often alleged to be deploying submarines and naval bases. As the intentions of China are not very clear, India wants to remain on guard, fully prepared to face any kind of Chinese naval expansion or any sort of security threat that might come up.[23]

Although India has not directly made any such claims in any of its white paper documents, the underlying threat is still lurking and is quite well understood through the demeanour of the Indian navy, deployed in this sector. Presently, India is very sure of its desire to attain the position of the 'net security provider' herein, but somehow is not able to trust the existing situation of the advancing Chinese naval force. This conception was used by the United States of America in 2009 for India. Given India's acceptance of the presence of traditional security concerns, the country was now formally claiming its potential for regional security. This nomenclature is more about not being the 'net provider of security', where the overall security and stability of the region would be taken into consideration.[24]

## Strategic Competition

Despite the fluidity of new issues, actors and alignments, Indo-Pacific geopolitics is mainly debated around the axis of the US–China strategic competition. Claiming their turf, both China and the United States have sought to cast and recast their regional alliances and imaginations. Prima facie, China's economic rise has disrupted the US-led status quo in this region.

At this juncture, China's growing footprint has caused a deep sense of anxiety in the region.[25] China's navy has actively been making inroads into the Indian Ocean in the recent years. Apart from creating friendly relations with the littoral states using maritime diplomacy and other tools, the Chinese navy today is a frequent guest at the ports of Karachi, Colombo and many other Southeast Asian countries. In addition, the Chinese navy has conducted numerous exercises well beyond its traditional sphere of influence, indicating a clear intent on its part to become a major player in this region.

Indo-Pacific visions of most other powers also remain sensitive to a balance between Washington and Beijing. US-led conventional security arrangements must contend with novel China-led economic alignments. Even the supposedly pro-US ASEAN has been amply cultivated and engaged by China's economic lure and has failed to stand up against China's increasing construction of artificial islands in the disputed South China Sea. This shows that the US- and ASEAN-led conventional multilateralism of this region has fallen prey to the US–China strategic competition. Indeed, the persistence of US–China tensions—primarily involving their economic and technological competition—have come far enough for new regional alignments to gather enough momentum to deserve a serious assessment of their new templates and trends.

The 2016 US withdrawal from the Trans-Pacific Partnership followed by the devastating pandemic has fuelled speculations of China's post-pandemic preponderance reinforced by the Regional Comprehensive Economic Partnership (RCEP) of fifteen Indo-Pacific nations led by China that concluded in 2020. This witnessed the United States resurrecting the Quadrilateral Security Dialogue in 2017, which has shown rapid thematic and vertical growth from senior officials' talks to ministerial meetings and their first Quad Leaders' Summit in March 2021. The region has seen two parallel networks emerging: a US-led security network versus a China-led prosperity network; both increasing, overlapping and contesting for pre-eminence. The US 'pivot' to this region, driven by China's rise, had begun with President Obama's Indo-Pacific formulation. It was followed more vigorously by his successor, Donald Trump, who announced the renaming of the US Pacific Command as the Indo-Pacific Command in June 2018; this was followed by the US Indo-Pacific Strategy Report in June 2019. President Joe Biden was equally quick to reaffirm his focus on this region. Hence, it seems that the US–China strategic competition is here to stay. In this situation, what comes across as a viable circumstance is the strengthening of multilateral institutions within the region.

## Is Multilateralism the Way Ahead?

The process of organising relations between groups of three or more states seems to be evident within the Indo-Pacific to maintain the balance of power and rules-based order. Beyond that basic quantitative aspect, multilateralism is generally considered to comprise certain qualitative elements or principles that shape the character of the arrangement or institution, suitable to counter a single nation's domination. A few aspects of this notion that may be applied to the Indo-Pacific are:

1. **Indivisibility:** It is a collective system, especially when the security of a particular grouping is concerned. There is a notion of the indivisibility of interests. In security arrangements, peace is treated as being indivisible, such that no participating member can be at war while others are at peace.
2. **Diffused Reciprocity:** Multilateralism is considered to give rise to expectations of diffuse reciprocity among participants. In situations characterised by diffuse reciprocity, there is an expectation that there will not be an equivalence of obligations or concessions in any one exchange, but, rather, a balance over an ongoing, potentially indefinite, series of exchanges with a group of partners.
3. **Dispute Settlement:** Having a system of dispute settlement enables participating countries to treat their interests as indivisible and to accept relations of diffuse reciprocity; they know that should the expected benefits not be forthcoming because of noncompliance by other participants, there is a mechanism through which redress may be sought. This happens mainly through compliance.
4. **Durability and Influence:** More controversially, it has been argued that multilateral institutions may be inherently more stable than other forms of organisation in that the principles underlying them appear to be more durable than other arrangements and more able to adapt to external changes.

## Conclusion

Since the time of Alfred Thayer Mahan, the idea of conventional security has changed. Technological advancements have made the doctrines far more complicated in nature,[26] which might not be sustainable in the long run. Nonetheless, the traditional maritime strategists argue that technology cannot affect tactics and strategy. It is about the achievement of superior sea control with cohesive multilateral action. How countries behave in a particular area depends much upon the historical ties that they might share as well. For India and China, this relationship is not quite pleasant. India has generally viewed China through the lens of suspicion. This reaction may be also forwarded as a generic reaction of the other major countries here as well. One of the reasons for this is the force China has been using to control its surrounding in the Indo-Pacific. One of the major paradoxes that has developed here is the reaction of the smaller islands and local waters, which will be used as 'bastions' for nuclear armed submarines. How these smaller islands will respond in this game or whether they have no choice but to take sides in this domain is a question that will remain unanswered till any such development takes place. As of now, they are receiving the fruits of development of bigger powers likes India or China. Thus, in the long run, such smaller islands will be key strategic players in the multilateral setup, helpful in developing capabilities, which countries must refrain from using for all the wrong purposes. It is doubtful whether India and China will ever come together to frame strategies for the region's wellbeing, but the point lies in respecting each other's space and moving towards collaborative efforts that will stabilise trade, political conduciveness and a strategically sound environment for the good of nations at large.

## Endnotes

1 Mercy A. Kuo, "The Origin of Indo-Pacific as Geopolitical Construct," *The Diplomat*, 2018.

2 Ash Rossiter and Brendon J. Cannon, eds., "Conflict and Cooperation in the Indo-Pacific: New Geopolitical Realities," *Routledge Studies on Think Asia*, 2020: 2.

3 Harsh Pant, "India, BRI and India's Indo-Pacific Strategy," *Infrastructure, Ideas And Strategy In The Indo-Pacific*, 32, (2019), https://henryjacksonsociety.org/wp-content/uploads/2019/04/HJS-Infrastructure-Ideas-and-Strategy-in-Indo-Pacific-web.pdf.

4 Maj. Patrick Applegate, "Strategic Deterrence," *Indo-Pacific Defense Forum*, 2018, Strategic Deterrence | Indo-Pacific Defense Forum (ipdefenseforum.com).

5 Gurpreet S. Khurana, "India's Maritime Strategy: Context and Subtext," *Maritime Affairs: Journal of the National Maritime Foundation of India* (Routledge, 2017), 1–2.

6 David Brewster, "An Indian Sphere of Influence in the Indian Ocean?" *Security Challenges* 6, no. 3(2010): 1, https://www.jstor.org/stable/26459796?seq=1&cid=pdf-reference#references_tab_contents.

7 H.E. Mr. Shinzo Abe, *Confluence of the Two Seas*, Speech by Prime Minister of Japan, at the Parliament of the Republic of India, (2007).

8 Media Center, Ministry of External Affairs, Government of India, "Prime Minister's Keynote Address at Shangri La Dialogue (June 01, 2018)," Speeches and Statements, https://www.mea.gov.in/Speeches-Statements.htm?dtl/29943/prime+ministers+keynote+address+at+shangri+la+dialogue+june+01+2018.

9 Gurpreet S. Khurana, "The Focus is on the Indo-Pacific," in *Maritime Perspectives*, Vice Admiral Pradeep Chauhan and Captain (Dr) Gurpreet S. Khurana, eds., (National Maritime Foundation, 2019).

10 Indian Navy, Government of India, "Indian Maritime Security Strategy-2015," https://indiannavy.nic.in/content/indian-maritime-security-strategy-2015

11 Dhiraj Kumar, "Indian Ocean Region (IOR): India as a Net Security Provider - The Way Ahead," The United Service Institution of India, April–June 2019, https://usiofindia.org/publication/usi-journal/indian-ocean-region-ior-india-as-a-net-security-provider-the-way-ahead/.

12 Kumar, "Indian Ocean Region (IOR): India as a Net Security Provider - The Way Ahead," 1.

13 Kumar, "Indian Ocean Region (IOR): India as a Net Security Provider - The Way Ahead".

14 C. Raja Mohan, *Samudra Manthan: Sino-Indian Rivalry in the Indo-Pacific* (Oxford University Press, 2013), 92.

15 Deepa Gopalan Wadhwa, "Regional and Sub-regional Constructs within the Indo-Pacific," *National Security Essays*, 2, no. 3, Vivekananda International Foundation, national-security-vol-2-issue-3-essay-Dwadhwa.pdf (vifindia.org).

16 Ministry of Foreign Affairs, Government of Japan, "A New Foreign Policy Strategy: Free and Open Indo-Pacific Strategy," Microsoft PowerPoint - インド太平洋戦略（英語）(emb-japan.go.jp).

17 Joseph Tertia and Anak Agung Banyu Perwita, "Maritime Security in Indo-Pacific: Issues, Challenges and Prospects," President University, 2018, 1.

18 Maherbaanali Sheliya and Hitakshi Joshi, "India's Maritime Wall in the Indo-Pacific Region," *Journal of International Relations*, 2019, http://www.sirjournal.org/research/2019/7/1/indias-maritime-wall-in-the-indo-pacific-region

19 Sheliya and Joshi, "India's Maritime Wall in the Indo-Pacific Region".

20 The Department of Defense, Government of the United States of America, *Indo-Pacific Strategy Report: Preparedness, Partnerships, And Promoting a Networked Region*, 2019, 7, https://media.defense.gov/2019/Jul/01/2002152311/-1/-1/1/DEPARTMENT-OF-DEFENSE-INDO-PACIFIC-STRATEGY-REPORT-2019.PDF

21 Khurana, "India's Maritime Strategy: Context and Subtext".

22 Rajesh Rajagopalan, "Evasive Balancing: India's Unviable Indo-Pacific Strategy," *International Affairs* 96, no. 1(2020), https://academic.oup.com/ia/article/96/1/75/5697517.

23 Rajagopalan, "Evasive Balancing: India's Unviable Indo-Pacific Strategy".

24 Khurana, "The Focus is on the Indo-Pacific".

25 Joshy M. Paul, "China's Naval Strategy Towards the Indian Ocean Under Xi Jinping," _*Air Power Journal*,

Vol. 16, No. 14, Winter 2021 (October - December), accessed at https://www.google.com/url?sa=t&source=web&rct=j&opi=89978449&url=https://capsindia.org/wp-content/uploads/2022/04/Joshy-M-Paul.pdf&ved=2ahUKEwiJ6tCV3s6IAxUnUvUHHcRGF6sQFnoECCoQAQ&usg=AOvVaw3ezSE9k4q1AY8LQf65pmLB.

26 Rahul Roy Chaudhury, Op. cit. p. 121

# Neo-Symbiotic Reality in India's Foreign Trade: The Case of Thailand, 2014–2022

***Surajit Mahalanobis***

## Introduction

This paper uses the Regional Comprehensive Economic Partnership (RCEP) as a tool to understand India's foreign relations and the Free Trade Agreement (FTA) with Thailand. The paper begins with an understanding that the RCEP in its current charter is a trap for India. Though expounded by one of India's best friends among countries in the South Asian region, Thailand, with an ambitious programme of creating a win-win platform of trade among the member-states, the charter created by the collective opinions apparently did not have what India expected to have. Certainly, going by Thai foreign policies with regards to India, one may assume that Thailand too would seldom want to frustrate India's expectations.

The scrutiny of the charter showed a deficit prospect for India. It was expected that India would step out of the RCEP platform for foreign trade with a view to forging ahead with its existing FTAs with the ASEAN states for mutual benefit to the domestic industries of both countries. Ironically, so far, India's performance at FTAs has not been bright either.[1] India's experience with FTAs as offshoots of the gateway to the WTO's Regional Trade Agreements (RTAs) are as under:[2]

- India's exports to FTA countries have not outperformed overall export growth or exports to the rest of the world.

- FTAs have led to increased imports but not increased exports[3].
- India's trade deficit with ASEAN, Korea and Japan has widened even post-FTAs[4].
- According to Economic Survey 2016–17, the FTAs have had a bigger impact on metals on the importing side and textiles on the exporting side.
- A 10% percent reduction in the FTA tariffs for metals increases imports by 1.4 percent.
- India's exports are much more responsive to income changes than price changes, and thus a tariff reduction/elimination does not boost exports significantly.
- Utilisation rate of RTAs by exporters in India is very low (between 5 and 25 percent).

Currently, with 14 RTAs in force and a dozen more under negotiations, the total Indian exports to ASEAN, South Korea and Japan till 2019 have only increased the trade deficit to India.[5] With 11 RCEP states, India's trade deficits are over 74 percent. This is because in an FTA trade pact India would not only get the opportunity to export on a regime of tax ease, but also have to give the FTA partners access to its own markets with a similar tax-ease regime. The import of goods or services will be treated as inter-state supplies and subjected to an integrated tax regime; this means while the IGST on import of services would be leviable under the IGST Act, IGST on imported goods would be levied under the Customs Act, 1962 or the Custom Tariff Act, 1975.

In general practice, it is believed that this makes the imported goods cheaper than the competing domestic products. In cases of the manufacturing sector, India's FTAs with China, Japan and South Korea have resulted in a balance of trade heavily against India's interests in each case, especially because of the cheap productions of Chinese raw materials and finished goods. Indian industries and businesses follow their own understanding about the cost of production and pricing. Nothing else (such as geo-political interests, geopolitical strategies, civilisational connects, etc.) matters other than corporate interests in importing cheap raw material and profitability. If an entrepreneur gets a window of cheaper raw material somewhere other than its FTA partner country, the business dynamics advise that they should take that opportunity with a view to prove higher profitability.

This has been the principal idea behind the success of Chinese raw materials in almost all world markets. Hence, the main anxiety is how to compete with Chinese raw materials and goods in any RCEP market. Everywhere the countries use them and face the challenges of profitability of their own domestic products. If India had joined the RCEP, the imports of Chinese goods would have double routes to India, directly from China and through the Chinese raw materials used in the ASEAN countries' finished goods. The dual import flood would have made India's domestic products not only costlier than others, but also would have reduced India's production (manufacturing and agricultural) further. This would have only increased India's imports and reduced the scope of export. The end result would have made Chinese products win major shares everywhere.

What happens when such products enter India through FTA routes, and when the Chinese cheap raw materials are used to manufacture products in India? The answer is simple; the cost of the imported products in India becomes cheaper than those produced by domestic entrepreneurs, even as Indian products using cheap Chinese raw materials would have remained higher than those imported due to the tax ease.

However, even without joining the RCEP, India is already suffering a negative balance of trade with 11 RCEP countries.[6] Since the early 1990s, RTAs have dominated the world trade.

After the WTO was formed in 1995, RTAs quickly multiplied. From 1995 to 2005, RTAs jumped from 58 to 188. At present, 456 RTAs (RCEP including) are in force globally. Of them, 14 are in India with a dozen more on negotiation tables.[7]

## Other Disadvantages

These apart, should India join the world's largest trade group a number of other issues would crop up to challenge India's capacity building. We may take a look at the list below:

1. Indian enterprises would likely lose the competitiveness in their own markets.
2. Indian investment funds would be diverted to procure imported goods and halt manufacturing and R&Ds. These would defeat the spirit of *Atmanirbhar Bharat* and *Make in India.*
3. A national habit would develop to use foreign goods rather than India's own.
4. That would eventually create dependency, just as it happened in British India.
5. With the capital base for R&Ds reduced, the original Indian manufacturing skills would get blunted if the entrepreneurs from foreign companies did not employ Indian skills for their economic growth.
6. The entire national ethos would get into an abysmal morass of *dependencia* in the absence of Indian originality.
7. The sectors that would be most impacted are manufacturing, R&D and agricultural research.

Therefore, it can be fairly assumed that the RCEP is a byproduct of structural realistic manoeuvres against India's interests in international relations, just another face of the Belt and Road diplomacy started by China in 2013. By joining it, a country generally independent by political structure gets into a slavish dependency due to immoral economic structural realistic manoeuvres. Imagine, this is happening at a time when the people of the world have effectively shaken off protectionism and Marxist principles dominate the economic world.

Ironically, the RCEP's charters and vision statements in general imply accommodating the Ricardian reality of comparative opportunities, but in practice that is not likely to happen.

Chances are the RCEP in the long run would prove what Nobel Laureate Paul Krugman observed, that there is much of the elite defence of globalisation, which is basically dishonest, due to

> …false claims of inevitability, scare tactics (protectionism causes depressions!), vastly exaggerated claims for the benefits of trade liberalization and the costs of protection, hand-waving away the large distributional effects that are what standard models actually predict.[8]

India's commission of the National Institution for Transforming India, or Niti Aayog, has already observed that joining the RCEP means further devastating India's own domestic economy.[9]

Though prophets of doom lament that India has missed an opportunity to level-play in the world's largest economic partnership bloc (as the RCEP shapes into) by refusing to join it, they seem to fail to see the structural realistic moves which, as a side effect, evolve against India's economic interests.

The fundamental reason is: In the structural realist strands, there is an 'if-then' environment in foreign policies. This has been variously defined by Oran T Young, Kenneth N Waltz, Stephen M Walt and John J Mearsheimer at various points of time as a structural realist environment. The behaviours of the protagonists create conditions and counter conditions to justify their stands while creating the spectres of defensive or offensive realism and simmering tension in relations. The tension or fear of future disagreement leads to a conflict, which the realists believe inevitable due to the anarchic nature of international relations, does not mitigate economic and commercial interests in relations.

If soft power such as trade relations, microeconomic enterprises and people-to-people contact alone could have constructed faith and social bonding between states, then definitely the Galwan Valley incident on 15 June 2020 on the Line of Actual Control on the Tibetan border of India with China would not have occurred. Nor would China have continued to explain its forward positions on Indian borders with sly arguments, trying to distract the world from its core intention. After all, China is one of India's leading trading partners, eliciting very high revenues from the Indian market. Technically and ideally, China should have been India's best friend, which never happened, and definitely never will happen after the Belt and Road Initiatives (BRI) have been pressed into its foreign policy. This is because the BRI concept mirrors structural realistic intents, which no country, however friendly with China, would appreciate; accepting these moves would only ensure the absence of fear of Chinese military aggressiveness.

Indeed, China has a great ancient civilisation. The country has immense capabilities of mass production almost in all fields of economy. Its people are bred in civilisational ideals, patriotic zeal and nationalist warmth. They can make great friends, when and if they want. If China drops its geo-political ambitions—expressed through territorial claims around its neighbouring states—and its geo-strategic muscle flexing, it would emerge as one of the most beautiful places for the world. Sadly, this is not the case. China harbours a determined mind to the contrary for its international goals, and today has emerged as a cause of worry, not friendship.[10]

In trading with India, it has successfully been able to turn the balance of trade heavily against India's interests. Due to lack of alternate opportunities, Indian businesses have to accommodate Chinese raw materials for their manufacturing. This dependency upon Chinese supplies needs to be contained by many areas of Indian business. This is one reason why economic relations with China could not be broken even after the deadly Galwan Valley conflict, despite astute efforts by the government led by Narendra Modi.

Therefore, neo-realism does not ensure peace in any of its avatars or extension. The fear of war or conflict with China always lurks in the Indian ethos. As for the Chinese, the fear of conflicts seems elusively selective, because only a few directly involved in the conflicts seem to be aware of the consequences; the masses do not quite know how their leaders in Central Command behave about the Indian borders or their BRI diplomacy beyond what China's state-controlled media want them to know.

The Chinese authorities' mind is important in the current form of the RCEP. The Chinese geopolitical mind is mooted through the backdoor in the RCEP charter. In such structural realist behaviour within FTA economies, the clear future winner is one country—China. Therefore, if the RCEP is interpreted as an expression of regional integrity through trade practices, it is calling short of extended neo-realism, which is likely to end in inevitable conflict situations.

The reason is, the real symbiosis happens through civilisational bonding in an environment of people-to-people contact, in which peace is understood not as the absence of war, but as absence of the fear of war or conflicts. It is well explained in a few words by Rabindranath Tagore: 'Where the mind is without fear (of conflict or war) /and the head is held high (with equal opportunities in jobs, projects offer, and revenue generation)',[11] where, in bilaterals, trilaterals, quadrilaterals or multilaterals, opportunities are created equal with 51:49 profit-share, if not 50:50.

## Symbiotic Realism in State Policies

This paper aims to prove that in RCEP-type environments, the fear of future conflicts cannot be ruled out; thus, symbiotic realism as proposed[12] cannot exist in its full spectre. Symbiotic realism can only connect people to people under the shadow of war machines and military lurking in the backwaters. That means, in the RCEP agreements, what emerges is only symbiotic realism under the shadow of future fear.

In the multipolar world today, no states can afford to be dependent in geopolitical or economic terms. A novel approach to symbiosis among states is required. There needs to be a *neo symbiosis* that is based upon tradition of relations and trust, which can be a stronger tool for lasting peace. There, civilisational bonding is possible or can be cultivated without banning ethics and morality. Indeed, ethics and morality are to be given a chance in the context of national interest. Despite not joining the RCEP, India can forge neo-symbiotic realistic relations with countries rather steadily for equal opportunity of growth through bilaterals, trilaterals, quadrilaterals or multilaterals, rather than agreeing to sign up with motifs shadowed by future violence.

This paper takes up Thailand as an FTA state of India for a case study to explain *neo-symbiotic realistic* relations as a model for win-win bilaterals. It also pinpoints that, in its current status, the RCEP intends to emerge as a tool to open discussions not on the ongoing neo-realist relations as a policy, but on *neo-symbiotic realism*, though not understood.

This paper rejects the notion of Waltzian neo-realism as an extended model for symbiosis. It proves that the make-belief neo-realist extensions often assumed by some scholars as symbiotic realism, are not the essential ingredients of *neo-symbiotic realism* that this paper aims to propose. It is because this paper aims to prove that neo-symbiotic realism is a positive aspect of international relations and does not emit negative impressions in the long run. This the Waltzian neo-realism does not achieve.

For all this, this paper adopts analytical methods for drawing inferences from concepts put on the table. It is based upon selective readings of primary institutional and secondary sources. It aims to prove its points with plausible original arguments in support of the available facts and figures.

## Neo-Symbiotic Realism Explained

In 2007, a scholarly interpretation emanated from the Geneva Centre for Security Policy (GCSP) using an idea called 'symbiotic realism'. The arguments explain 'the difficulty of engaging in moral behaviours in the absence of an overarching just authority or a responsible hegemon'.[13] It argued that realism identified only some motivators of human nature and of states. There is a substrate human nature which requires recognition of the importance of perceptual frameworks and norms, which is not understood in realism. The argument draws from neurobiological traits to contend that insights provide 'a more complete picture of predilections of human nature and have important implications not only for how we conceive of individuals and states, but also for how we identify relevant actors and the significance of international anarchy.'[14] However, though the analysis preconditions traditional liberal rights at the individual level of a hegemon to incorporate freedom from fear and want, prescribes balancing behaviour and asks the responsible hegemon to accommodate interests of other states by avoiding threatening behaviour, the entire premise has the destructive might of the responsible hegemon in individual behaviours. It does not ask for equity in relational behaviours, emboldened by the confidence that the powerful state's approach is without the show of strength in relations. The mind remains caged in forethinking of the powerful partner's intentions, as in the case of China.

Thus, symbiotic realism, as expounded by GCSP scholars, also indirectly mirrors an extension of structural realism, in line with Waltzian micro-economic relational exercises. The argument[14] virtually hovers round the essentials of Waltzian neo-realism, anxious to put American hegemony back in the world order, that is, a rigorous and investment-prudent socio-political idea bereft of a modular solution with moral responsibilities in international relations.

This book proposes a neo-symbiosis in relations which turns into constructive realistic civilisational bonding between or among states. Such bonding should be built upon the bricks and mortars of civilisational understanding and faith, trust and an equal-opportunity reciprocated economy that create an environment of peace without the fear or conflicts or war. This is possible, but the book chooses to remain silent about it.

Indeed, a new type of symbiosis outside the influence of 'the responsible hegemon' has been made possible by a few states among themselves already in the world through FTAs. When these states entered their respective FTAs, they did not know or term their behaviour an expression of neo-symbiotic realism, where fear does not exist about the intention of the 'responsible hegemon' and the heads (individual dignity) of the parties are also held much higher in dimensions than earlier times. We have examples in the relations of the USA and Australia; the USA and Canada; the USA and the UK; the Kingdom of Saudi Arabia and the United Arab Emirates; India and Bhutan; India and Sri Lanka; India and Thailand; India and Laos; and India and Cambodia, among others. Truly, real symbiosis goes into the civilisational ethos and does not pretend to be a behaviour of the centre as a 'responsible hegemon', putting the periphery under the shadow of mighty fear, silently lurking in backyards. The real symbiosis does not create the concept of 'the responsible hegemon' at all; it creates the term responsible partner, instead. This has been the case in the relations of India with Thailand, Laos, Cambodia and Sri Lanka, among others in different parts of the world. Seldom is there any fear of conflict or discordant note audible in these bilateral relations. The relations based upon such neo-symbiotic realism do not get shattered even by tricky microeconomic prospecting—as China recently tried with Nepal against India over the river Kali that often attempted to break India's civilisational bonds with Nepal.

It is a neo-symbiotic move, a form of realism, because it aggressively quells the fear syndrome of structural realism or pseudo-symbiosis as explained in symbiotic realism.[15] While doing so directly or indirectly, the neo-symbiotic move counters the neo-realist concept of lateral inevitable conflict on the pretext of national security and national interests, and does so by developing people-to-people contact, cultural bonding and mutually equitable commercial interests, creating assets in each other's country (say 50:50 or 49:51 share of trading) through the route of FTAs or RTAs, thus keeping the dignity of both countries' people and sovereignty. These become easy when cultural similarities meet civilisational bonding. Neo-symbiotic relations essentially and aggressively move against the fear of conflict or war to forge a realism of anti-war and anti-conflict.

However, neo-symbiotic realism is not a mere neo-liberal thought that promotes idealistic trust in humanity. Neo-symbiotic realism brings home a sense of morality in mutual policies too, by which the trust in humanity becomes a natural process for furthering relations. The classical or structural (Waltzian) realists in all forms, mild or hard, have rejected morality and upped the fear syndrome by the definitions of defensive and offensive realism. Even in the peacetime relations of Israel and Palestine, Waltzian structuralism has been seen developing economic opportunities for Palestinians, yet all under the military shadow of Israel. Israel's structural encircling of Palestine cannot be missed, as the military might silently dictated the time of peace without war, meaning actually un-peace in the minds of the people of both states. For Israel, it has always been the basic intent that worked behind the theories of Alfred Mahan, MackInder, Morgenthau and EH Carr, that is, supremacy over Palestine on the pretext of national interest and without morality. Thus, structuralism expanded into symbiotic realist behaviour, as a mark of denial of the intent for perpetual coexistence, a reality which the UNO system and the majority states of the world, including Israel's allies the UK and the USA, do not officially want.

Therefore, the prescribed symbiotic realism is not essentially anti-war or anti-violence, whereas neo-symbiotic realism empowers itself from the functionalists' or neo-functionalists' or neo-liberal thoughts, but rejects sloppiness in unsubstantial idealism and/or hegemonic statecraft. It draws strength from mutually equitable FTAs and RTAs for national security and national interests (in national economy and national power). It keeps up its realism with a feeling of trust from a position of strength, as a partner in development, and not by muscle flexing. Thus, neo-symbiotic realism counters adversities caused by structural realism. As it functions from the position of equitable strength developed through mutual connects in relations, none of it becomes a hegemony.

Let's draw an example here: Suppose country A creates a marine string of pearls around a group of countries, atolls and islands against its assumed targeted future foe country B, and takes unto its fold of converging policies some common lucrative ambitious goals (close or remote), country B has the option to apply neo-symbiotic realism to quell the moves of country A. Country B has the option to build up its capabilities through R&D activities, fiscal prudence and improving defensive muscles to forge a new symbiosis with the nearby states around which the string has been formulated through FTAs and RTAs with the states. It is possible, because FTAs between culturally and civilisationally different countries cannot be stronger than an FTA between civilisationally connected countries. Country B will create anti-war and anti-conflict symbiosis with countries within the string of pearls, to counter the structural realistic motif of country A.

The challenges to GCSP-sponsored symbiotic realism evolves in nations trying FTAs or RTAs with different civilisational connections. A degree of uncertainty always lurks in such relations, because cultural assimilations are very arduous to effect. The lurking fear may extend to periods when the current one would disseminate in the passage of time, as nothing is permanent in the international world order. Yet, neo-symbiotic realistic relations would last between or among countries with civilisational connects, building up ingredients of symbiosis despite the anarchic world order. After all, most countries want peace without the fear of future conflict in any form. The realism is always, as has been, in practice when some major powerful countries want to expand their hegemony under the pretext of national interests.

## Neo-Symbiotic Realism between India and Thailand

Thailand's symbiosis with India is a case in point for detailed understanding. The government of India's foreign policy has adopted *neo-symbiotic realism* with Thailand in the ASEAN region without terming it as such or even without knowing it to be so. The 'Act East' policies have helped India and Thailand in forging a bond for mutual growth. It may be understood as neo-symbiotic relations evolving a realism upon civilisational friendship as opposed to structural realistic friendship for economic advantage or economic one-upmanship. The potentials in India and Thailand's relations are enormous and cannot be stymied by any force strategically stronger than both India and Thailand.

Tracing the interaction of the leaders of India and Thailand proves an intense understanding of the two states about each other. Located in each other's extended neighbourhood, the two countries share a maritime boundary in the Andaman Sea.

India's bilateral relations with Thailand are rooted in history, age-old social and cultural interactions and extensive people-to-people contact.[16]

## Reference Number to Change from Hereunder

Buddhism reflects a direct link of people-to-people interactions for and in extensive travelling into each other's country. It's more a cultural trait in Buddhism than religious. Hindu cultures are traced profusely in the general lifestyle of Thai people in family names, drawing from ancient Indian Ramayanic connects, behavioural symmetry and in the professional worlds of Thai architecture, arts, sculpture, dance, drama and literature. The Thai language incorporates Pali and Sanskrit influences.[17] A large Indian diaspora living and working in Thailand makes a distinct link of civilisational influence.

A constitutional monarchy, the kings of Thailand are essential figures in all nation-building and national ceremonial events, as they prove the concept of *Rajarshi* in ancient Indian Ramayanic models. Thailand has had nine kings so far in the ruling Chakri dynasty, all named as Rama, after the concept of *Maryada Purushottama* Rama, an incarnation of Bhagavan Vishnu. In matters of serious crisis, legendary Thai King Chulalongkorn and his grandson Bhumibol, revered in the country as Rama V and Rama IX, were the most astute architects for peaceful coexistence of their people. They learnt the techniques of Western civilisation to construct their nation and infused Indianness in every aspect of Thai culture.[18] The ethos of Thai society finds deep connection with Ramchandra *Maryada Purushottama.* Scholars report that every important member of the royal family has learnt Ramayana in the Thai language, known as *Ramakien* or *Rama Kriti*.[19] The Ramayana, Indian Hindu trinity and sculptures are fundamental links between the royal family and the people. The popular ethos, therefore, has meandered into a conscious understanding of the ancient civilisation and culture of their immediate neighbourhood, the cultures of lands on the Andaman Sea, besides of India and Indianness. This has been possible because the land of *Siam*, today's Thailand, has intensely imbued its people with the ethos of the Hindu scriptures and cultural traits. This is an example of civilisational linkage.

India cannot overlook this natural civilisational bond. In the past two decades, with regular political exchanges, growing trade and investment, India's ties with Thailand have evolved into a comprehensive partnership. India's erstwhile Look East Policy (LEP) was rather a belated manifestation of India's geo-economic bonding with Thailand through the platform of the ASEAN, because much before the Narasimha Rao government's LEP was adopted as a policy, Thai and India connections were soundly on course.

Today's 'Act East' policy has been complemented by Thailand's 'Act West' policy in bringing the two countries closer. Yet, both countries' geo-economic overtures are comparatively recent and never interfered with the heritage bonding, which has been natural and silent, underpinning the ethos shaped by the fusion of Pali and Sanskrit influences.

Today, Thailand is one of the originators of the regional partnership linking South and Southeast Asia. Joining Thailand, India cooperates closely in the ASEAN, East Asia Summit (EAS) and Bay of Bengal Initiative for Multi-Sectoral Technical and Economic Cooperation (BIMSTEC[19]) groupings as also in Mekong Ganga Cooperation (MGC), Asia Cooperation Dialogue (ACD), Indian Ocean Rim Association (IORA) and Ayeyarwady-Chao Phraya-Mekong Economic Cooperation Strategy (ACMECS). The India-ASEAN Agreement on trade in goods was implemented in January 2010 and the India-ASEAN FTA in services and investment was signed in September 2014 and came into force in July 2015.

High-level exchanges of dignitaries visiting Thailand have been former Vice President Dr. Zakir Hussain in 1966; former President V.V. Giri in 1972, former Prime Minister Rajiv Gandhi in 1986; former Prime Minister P.V. Narasimha Rao in 1993; former Prime Minister Atal Behari Vajpayee in 2002 and 2003; former Prime Minister Dr Manmohan Singh in 2004, 2009 and 2013; former Indian Vice President M. Hamid Ansari in 2016; and current Prime Minister Narendra Modi from 2016 to the present.

Thai dignitaries were rather more frequent to India, particularly at the Buddhist sites. Though Thai people's visits to India have been highly voluminous for centuries, the dignitaries visiting India during the recorded late-20$^{th}$ century onwards are as under:

- HRH Princess Maha Chakri Sirindhorn in 1987, 1996, 2001, 2004, March 2005, November 2005, March 2007, Aug 2007, March 2008, February 2009, August 2009, March 2011, October 2011, February 2014, July 2014, November 2016; Mar 2017, July 2017, November 2018 and February 2020.
- Prime Minister Gen. Prayut Chan-o-cha on 16-18 June 2016, 24-26 January 2018.
- HRH Princess Bajrakitiyabha in November 2011 and June 2015.
- HRH Princess Chulabhorn in February 2013, February 2015 and February 2020.

- Prime Minister Yingluck Shinawatra on 24–26 January 2012 and 20–21 December 2012.
- Former Prime Minister (2008–2011) Abhisit Vejjajiva in April 2011.
- Crown Prince Maha Vajiralongkorn (Now HM King Rama X) in December 1998 and Nov 2010.
- Prime Minister Somchai Wongsawat in November 2008.
- Prime Minister Surayud Chulanont in June 2007.
- Prime Minister Thaksin Shinawatra in November 2001, Feb 2002 and June 2005.
- Gen Chatichai Choonhavan in March 1989.

The high-level visits and meetings have taken place on a regular basis between both sides.

In the recent times, Prime Minister Narendra Modi, accompanied by External Affairs Minister Dr. S. Jaishankar and Commerce and Industries Minister Piyush Goyal, visited Thailand from 2–4 November 2019 to attend ASEAN related summits (16th ASEAN India Summit, 14th East Asia Summit, the 3rd RCEP Summit and related events).

Modi had a bilateral meeting with his Thai counterpart Gen Prayut Chan-o-cha on November 3. During the visit, Modi addressed a community event 'Swadee Modi' on November 2, which was attended by around 5000 persons of the Indian community. He also released a special commemorative coin to mark the 550th birth anniversary of Guru Nanak Dev and Thai translation of Tamil book *Thirukkural*.

Thai Princess Maha Chakri Sirindhorn is a regular visitor to India (20 visits). A member of the International Advisory Panel of Nalanda University and recipient of the Indira Gandhi Prize for Peace (2004), the Padma Bhushan (2017) and the World Sanskrit Award (2016), she visited Delhi, Uttarakhand and Telangana recently (from 10–14 February 2020).

Another Thai Princess Chulabhorn visited India from 14–23 February 2020. She attended the commemoration of the 10th anniversary of Chulabhorn Hospital at Wat Thai Bodh Gaya. She also visited Kushinagar and Delhi during her stay in India. She is a recipient of the Padma Bhushan for her profound knowledge in Indology. She was awarded the first World Sanskrit Award by the Vice President of India on 21 November 2016.

## Economic Relations

Rooted in history as mentioned above, India's 'Act East' symbiosis prompted Thailand to reciprocate with 'Act West' since 1996.[20] Though the bilateral trade has a favourable balance for Thai companies, the two-way trade promises steady growth. In the ASEAN region, Thailand ranks as India's fifth largest trading partner after Singapore, Vietnam, Indonesia and Malaysia. The growing ties between the two countries have come at a time when the expected integration promises geopolitical connectivity unlike the Chinese BRI, economic links and cultural and educational ties.

The fast-growing Indian market remains attractive for Thai investors, given the vast opportunities available in infrastructure, tourism and retail industries. India continues to remain an interesting market for the export of goods from Thailand. Currently, Thai goods have benefited from a tax reduction under ASEAN-India FTA in goods, which came into effect from 1 January 2010, and resulted in the flow of more goods into the Indian market. An Early Harvest Scheme (EHS) covering 83 products under the proposed India-Thailand FTA, in place since September 2004, has already resulted in phenomenal growth in our bilateral trade.

## Defence Relations

The MoU on Defence Cooperation between India and Thailand was signed on 25 January 2012.

Since 2015, India has been participating in Ex-Cobra Gold, the largest Asia Pacific Military exercise as 'Observer Plus' category. India fields its engineers, observers and medical delegations in the exercises in Thailand. Bilateral exercises are held annually between the armed forces of both countries.

The other ongoing defence cooperation initiatives comprises of bi-annual joint maritime patrolling by the navies of both countries, annual staff talks, subject matter expert exchange visits and training of officers at each other's institutions.

## Economic and Commercial Partnership Bilateral Trade

As a result of the reduced tariff rates and new initiatives adopted by India and Thailand, trade between the two countries has increased impressively in recent years. Data from the Ministry of External Affairs of India presents a picture as below that illustrates a mutual understanding augmented to mutual support.

**Table 1 Amount in billion US$**

| Years | Total Trade | Thai Export to India | Thai Import from India |
|---|---|---|---|
| 2014 | 8.66 | 5.62 | 3.04 |
| 2015 | 7.92 | 5.30 | 2.62 |
| 2016 | 7.72 | 5.15 | 2.57 |
| 2017 | 10.39 | 6.49 | 3.90 |
| 2018 | 12.46 | 7.60 | 4.86 |
| 2019 | 12.12 | 7.30 | 4.82 |

*Source: Embassy of India, Bangkok, 2022*[21]

Major Indian companies present in Thailand are Tata Motors, Tata Steel and Tata Consultancy Services; Indorama;

Aditya Birla Group; Tech Mahindra; Sun Pharma; Dabur; Lupin; NIIT; Kirloskar Brothers; Larsen & Toubro; Punj Lloyd Group; Precious Shipping PCL; Usha Siam Steel Industries PCL and others.

Leading Thai companies in India are in the fields of agro-processing, construction, automotive, engineering and banking, which have growing business prospects in India. Some very important companies are:

- Charoen Pokphand Group
- Thai Union Frozen Products PCL
- Stanley Electric Engineering India Pvt. Ltd.
- Thai Airways International PCL.
- Minor Group of Companies
- Rockworth PCL
- Precious Shipping of Thailand
- Delta Electronics (Thailand) PCL
- Siri Thai Superware PCL
- Bangkok Airways
- Siam Cement Group
- Ital Thai Development PCL
- Dusit Group
- Thai Air Asia
- ONYX Hospitality Group
- Pruska Reality
- Thai Summit

Memoranda of undertaking between the Port Authority of Thailand and Navayuga Container Terminal (Krishnapatnam Port), Kolkata Port Trust, Chennai Port Trust and Visakhapatnam Port Trust were signed in 2019.[22]

The understanding between the two countries has deepened in the prism of mutual cooperation. Thus, the companies of two countries recruit from the respective local workforce, issue contracts on their suitability preferably to the capable contractor companies from within the country they operate in and create smooth mutual servicing in a prism of symbiotic bonding. The growth is reciprocal.

The Thai experience proves that neo-symbiotic realism is an anti-thesis of structural realism, the latter being the euphoric name of neo-realism. Neo-symbiotic realism seamlessly works to ensure strength in relations that has the potential for a lasting understanding and order in the run up for lasting peace in the relational systems. Successful outstretching of neo-symbiotic realism promises lasting peace in the world systems, without the fear of violence or war, or any perceived threat of war or violence. Neo-symbiotic realism promises to ensure a peace not by the absence or perceived threat of war, but by ensuring an inheritance of peace developed over civilisational outreach. Neo-symbiotic realism is far stronger than what we understand as soft power. Soft power preaches and remains mere wistful thinking. Because underneath soft power realism or neo-realism lurks the perceived fear of violence, within the phase of absence of war.

Neo-symbiotic realism is a stronger output of hard diplomacy with proactiveness and people-to-people constructivism, which cannot be deterred by violent geopolitics. In fact, in such people-to-people constructivism, wars would seldom happen. The neo-symbiotic realism bolsters to work for attaining unenviable relations to conquer the perceived threat of war. If the absence of war is no peace, then the absence of the perceived threat of un-peace is definitely peace. Neo-symbiotic realistic relations have the potential to attain this goal of permanent peace.

## Undercurrent of Neo-Symbiosis Created and Evolved

The undercurrent of civilisational traits in the ethos of a nation-state has enormous strength to stymie the discordant notes put up against mutual relational faith. This is neo-symbiosis, because it instils in the minds of the leaders and their people faith in mutual foreign policies, and also because it is much stronger a national feeling than what has been preached as (GCSP-sponsored) symbiotic realism.[23] A new symbiotic relation rejects it and also ignores the structural realism of the states' lineups, because it subtly offers a humane approach for both connections and business. Invariably, these two entail ethics and morality. Thus, realism with morality and ethics is possible, which Machiavelli and Hobbes ignored in the past. The world has witnessed realism in its cruellest forms over the millennia in over 5000 painful conflicts between the decimation of Cold War and the Galwan Valley conflict. Modified realism such as Waltzian neo-realism, soft power or GCSP-sponsored symbiotic realism could not stop these wars. Tensions in the world's conflict zones have not been mitigated. The fear of violence lurks everywhere. Countries are not keeping their heads high with a mind without a possible futuristic fear.

Another test case in point is the neo-symbiotic overtures among apparent adversaries in the Persian Gulf region, the Gulf Cooperation Council (GCC) states and Iran. Today's world has exciting examples to understand the neo-symbiotic overtures between people of Iran and the small traders in the Arab states of Oman, the UAE, Kuwait and Qatar, who 'smuggled'[24] consumer goods, medicines and essential computer accessories across the Persian Gulf to Iranians from 2012 to 2016. These 'smugglings' actually kept Iran's economic life thriving despite the West's sanctions, so much so that the USA had to issue cautionary notes to the allied Arab states against the 'smugglings'. The 'smuggling' actually defeated the US sanctions on Iran to a great extent. This was a neo-symbiotic overture, but never matured into neo-symbiotic realism. It is because the fear of violence or war always lurked in the relations, however benevolent the overtures rendered through supplies to sanction-ridden Iran by the Arab neighbours were. Also, the fear always lurked about US backlash for ignoring its sanctions on supplies to Iran.

Then US President Donald Trump was highly critical of the 2015 Joint Comprehensive Plan of Action (JCPOA) decisions of withdrawal of sanctions on Iran, arguing that Iran was slowly but decidedly falling to 'its knees'[25] due to the sanctions, which the JCPOA decisions denied, and the purpose of the sanctions was partly defeated.[26]

The inside story was that these 'smugglings' had helped Iran continue its resistance economy despite the sanctions. It was Iran's neo-symbiotic overture defeating a structural realism as the GCC's. During Ahmadinejad's presidency, the Iranian government was also discreetly appreciative of this humane 'smuggling', which can be assumed to be an aspect of the tool of structural realism. Symbiotic realism did exist in the smuggling relations of sanction-ridden Iran and its Arab neighbours across the Persian Gulf; however, because the distrust and the fear of war always lurked between standard Arab feelings about Iran's determination to ensure its rights to nuclear energy capabilities, the neo-symbiotic overtures of the traders of the two regions overturned the teeth of the sanctions. But it was only a new symbiotic overture, and not a neo-symbiotic realism, because the fear of backlash from either the USA or aggressive hostility from Iran was always lurking in the background. Therefore, it was an overture only, and not the realistic relation to last to remove the fear of conflicts.

A hard look into the story of 'smuggling' found that what the West called 'smuggling' has been the traditional trading between both sides across the Persian Gulf region by small traders seeking to turn their individual fortune through petty business. Historically, it originated from the centres of the

Musandam archipelago of Oman and the Fujairah (the UAE) on the eastern corner of the Strait of Hormuz. These across-the-Gulf merchandise navigation was a historical trade route of small and cottage industries in Iran particularly, and later by the Arab states on the Gulf's northern coasts.

The tip was a few miles south within the Fujairah emirate off the island Hormuz on the Strait. These navigational activities on the Persian Gulf from the Arab states toward Iran, that is from south to north of the Persian Gulf, started carrying essential commodities from the Arab lands of the UAE and Oman in particular, and Qatar and Kuwait later, to Iran to save the common Iranians' life. These overtures did not consider any sectarian divide or anti-feeling toward Iran because of the sanctions, such was the power of neo-symbiotic overtures.

Similarly, during the rule of the Iranian Shah, after his reinstatement by the CIA-sponsored 1953 coup, conservative Iranians fled to Arab lands to protect their dress code and to fight back the Westernised policies of the Shah from the Arabian lands. That was a show of neo-symbiotic realism.

Thus, the neo-symbiotic realism is essentially outside of the structural realism that is silently active in the world systems today, particularly in the Occident versus Orient discourses, or for example in the US versus Iran muscle-flexing episodes. Structural realism is the basic tenet of international politics in the conflict-ridden world. Neo-symbiotic realism is more real, touching the ground realities silently through people-to-people and business-to-business (B2B) situations, and morally in underpinning traits, in which mutual trust grows into a composite civilisational ethos. It creates its own civilisation and ethos. It becomes an enormous relation beyond which the governments can manoeuvre. It does not go rigidly by the states' official behaviours, but is carried out often within the bordering local connections or agreed B2B undertakings. It does not oppose the structural state policies in the world system, nor defuse the intensity of the state diplomacy, but creates within the states a strong animus to deny conflicts. Neo-symbiotic realism wields the potential to be the future of the world order.

## Taking Forward

Indian civilisational connections have been linear in the Southeast Asian region, stretching across the entire Indo-Pacific region. Of the countries in the region, Cambodia, Laos, Indonesia, Malaysia and the Philippines also connect with Thailand as essential natural partners, because these countries enjoy civilisational connections with India. Lord Rama is the ruling deity in the ethos of the states' polity in the region, symbolised through names and nomenclatures. Intensifying symbiosis with Thailand, Laos and Cambodia makes sense for India because that immediately connects Pali and Sanskrit, but the civilisational connects with Indonesia, Malaysia and the Philippines take the story of neo-symbiotic realism to a challenging height. It is because the discordant notes have been seeded in some of the relational overtures recently.

The symbiosis between India and Thailand merits to be extended into responsible partnership such as setting up join military and naval centres for mutual coordination in the Gulf of Thailand and the Andaman Sea.

India needs to take responsibility to help to protect Thailand and its SLOC in the event of any probable geopolitical misadventure. In the similar neo-symbiotic spirit, India must give respect as a responsible partner with mature moral and physical cooperation, while expecting Thailand to extend the same to Indian efforts. The aim of the neo-symbiotic realism is not just wishing away soft idealistic policies, nor is it an aspect of structural realism in which the structure of geo-political realism is governed by the 'if-then' hard realist adventurism or policies. It is also not a soft power policy tool, as is often termed in the discourses of international relations. Instead, neo-symbiotic realism in the current world system removes the lurking fear psychosis. It merits to be a solution to fear, in which states, small or large, powerful or middle power, should be able to posit their policies with dignity, with heads (dignity) kept high.

Though the neo-symbiotic relations of India with ASEAN states like Indonesia, Malaysia, Vietnam, Singapore and Myanmar is civilisational, that between India and Thailand is more seamless. Neither Indian scholars nor those in Thailand have ever defined the mutual understanding in their foreign policies as symbiotic. It has been possible for both India and Thailand, considering their civilisational heritage today.

To become neo-symbiotic, this bonding needs to be strengthened in all aspects of bilateral relations, from commerce to people-to-people engagements in production of goods and material, consumption of outputs from investments, fashion, lifestyles, from security cooperation to strategic military cooperation in the SLOCs, from cultural exchanges and communication through languages and literatures to the feeling of secure understanding. The Andaman Sea and the Gulf of Thailand need to find a common ground for naval exercises and experiments of the two countries.

## Conclusion

India-Thailand bonding thus posits perfect neo-symbiotic relations through civilisational connects. The peace understood in this bonding is not the absence of war or violence, but absence of fear of war or violence. Seldom in the near future will there be a scope of fear emerging from the ethos of the two nations. This bonding is all set to reach newer heights in times to come.[27]

It has left behind the clichéd refrain that soft power bonds countries, as that is rather an understatement. The soft power that Prof Joseph Nye proffered in 1990s, today does not prove a substantial force in most cases of international relations. Conflicts or disputes continue to happen despite soft power like diaspora pressures or trade bonding. If these could affect foreign policy towards permanent peace, then wars like in Ukraine, conflicts like in the Galwan Valley in Ladakh or violent fights between Azerbaijan and Armenia over territory of Nagorno-Karabakh—five wars that India had to fight against Pakistan—would not have taken place. There are umpteen simmering conflict zones in geographies today, none of which can be explained to be in peace without fear of conflict, sooner or later, but where the so-called soft power continues to work.

By taking such a cue from a model as the case of India-Thailand relations, it is possible to understand that the neo-symbiotic realism of the USA with Canada, Australia and the UK; Saudi Arabia with the UAE; and India with Nepal, Bhutan, Thailand, Cambodia, Laos, Indonesia, and the Philippines portends to grow mature enough to generate a peace without fear lurking in the back of the mind.

In fact, India would excel by adopting more plausible foreign policies by bonding with the BIMSTEC states through FTAs and RTAs with neo-symbiotic realistic overtures to sidestep the structural realistic overtures of China and others. Relations with Thailand is a solid step to exemplify how strong neo-symbiotic realism can emerge in the benefit of the states for sustainable peace without fear of conflicts or violence or war.

Thailand would excel similarly with its hereditary trending of astute foreign policies. It is time for both India and Thailand to Prove East and Prove West, rather than just 'Act East' and 'Act West', as a live example of neo-symbiotic realistic behaviour towards each other.

## Endnotes

1 VK Saraswat et al. "A Note on Free Trade Agreements and Their Costs, National Institution for Transforming India," Niti Aayog, 1–15, FTA-NITI-FINAL, chrome-extension://efaidnbmnnnibpcajpcglclefindmkaj/http://164.100.94.191/niti/writereaddata/files/document_publication/FTA-NITI-FINAL.pdf

2 VK Saraswat, "India's Experience with Free Trade Agreements (FTAs)," in A Note on Free Trade Agreements and Their Costs, National Institution for Transforming India (Niti Aayog), 6-7. chrome-extension://efaidnbmnnnibpcajpcglclefindmkaj/http://164.100.94.191/niti/writereaddata/files/document_publication/FTA-NITI-FINAL.pdf

3 Arjun Srinivas, "India's Brush with FTAs in Five Charts," *Mint*, March 1, 2022, https://www.livemint.com/economy/what-the-indo-asean-trade-pact-tells-us-about-ftas-11646115455300.html

4 Nandini Sarma, *Free Trade After RCEP, What Next for India?* New Delhi: ORF, 2020, https://www.orfonline.org/research/free-trade-after-rcep-what-next-for-india-64163/

5 Akarsh Bhutani, *India's Reluctance in Joining the RCEP — A Boon or a Bane in the Long-Run?* New Delhi: ORF, 2021, https://www.orfonline.org/expert-speak/india-reluctance-joining-rcep-boon-bane-long-run/

6 Bhutani, *India's Reluctance in Joining the RCEP — A Boon or a Bane in the Long-Run?*

7 Bhutani, *India's Reluctance in Joining the RCEP — A Boon or a Bane in the Long-Run?*

8 Paul Krugman, "Conscience of a Liberal," *New York Times*, 2016, https://archive.nytimes.com/krugman.blogs.nytimes.com/2016/03/09/a-protectionist-moment/

9 "A Note on Free Trade Agreements and Their Costs, National Institution for Transforming India (Niti Aayog)".

10 Manoj Kewalramani, "The Future as Foretold by Xi," *The Times of India*, 2022, https://timesofindia.indiatimes.com/

blogs/voices/the-future-as-foretold-by-xi-chinese-citizens-have-to-brace-themselves-for-tough-times-indians-for-a-more-aggressive-pla/

11 Rabindranath Tagore, "Where the Mind is Without Fear: Song No. 35," *Berne Convention: Gitanjali, The Song Offerings*, 1992, https://www.sacred-texts.com/hin/tagore/gitnjali.htm

12 Nayef Al-Rodhan, "The Future of International Relations: A Symbiotic Realism Theory," in *There Is a Future: Visions for a Better World* (Madrid: BBVA, 2012), https://www.bbvaopenmind.com/en/articles/the-future-of-international-relations/#:~:text=According%20to%20symbiotic%20realism%2C%20the,of%20nature%E2%80%9D%20(SON)

13 Nayef Al-Rodhan, *Symbiotic Realism: A Theory of International Relations in An Instant and An Interdependent World* (Zurich: GCSP, LIT Verlag GmbH & Co. KG Wien, 2007).

14 Al-Rodhan, *Symbiotic Realism: A Theory of International Relations*, 137–9.

15 Al-Rodhan, *Symbiotic Realism: A Theory of International Relations*, 137–9.

16 PhrmahaWutthipong Rodbamrung, "India-Thailand Relations: And Cultural Links in Soft Power Policy," *Thai Journal Online (ThaiJO)*, https://so04.tci-thaijo.org

17 Ministry of External Affairs, "India-Thailand Relations," *Government of India: MEA Briefs*, 2020, https://www.mea.gov.in/Portal/ForeignRelation/India-Thailand_Bilateral_Brief_Feb_2020.pdf

18 Anita Bose, *Ramayana: Footprints in South East Asian Culture and Heritage* (Kolkata: BEE Books), 34.

19 Ministry of Commerce and Industry, *India-Thailand Comprehensive Economic Cooperation Agreement (CECA) negotiations* (New Delhi: Government of India) https://commerce.gov.in/international-trade-trade-agreements-indias-current-engagements-in-rtas/india-thailand-comprehensive-economic-cooperation-agreement-ceca-negotiations/

20 Embassy of India Website, *India Thailand Economic and Commercial Relations*, Bangkok, https://embassyofindiabangkok.gov.in/eoibk_pages/MjM

21 Embassy of India, Overview in India Thailand Economic and Commercial Relations. https://embassyofindiabangkok.gov.in/index.php/eoibk_pages/MzE4

22 Embassy of India, Overview in India Thailand Economic and Commercial Relations. https://embassyofindiabangkok.gov.in/eoibk_pages/MTM2

23 Al-Rodhan, *The Future of International Relations: A Symbiotic Realism Theory* https://www.bbvaopenmind.com/en/articles/the-future-of-international-relations/#:~:text=According%20to%20symbiotic%20realism%2C%20the,of%20nature%E2%80%9D%20(SON)

24 Lin Noueihed, "Smuggling to Iran Rife in Dangerous Gulf Waters," *Reuters*, May 12, 2008, https://www.reuters.com/article/uk-oman-iran-smuggling-idUKL0624311920080512

25 "Iran Turns to Barter for Foods as Sanctions Cripple Imports," *Reuters*, February 9, 2012, https://www.reuters.com/article/uk-iran-idUKTRE8181Q920120209

26 Deborah Haynes, "US Sanctions 'Will Fail to Bring Iran to its Knees'," *Sky News*, November 5, 2018, https://news.sky.com/story/us-sanctions-will-fail-to-bring-iran-to-its-knees-11545819

27 S Jaishankar, "India's Time-Tested Relations with Thailand Poised to Move to the Next Level, says EAM Jaishankar," (Bangkok: PTI).
https://economictimes.indiatimes.com/news/india/indias-time-tested-relations-with-thailand-poised-to-move-to-the-next-level-says-eam-jaishankar/articleshow/93644557.cms

*Section IV*

# Covid 19: The Pandemic of Our Time

# Covid-19 and the Asia Pacific in its Early Years till the End of 2022

*Lipi Ghosh*

## Introduction

The Covid-19 outbreak brought the world to a standstill. The world faced a new Great Depression and global panic as the virus toll mounted. The undeclared cold war that has been gathering momentum shows its true face under the tedium of Covid-19, which had major impacts on international relations, especially in the Asia Pacific region, for the contemporary period. Apart from the USA and China's reciprocal allegations against each other about the origin of the coronavirus, relations among interregional powers have also become strained. The central directive of these relations are anti-Chinese feelings either at government or at civil society levels. This paper studies the issues of Covid-19 in the Asia Pacific and its impacts till 2022, the year when Covid-19 reached its end. This paper concentrates especially on the issue of vaccine diplomacy.

Southeast Asia reacted in different ways. Regional states went into different variations of a lockdown. Thailand declared a state of emergency. In the Philippines, President Rodrigo Duterte was granted emergency powers to combat Covid-19. In Cambodia, Prime Minister Hun Sen used Article 22 of the constitution to declare an emergency. Malaysia took stubborn control measures. The civil society of Myanmar termed the outbreak catastrophic. In Indonesia, the number of cases has been increasing daily and lockdown was declared. In Vietnam, lockdowns were implemented around Hanoi. Vietnam chaired ASEAN in 2020, and the annual meeting was postponed till 2021. All Southeast Asian governments were upset by this Covid-19 outbreak.

Interestingly, in actual manifestations, the Southeast Asian states' reaction was not anti- Chinese; rather, it was anti-Westerners. Thailand was the first to blame not China but 'dirty Caucasian tourists' for infecting Thailand 'because they don't shower and do not wear masks', according to Thai Health Minister Anutin Charnvirakul. The Cambodian Prime Minister Hun Sen visited Beijing in early February to showcase 'unbreakable friendship and mutual trust'.[1] In his presidential address on March 12, Duterte, the President of the Philippines observed that 'Chinese President Xi Jinping was ready to help and all we have to do is ask…'[2] In an interview on March 29, Singapore's Lee Hsien Loong said that 'blaming China for the spread of the Covid-19 pandemic is unfair'.[3] Definitely, the whole Southeast Asian region is looking for cooperative solutions.

In regards to the coronavirus, on February 5, China's Foreign Ministry listed '21 friendly countries' who had offered a 'friendly understanding' during the crisis, namely 'the Republic of Korea (ROK), Japan, Thailand, Malaysia, Indonesia, Kazakhstan, Pakistan, Germany, Britain, France, Italy, Hungary, Belarus, Turkey, Iran, the United Arab Emirates, Algeria, Egypt, Australia, New Zealand and Trinidad and Tobago'.

Noticeably, China was also working to control the damage to the Southeast Asian nations. In late February, it rushed to discuss the impacts of the outbreak with all its Southeast Asian partners in Vientiane, the capital of Laos, aiming to reinstate regional unity. The Vientiane ASEAN-China declaration of February 20, 2020 emphasised solidarity and the long-standing tradition of helping each other in difficult times. By stressing assistance at all levels, China succeeded in bringing ASEAN member-states closer than they themselves had actually contemplated.

Reviewing the situation in East Asia and the Pacific, however, one finds it to be mostly troubled. Out of 21 'friendly nations', Japan and ROK, the only two East Asian powers, were also largely upset. Covid-19 affected the North Korean economy too. Hong Kong's protest movement against China inspired a new surge and Taiwan also braced for the negative economic impacts of Covid-19. The same also escalated the China–Australia contest in the Asia Pacific.

So, the crucial question at the time was what the policies of these nations would be towards China in international relations, especially in the post-Covid scenario. As part of its economic stimulus package, Japan earmarked $2.2 billion to help its manufacturers shift production out of China. Of this amount, 220 billion yen ($2 billion) was for companies shifting production back to Japan and 23.5 billion yen for those seeking to move production to other countries.

According to *Daily NK* sources inside North Korea, trade with China came to an abrupt halt and a shortage of supplies quickly ensued. Sinuiju port and borders with China were closed. Rajesh Chandramouli reported that South Korean companies were keen to move out of China to India. The Korean consulate in Chennai has been working with a number of requests, both in preliminary and advanced stages.[4]

For Hong Kong, the highest risk sectors included tourism and service sectors. Though some have suggested that the civil unrest and social movement so prominent in Hong Kong will recede permanently, the actuality is that underlying grievances remain vigorous and once the pandemic settles, they will re-emerge as a fresh burst.[5]

Taiwan's tourism and aviation industries are struggling; most sectors faced heavy damage, and the government planned $2 billion assistance.[6]

The global pandemic has crippled the economies of Pacific island nations. Papua New Guinea, the Pacific's most populous country and Australia's largest aid beneficiary, had already been teetering on the edge of a health crisis. China's Covid-19 response presented a major challenge for Australia broadly in countering Chinese influence in the Pacific. Prior to the pandemic, Australia was in the process of instituting changes to its foreign policy by planning an AU$2 billion investment in the Australian Infrastructure Financing Facility for the Pacific (AIFFP). However, the global pandemic derailed and destabilised the plans.[7]

So, it was evident that the post-Covid-19 international relations would be considerably altered and may have a significant blowback for China. Tensions between superpowers like United States and China were already significantly impacting global trade and multilateral institutions. In spite of China and Southeast Asia's closeness, some changes may come up.

There are a couple of areas where China's interest was jeopardised. Firstly, the problems associated with China's ambitious Belt and Road Initiative (BRI) and One Belt One Road (OBOR) were dulled by this pandemic. Secondly, China's involvement in the Regional Comprehensive Economic Partnership (RECP) was bound to be affected.

The BRI needs to be understood in the context of the Trump administration's Free and Open Indo-Pacific (FOIP) strategy, which provided a counterpoint to China's increased penetration in the region through the BRI. Here, Malaysia has a crucial role to play. Malaysia wholeheartedly supported *ASEAN Outlook* published in 2019. The document stated that the Asia Pacific and Indian Ocean were closely integrated in security and economic structures and need restrained order. Malaysia insisted on a warship-free zone in Malaysia's adjoining seas. It was a clear-cut message to both China and the United States. But Mahathir's ostensible use of Japan to evade China may change under his successor Muhyiddin.

Through this perspective of Southeast Asia and the Asia Pacific, what will the role of India be in the Asia Pacific, especially in the context of her Act East policy ? One prime question of the Covid-19 period was whether Japan would now be more interested in India. Could India attract more Japanese investments? Which sectors could attract Japanese FDIs? Shinichi Seki, an economist at the Japan Research Institute, predicted that there would be a shift in the coming days, as there was already renewed talk of Japanese firms reducing their reliance on China as a manufacturing base.[8]

Regarding Southeast Asia, China has risen to become the largest source of imports for nine of the ten Southeast Asian countries. Also, it is an increasingly important export market for all ten. Will coronavirus turn this relationship upside down? Analysts are unanimous in predicting that the dampened demand will surely translate into an economic slowdown for the entire region. The ASEAN and BIMSTEC countries were very badly affected in tourism and related service sectors. Australia and Japan tried to persuade India, which had backed away from the RCEP talks, to rejoin to help balance China's role. The coronavirus could be a game changer for nations striving to catch up with the rest of the world. Southeast Asia should wake up and direct its own transformation. The region could find a silver lining to the turmoil if ASEAN starts to pose India as a serious alternative to China as a united bloc.

Prime Minister Modi took the lead both at the G-20 summit and in SAARC, advocating international cooperation to defeat Covid-19. This considers the fact Modi also needed to take a leading role in ASEAN & BIMSTEC, which are parts of India's Act East policy. India's non-participation in China's BRI makes it more important for India to strengthen its own strategic and economic ties in Southeast Asia.[9]

With fellow Asian nations, Beijing might employ a mixture of assertive and non-assertive approaches. A 'low-profile' approach might be visible on conflicting issues like the South China Sea and East China Sea, as well as the boundary disputes with India for some time, even though nothing is changing Beijing's claim and posturing.

Overall, a moderate approach combined with both assertive and non-assertive posturing is likely to emerge in Asia. Holding relatively stable relations with India will become a priority, even though Beijing would be mindful of New Delhi's growing partnership with the US and India's rising Indo-Pacific profile.

## Vaccine Diplomacy

India launched the world's largest Covid-19 vaccination drive. India's vaccine diplomacy put it in direct competition with China, which has made no secret that vaccine distribution is linked to its broader geopolitical ambitions. In fact, it even explicitly included vaccine distribution in its broader Health Silk Road initiative, which aims to bolster China's international soft power.

If the government of India can ensure that its domestic vaccine requirements are being adequately met, as seems to be the plan, there is little possibility of political blowback for Modi sending vaccines elsewhere. Meanwhile, the foreign-policy benefits in strategic areas could be great. For instance, India is keen on mending its ties with Bangladesh. New Delhi's controversial citizenship law enacted last year and the news of $40 billion in investments from China to Bangladesh had strained ties between the two nations. The Covid-19 vaccine could lessen the strain.

Similarly, vaccine diplomacy provided an opportunity for India to resolve outstanding issues with Nepal. Relations between the two countries recently hit a new low when they entered a heated exchange over the Kalapani territory, an area situated at the strategic China-Nepal-India tri-junction. Bhutan was the first country to receive a shipment of Covid-19 vaccines on 20 January, 2021.

In Indian Ocean countries like the Maldives and Mauritius, India's vaccine diplomacy helped foster stronger ties in the region, and offset China's growing influence attributable to its financial investments and social-development projects. India needed more than a billion doses to protect its own population, but it also aimed to offer 20 million doses to neighbouring Nepal, Bangladesh, Sri Lanka, Afghanistan, the Seychelles and Mauritius by spring. It then distributed vaccines to Latin America, Africa and the former Soviet Republics. Many of the recipient countries signed so-called vaccine pacts with India on a government-to-government basis to finalise the number of doses and determine whether they would be provided.[10]

Clinching vaccine deals in South Asia as well as the global South could boost India's regional standing, particularly with countries like Nepal, Sri Lanka and Bangladesh, with whom ties have soured for various reasons. Tensions between Nepal and India escalated over territorial claims in the disputed Kalapani region and relations with Bangladesh soured after the passing of the Citizenship (Amendment) Act 2019 and the National Register of Citizenship Bill. In December 2020, however, India's Prime Minister Narendra Modi and his counterpart in Bangladesh, Sheikh Hasina, discussed the vaccine deal virtually, marking their first talks since last year's drift.[11]

Regarded as the world's vaccine manufacturing hub, India also shipped 10 million commercial units to 17 neighbouring states, West Asia, Africa and Latin America early this year.[12]

With the 'Vaccine Maitri' (*maitri* is Hindi for friendship) diplomatic mission launched on 20 January 2021, India is aiming to bridge the world's vaccine divide. The mission includes vaccine gifts to neighbours in need Bhutan (0.15 million doses), Maldives (0.1 million), Nepal (1 million), Bangladesh (2 million), Myanmar (1.5 million), Mauritius (0.1 million), Seychelles (0.05 million), Sri Lanka (0.5 million), Bahrain (0.1 million) and Oman (0.1 million). Other beneficiaries of India's strength in vaccine production are the Caribbean Community (CARICOM) countries (0.5 million doses), Nicaragua and the Pacific Island states (0.2 million doses each). India will also supply affordable vaccines to Saudi Arabia, Canada and Mongolia. Under the GAVI-COVAX alliance, India hopes to supply 10 million doses to Africa and 1 million to UN health workers.[13]

## Conclusion

India's vaccine diplomacy put her in direct competition with China, which made no secret that vaccine distribution is wrapped up in its broader geopolitical ambitions. In fact, it even explicitly included vaccine distribution in its broader Health Silk Road initiative, which aims to bolster China's international soft power.

The quality and efficacy of Chinese vaccines have been questioned due to concealment of test data and lack of transparency in information. Recent reports have revealed that Brazil—which was initially planning to deploy China's Sinovac—raised concerns about the efficacy and safety of the vaccine and ultimately decided to opt for India's Bharat Biotech. Such outcomes will help India position itself as the more responsible global power. Simply put, India has a longer track record of supplying medicines and vaccines to the rest of the world, especially to low- and middle-income countries.[14]

Nevertheless, China has one big advantage over nearly every other country: It has largely been able to control the pandemic within its borders, and its economy is mostly back on track. That means China can potentially devote more diplomatic attention and resources to its global vaccine outreach. However, unlike India, there is little transparency about the safety of efficacy of Chinese vaccines. The Brazil case shows the problems that can cause.

We need to see the world in peace and not in conflict. Covid-19 reduced the pace of quarrels and it became time for India to maintain a balance in diplomatic relations in the Asia Pacific, along with her superior image by following tenets of tolerance, flexibility and guidance in midst of the biggest humanitarian crisis. For ages, Indian philosophy has showed ways to mankind; India also showed a *true path* to the world.

## Endnotes

1 http://www.xinhuanet.com/english/2020-02/05/c

2 Sophie Boisseau du Rocher, "What COVID-19 Reveals About China-Southeast Asia Relations," April 8, 2020.

3 Boisseau du Rocher, "What COVID-19 Reveals About China-Southeast Asia Relations".

4 Lipi Ghosh, "Affliction and Asia," *The Statesman*, April 25, 2020.

5 Brian Wong, "Hong Kong's Protests Amid COVID-19: A Dying Movement or a Halted War?" *The Diplomat*, April 10, 2020.

6 Nick Aspinwall, "Taiwan Braces for Economic Impact of Global Coronavirus Outbreak," *The Diplomat,* March 6, 2020.

7 Philip Citowicki, "COVID-19 Escalates the China-Australia Contest in the Pacific," The Diplomat, April 10, 2020.

8 "Japan Will Pay Its Firms to Leave China, Relocate Production as Part of Coronavirus Stimulus Package," News18.com, April 9, 2020.

9 https://www.narendramodi.in/prime-minister-narendra-modi-s-interaction-with-saarc-leaders-on-fighting-coronavirus-548793

10 Harsh V Pant and Aarshi Tirkey, "India's Vaccine Diplomacy: The World's Pharmacy is Looking to Inoculations to Build Friendly Ties Around the World—and Compete with China," FP, January 22, 2021.

11 Jyoti Sharma and SK Varshney, "India's Vaccine Diplomacy Aids Global Access to Covid-19 Jabs," *Nature India*, February 17, 2021.

12 https://www.ncbi.nlm.nih.gov/pmc/articles/PMC9620874/

13 Marjan Mohamadi et al., "COVID-19 Vaccination Strategy in China: A Case Study," *Epidemiologia* (Basel) 2, no. 3(2021): 402–25, https://www.ncbi.nlm.nih.gov/pmc/articles/PMC9620874/

# Populist Political Communication in India during Covid-19: A Comparative Study of National and Regional Political Leadership's Messaging in Response to the Pandemic

*Ambar Kumar Ghosh*

## Introduction

The phenomenon of populism emanates from a deep-rooted crisis of representation and unfulfillment of popular aspirations manifested despite the tall promises of electoral democracy. The centrality of populism lies in a fluid creation and invocation of a category called 'the people' as a political subject, especially in a situation that is perceived as a political, socio-economic or cultural 'crisis' of democracy.[1] Populism identifies the will of 'the people' with justice and morality, according legitimacy to its cause.[2] Therefore, it denotes a set of ethical political actions underlining 'crisis politics' that is 'redemptive' in nature for the 'true emancipation of the people' as a departure from 'routine politics' of 'pragmatic' incrementalism in institutional democracies.[3] The Covid-19 pandemic—as an unprecedented crisis that has had far-reaching and overarching implications on human lives across the globe—created a conducive opportunity for the further consolidation of populist politics. As the pandemic cloaked the whole world in uncertainty, fear, unprecedented health and socio-economic crises, many countries witnessed the consolidation of populist leaders concentrating power in their hands to 'salvage' the crisis situation as the 'saviour'.[4]

India, as one of the nations with a massive population density and a robust electoral democracy with a federal system, becomes an extremely important case study to understand the democratic leadership's response in dealing with the Covid-19 pandemic.[5] Also, in the culture of India's democratic politics that has given rise to 'strong' leaders with charismatic personality cults at the national and state levels, who are often categorised as populists, analysing the leadership's conduct during the pandemic is extremely interesting.[6] This is because the Covid-19 pandemic gave scholars a rare window of opportunity to understand what forms and levels of populist political tools are used by the political leadership in India to confront a crisis situation like the pandemic. Unmediated communication between the leader and 'the people' by subverting the institutional bulwarks of democracy like legislature, political party's organisational arrangements, governmental hierarchy and federal structure, is one of the key elements of a populist leadership's communication style.[7] This paper confines itself to studying the nature of political communication and messaging during the pandemic of three prominent leaders in India: the country's Prime Minister and leader of the national ruling Bharatiya Janata Party (BJP) Narendra Modi; CM of West Bengal and founder-president of the regional party All India Trinamool Congress (AITC) Mamata Banerjee; and CM of Delhi and founder-leader of the Aam Admi Party (AAP) that presently occupies power in two states in India, Arvind Kejriwal.[8] While the importance of studying Modi as the head of the national government is understandable, the rationale of looking at select state-level case studies—Mamata Banerjee and Arvind Kejriwal's political styles during Covid-19 is that these leaders are also often touted as populists,[9] and they are powerful regional leaders who have successfully challenged the ascendency of the Modi-led BJP in the state-level electoral contests in Bengal and Delhi. In this context, first, the paper will assess whether the national and state leadership's political messaging during the pandemic facilitated unmediated political communication between the leader and 'the people' by bypassing the institutional bulwarks of constitutional democracy. Second, the paper will seek to understand whether such a political communication facilitated centralisation of power by the Centre as well as state and how it impacted the federal political structure of India. Lastly, the paper will evaluate if such political communication coincides with populist polarised political constructs like 'virtuous homogenous people' and the 'corrupt and debilitating other' or 'enemy' in the war-like rhetoric to fight against the pandemic.[10]

## Defining Populism

Populism encapsulates a condition that ostensibly demands a revulsion of the conventional mainstream discourse of institutional democratic politics that is accused of embodying moral erosion, illegitimacy and inefficiency.[11] Hence, it purportedly attempts/claims to build a mass-based democratic movement by mobilising a considerable section of the populace to elicit support for a morally higher political discourse that would replace the remnants of a decadent system with an arrangement that is truly representative of the interests of the 'authentic people'. So, broadly speaking, populism as a political project emerges apparently to offer a corrective to the depravations of representative democracy.[12] However, populism as a seemingly cathartic political project to refurbish the ideals of truly representative and participatory democracy is itself perceived by its critics as a 'potential usurper' of the vestiges of liberal democratic institutions and processes.[13] This is the point of contradiction between what the populist political discourse claims to be and actually delivers in the cause of popular sovereignty within the framework of constitutional democracy. However, scholars have cautioned that populist politics shouldn't be misconstrued as one of the pathological pitfalls of democracy.[14] Rather, the populist style of politics is inextricably linked with the very functioning of democracy.[15] It is noteworthy that though this paper delves into the nature of populist leadership in democracy, the populist political style has also been adopted by non-democratic authoritarian leadership in many countries in the world.[16]

The populists tend to resort to tactical manipulation of the masses by fanning emotive grievances that have a deep impact on the foundation of the democratic system in significant ways. First, populism's creation of the 'people' and the 'other' often paves the way for political polarisation and social disharmony, leading to unrest in multicultural and diverse societies.[17] Second, populist political appeal's tendency of creating a linear definition of 'people' whom it considers as its target social base for political support undermines the existence of plurality of views, constituencies and political actors in robust multi-party democracies. The populist leadership asserts itself as a sole embodiment of the interest of 'the people' and demonises the political opponents as the 'enemy' of the nation or society. Third, the populist political appeal accords importance to popular elections as the ultimate marker of legitimacy in a democracy and systematically suppresses the institutions, procedures and rule of law that constitutes the integral core of a democratic political system.[18] Fourth, it creates a perennial condition of a mythical moral war against the 'other' for the salvation of 'the people' and the nation led by the charismatic leader who can harbour 'authoritarian' tendencies by supressing opposition and dissent. , Dramatic one-sided emotive communication from the leader to their people can create a situation of politically ignorant 'audience democracy'.[19] Fifth, the distribution of material goods by the leader to their people, seen as an important element of populism, creates a situation of mass clientelism, where people become extremely dependent on the populist regimes for essential goods necessary for survival .[20]

## Populist Political Communication

Populism scholars have given great attention to the forms of populist political appeals prevalent in democracies across the world. Populism is seen from an ideational (Mudde), politico-strategic (Weyland) and socio-cultural (Ostiguy) perspective.[21] Broadly speaking, populism thrives in a socio-economic and political condition of 'crisis' that makes it conducive for a personalistic leader to seek support and exercises government power based on direct, unmediated, uninstitutionalised support from large numbers of mostly unorganised 'disgruntled' followers. The political appeal of populism is often regarded as a form of political culture or approach based on a 'thin-centred ideology' or 'empty signifier' without any definite concrete doctrinaire.[22] So, the populist political style can be structured in any particular way to ensure the representation of whatever political content it seeks to articulate. The political communication between the populist political leader and the people whom the leader considers the core electoral constituency and seeks to represent is the key element that shapes the discourse of populist politics. Such a communication has three integral parts. First, the leader has to create a 'people' as a moral and virtuous entity based on some specific socio-cultural or economic identity whose interest he claims to solely represent, delegitimising other leaders or parties. Such a definition of people is exclusive and keeps the sections whom the leader demarcates as the 'enemy' or the 'other' outside the legitimate and moral imagination of the people.[23] Second, the leader has to possess the charisma to establish his emotive relationship with 'the people' by instinctively relating to their interests and claim to be their sole representative. Third, the leader is the sole custodian of the people's interest, directly communicates with the people, distributes material welfare to them and delivers governance overshadowing the rule-based institutions of democracy.[24]

## Populism and Indian Democracy

India, with its multi-party electoral democracy and federal polity, has witnessed many kinds of populist political appeals. Political leadership in India has been characterised by direct, personalised appeals to 'the people' by leaders who deploy particular socio-economic and cultural registers to secure and maintain political power by circumventing political intermediaries and organisational structures and by subverting institutions of democracy.[25] Hence, in the Indian context, populism can be traced both as a distinctive form of political strategy and politics conducted within an ideational and socio-cultural register grounded in a 'plebeian grammar'.[26]

The culture of hero worship and mass adulation of charismatic leaders has historically been the modus operandi of Indian politics, making it conducive for crafting effective populist appeals.[27] Studies on populist leadership styles in India have highlighted three major strands of populism. First, former Prime Minister and Congress leader Indira Gandhi, after the split of her party in 1969, created her charismatic personality cult by effectively defining 'the people' as encapsulating the 'poor and marginalised sections' against the vested interest of landed gentry, capitalists and conservatives whose interest she claimed was safeguarded by her political opponents. She overshadowed the institutional mechanisms of her party and government in order to create a direct unmediated appeal to the people.[28] Second, the populist tendency found a communal Hindutva flavour in the political appeal of BJP leader Narendra Modi in his earlier stint as CM of Gujarat and, since 2014, in a different avatar as the Prime Minister of India. The Hindutva populism led by Modi created an electorally rewarding ethnic majoritarian imagination of Hindus as the 'authentic people', and attempts have been made to marginalise the minority Muslim community as the 'other' who are allegedly safeguarded in the name of 'pseudo-secularism' by the hitherto ruling elite led by the Congress party, liberal English-speaking media and civil society at the cost of the Hindu majority.[29] Such majoritarian populism after capturing governmental power has shown the propensity of authoritarian tendencies led by strong leaders like Modi, reminiscent of Indira Gandhi's political style. Third, charismatic regional leaders of Tamil Nadu like Karunanidhi, MGR and Jayalalitha and Andhra Pradesh's T Rama Rao made their populist appeal on the basis of their ethnic, linguistic and regional pride, mainly to the middle and intermediate castes for massive mass mobilisation against the Brahmanical culture,[30] Hindi imposition and central government's domination. The newer regional parties, such as the TMC in Bengal led by its charismatic leader Mamata Banerjee[31] and AAP led by Arvind Kejriwal, also offer different variants of populist leadership and governance patterns based on a strong personality cult and distribution of material goods in the name of the leader.[32]

## Populism During the Covid-19 Pandemic

The sudden outbreak of the unprecedented and unforeseen crisis like the Covid-19 pandemic that brought the entire world to a standstill has called for bold leadership in countries across the globe. The unknown nature of the crisis triggered an unimaginable sense of life and livelihood insecurity amongst the people and understandably looked up to the state and its leadership for respite and guidance. Such an unconventional crisis situation made it conducive for populist leaders to consolidate and reinforce their popular appeal amongst their political constituencies.[33] However, to be fair, the urgency of the situation also posed a challenge for leaders across the globe, populist or otherwise, as they had to deliver material as well as emotional support to their citizens to sail through such uncertain times of unending human suffering.[34] However, amidst such an unprecedented contingency, the populist political appeal becomes crucial in three ways. First, as populism is premised upon the 'politics of crisis', the Covid-19 crisis that demanded the temporary suspension of all institutional forms of political communication like legislative debates, cabinet consultations, party meetings and bureaucratic deliberations opened up the space for the leader to occupy the centre stage of governance and make unmediated direct appeals to the people. Society looked up to the topmost leadership for guidance, motivation and material resources like healthcare and subsistence support during the period of lockdown and rise of Covid-19 cases especially during the ugly waves of coronavirus infections. Such a situation enabled a condition for the leader to project himself as a saviour who alone can act as the panacea for the people in distress. Second, as populism thrives on the antagonistic division of the 'people' and the 'enemy outsider', social prejudices against groups like the poor, migrants and ethnic minorities could be politicised for creating the 'other' as the 'carriers of the virus'. Third, as the state became the ultimate arbiter and regulating mechanism for ensuring the survival and safety of the people, the patrimonial state could deliver health and economic governance as a direct gift to the people from the 'benevolent' populist leader, further bolstering his charisma.[35]

Bearing such conditions in mind, it will be interesting to look at the populist communication styles of three political leaders in India. Prime Minister Narendra Modi, who is often touted as the national populist, has been perceived as the national face of India's fight against Covid-19. CM Mamata Banerjee and CM Arvind Kejriwal are often recognised as regional populists and the most vocal opposition leaders and major political rivals of the Modi-led BJP who harbour national political ambition. Also, it would be interesting to compare national-level and regional-level populist communication during Covid-19 and how it is shaped by India's federal dynamics. Communication of political leaders can be categorised into two distinct forms for analysis: First, the verbal communication by referring to the speeches, interviews, press conferences and public statements of the leaders. Second, the symbolic or performative modes of communication in which discursive analysis of leader's countenance, gestures and appearances are taken into account. For the analysis in this paper, both forms of communication—verbal as well as symbolic—by the select leaders will be considered. The analysis delves into three forms of populist repertoire in leadership communication in India during the Covid-19 pandemic.

## 1. *Patrimonial and Intimate Leader*

As Covid-19 started to manifest its presence in India from mid-March 2020, the pandemic became the focal point of the topmost political leadership communication both at the central and the state level. It is important to note that despite the reports of Covid-19 outbreak in other countries since early January, India's administration didn't appear to take major tangible efforts towards it until mid-March, when it had already been aggravated to some extent across the world.[36] Though a few state governments took some pre-emptive steps, it is only after mid-March that the Indian political leadership at the national and state levels took concerted steps towards battling the spread of Covid-19. In the initial period of the pandemic, PM Modi, as the face of India's national fight against the pandemic, made periodic televised appearances in order to inform the citizens about the enormity of the crisis and motivate them to take appropriate steps to collectively fight the virus.[37] Modi's mode of communication was in form of monologues taking up the role of motivating, uniting and encouraging the citizens to stay vigil and put up collective cooperation to fight the pandemic. In his widely viewed 'Janta Curfew' speech on 19 March 2020, he applauds the people for cooperating with the government in the fight against Covid-19 till then and alludes that as the people of the country always have listened to him, they should also adhere to the Janata Curfew by staying indoors and exercising social distancing to win the 'war' against the Covid virus.[38] He harped on *sankalp* (resolve) and *sayyam* (patience) for the people to unitedly fight the pandemic. Modi's televised addresses focused on emotive appeals to the people to mobilise support and embolden the collective spirit of a nation as a whole in order to navigate through the crisis, make a symbolic gesture of national unity and togetherness and pay tribute to the country's health workers for their tireless service at that time. PM Modi appealed to the nation that 'On March 22, at 5 pm stand at your doors and windows for five minutes and clap or ring a bell to salute people who are serving the nation tirelessly'.[39] Modi's speeches harped more on the abstract ideas of national resilience and capacity for economic self-reliance (Atmanirbhar Bharat), while his proclamations were largely bereft of details about the health infrastructure or the government's blueprint for fighting the pandemic.[40] These intricacies of the governmentality of the pandemic were left to other ministers and bureaucrats in their relatively regular press briefings.[41] Such a mode of proselytising unidirectional communication that laid down the broader direction and sought to offer psychological support and guidance can be categorised as a patrimonial leadership communication by a 'messiah-saviour' populist leader who is capable of transcending beyond the vagaries of everyday necessities of the crisis. However, the strongman element in populist leadership could be demystified as India entered into more severe phases of the pandemic. Modi's televised addresses and the central government's initial centralising approach that triggered the sudden lockdown faded out subsequently as infection rates started increasing across the country. The omnipresence of the saviour strong leader was marked by withdrawal and relative stepping back as the centre conceded major decision-making power regarding lockdowns and procurements of medical equipment to the state leadership.[42] During the worst Covid crisis of the raging second wave in April 2021, Modi made a very short and largely precautionary and motivational televised address to the nation. He was seen present in the election campaign rallies in the election-bound state of West Bengal, addressing huge crowds and delivering speeches in the campaign trail.[43] During this time, the country suffered massive oxygen shortages, unavailability of hospital beds and life-saving drugs and a large number of Covid casualties.[44]

West Bengal CM Mamata Banerjee, who has had carved a political distinction as a street fighter and close mass connector, attempted to project more direct communication with the people during this period. She was witnessed on the roads and in the markets, educating people regarding social distancing norms.[45] Delhi CM Arvind Kejriwal and Banerjee also kept visiting hospitals to review medical preparedness. Moreover, both Banerjee and Kejriwal,[46] along with other CMs, were found attending regular press conferences to apprise the people of their state on the status of the Covid situation, revised guidelines, state's preparedness and the governmental actions being taken to control the situation.[47] In Mamata's case, in an unprecedented move, administrative meetings on Covid were also televised and followed by press conferences.[48] However, such channels of accountable communication during the crisis were accompanied by selective silence or denial of alleged suppression of Covid deaths in Bengal and discrepancies in data on Covid-19 infections that has led to scuffles with the centre.[49] The Delhi government's inability to fully utilise the Maholla Clinics as pointed out by the Delhi High Court was met with a studied silence from CM Kejriwal.[50] However, the overall tendency of the CMs of both states to constantly remain visible in public view and communicate about the nitty-gritty of the pandemic management created an intimate, highly tangible and involved manner of both symbolic as well as verbal communication from the leadership for the respective states.

## 2. *The Creation of the Political and the Socio-Cultural 'Other'*

The typical populist political strategy of creating a homogenous category of virtuous people in opposition to the 'alien or enemy outsider' was visible in the communication of Modi at the national level and Banerjee and Kejriwal at the state level during Covid-19. Such a project of 'otherisation' occurred both at the political and socio-cultural level. At the political level, the CMs of the opposition parties like Banerjee and Kejriwal, as vocal critics, accused the centre of vendetta politics and non-cooperation in the fight against the pandemic.[51] They alleged that the centre was halting crucial funds needed by their state governments, was not appropriately distributing medical equipment including medicines and oxygen and was slow on procurement and adequate distribution of vaccines.[52] In return, Modi government accused the opposition-ruled states of deliberately not cooperating with the centre, raising false alarms of requirement of oxygen, medicine, vaccines and unavailability of funds and deliberately spreading the virus by sending migrant workers back to their native villages in order to embarrass the central government.[53] The state governments, especially Banerjee, vociferously protested the centre's move to send central inspection teams to opposition-ruled states for review of Covid-19 preparedness, as she apprehended that such a team has been sent with ulterior motives to belittle her efforts of fighting the pandemic and to play vendetta politics.[54]

In the socio-cultural sphere, after the Tablighi Jamat congregation in Delhi in March 2020, the proponents of anti-Muslim rhetoric as part of Hindu right-wing propaganda started to stigmatise Muslims as 'carriers of the virus' or 'super spreaders', triggering violence against Muslims in many parts of the country.[55] This narrative coincided with the Hindutva right-wing's broader political narrative that espouses the 'otherisation' on religious minorities.[56] The social ostracisation was not only based on communal prejudice but also included ethno-racial attacks in the early period of the pandemic.[57] The virus originated from China, and there were incidents of harassment of northeastern citizens, especially students living in north India and other states, for their facial resemblance to Chinese nationals.[58] Such national-level prejudices were accompanied by sub-national jingoism as both CMs Banerjee and Kejriwal 'othered' people from outside the state as potential carriers of the virus or non-natives of the state.[59] They were also discriminated against in matters of medical treatment for non-natives in the state, as attempted in New Delhi.[60] Banerjee also allegedly dubbed the trains carrying migrant workers 'Corona Express' in a statement explaining the complete lack of Covid protocol on the part of the centre while the migrant workers were being sent back home.[61]

## 3. *Symbolic Forms of Political Communication*

Typical of the populist political strategy, the making of the personality cult of the leader as an 'embodied sovereign', 'infallible strongman' and benevolent 'saviour of the people', took place during Covid-19. All crucial announcements related to the Covid-19 pandemic starting from the lockdown announcements, crucial governmental steps and vaccines were made by the topmost leadership. The need for the leaders to be at the forefront of every policy decision related to Covid-19 was the typical ubiquity that the cult-making of populism requires. The vaccine certificates have the PM's picture on it, the funds were called the PM-CARES and CM Relief funds and all welfare schemes of the central and state governments were carried out in the name of the leader, be it the PM or the CMs.[62] Hence, the need for visibility of the populist leader during a crisis as monumental as Covid-19 was to reinforce the prerequisite of the leader to appear all-pervasive and successful in managing the crisis.[63] Even at the state level, similar efforts to project and attribute all governmental initiatives during the pandemic to the topmost leaders, Banerjee in Bengal and Kejriwal in Delhi, were witnessed throughout the crisis.

## Conclusion

The study revealed three major trends of populist communication during a crisis situation like Covid-19. First, during such an unprecedented crisis, the propensity of populist leaders to further consolidate their personality cult as 'only saviours/messiahs' capable of mitigating the crisis was further reinforced. Second, as the crisis aggravated, the insidious populist design of antagonistic politics to attribute the blame to the 'other', was seen in full swing both from central as well as state leadership. Lastly and most importantly, the zealousness of the populist administrator to advance their performative politics of visibility and heroism have often compromised the immediate administrative needs that a diffused institutional structure with a trained bureaucracy is better equipped to handle than personal arbitrary interventions by the highest political leadership. Hence, the imperative of swift and efficient governance becomes the biggest casualty of populist machismo during a crisis like Covid-19. However, the visibility of the leadership also ensured, to some extent, the much-needed political accountability during a critical crisis like the Covid-19 pandemic. Moving further, more nuanced studies on India's populist political communication during crisis like COVID-19 should be taken up ton have a more comprehensive understanding of populism during crisis.

## Endnotes

1 Cristobal Rovira Kaltwasser et al., eds., The Oxford Handbook of Populism (Oxford: Oxford University Press, 2017).

2 Murray Hausknecht, "Populism as Bogey-Man," Dissent (1956), https://www.dissentmagazine.org/article/populism-bogey-man/

3 Margaret Canovan, *Trust the People! Populism and the Two Faces of Democracy, Political Studies*, Volume 47 Issue 1, (1999).

4 https://www.institute.global/insights/politics-and-governance/pandemic-populism-analysis-populist-leaders-responses-covid-19

5 https://theloop.ecpr.eu/narendra-modi-indias-vulnerable-strongman-populist-leader/

6 https://www.theindiaforum.in/politics/emotional-burdens-personality-cult

7 Christophe Jaffrelot and Louis Tillin, "Populism in India," in *The Oxford Handbook of Populism,* eds. Christobal Rovira Kaltwasser, Paul Taggart, Paulina Ochoa Espego and Pierrie Ostiguy, Oxford University Press,(2017).

8 Proma Ray Chaudhury, "The Political Asceticism of Mamata Banerjee: Female Populist Leadership in Contemporary India," *Politics & Gender* 18, no. 4 (2022): 942–77.

9 https://www.indiatoday.in/elections/delhi-assembly-polls-2020/story/populism-mixed-with-soft-hindutva-makes-arvind-kejriwal-1645626-2020-02-12

10 https://blogs.lse.ac.uk/government/2020/12/07/populists-have-attacked-pluralism-its-time-to-restore-democratic-public-debate/

11 Gregor Fitzi, Jurgen Mackert and Bryan S. Turner, *Populism and the Crisis of Democracy Volume 3: Migration, Gender and Religion* (Routledge, 2019).

12 Francisco Panizza, ed., *Populism and the Mirror of Democracy* (Verso, 2005).

13 Jan Werner Muller, What is Populism? (University of Pennsylvania Press, 2016).

14 Ernesto Laclau, On Populist Reason (Verso, 2005).

15 https://www.wilsoncenter.org/publication/populism-really-problem-for-democracy

16 https://ses.library.usyd.edu.au/handle/2123/18429

17 Kurt Weyland, "Populism as a Political Strategy: An Approach's Enduring — and Increasing — Advantages," *Political Studies*, 69, no. 2(2021).

18 Annika Werner and Heiko Giebler, "Do Populists Represent? Theoretical Considerations on How Populist Parties (Might) Enact their Representative Function," *Representation: Journal of Representative Democracy* 55, no. 4(2019): 379–92, DOI: 10.1080/00344893.2019.1643776

19 Benjamin Arditi, "Populism, or, politics at the edges of democracy," *Contemporary Politics* 9, no. 1(2003), 17–31.

20 Koen Abts and Stefan Rummens, "Populism versus Democracy," *Political Studies* 55, (2007): 405–24.

21 Kaltwasser et al., *The Oxford Handbook of Populism.*

22 Laclau, *On Populist Reason.*

23 Jakob Schwörer, *The Growth of Populism in the Political Mainstream: The Contagion Effect of Populist Messages on Mainstream Parties' Communication* (Springer, 2021)

24 Pavan Kumar Malreddy, "Dicoursing Populism: Types, Typologies and Contexts," Kairos: A Journal of Critical Symposium 5, no.1(2020).

25 Jaffrelot and Tillin, "Populism in India".

26 Ajay Gudavarthy, *India After Modi: Populism and the Right* (New Delhi: Bloomsbury, 2018).

27 Andre Beteille, *Democracy and Its Institutions* (Oxford University Press, 2012).

28 https://carnegieendowment.org/posts/2017/03/populism-remixed?lang=en

29 https://home.watson.brown.edu/news/2021-07-06/populism-and-hindu-nationalism-india

30 https://www.files.ethz.ch/isn/138126/WP15.pdf

31 Chaudhury, "The Political Asceticism of Mamata Banerjee: Female Populist Leadership in Contemporary India".

32 https://www.thequint.com/opinion/aap-kejriwals-tryst-with-hindutva-from-hanuman-chalisa-to-ram-mandir

33 https://cepr.org/voxeu/columns/populism-and-covid-19

34 https://www.ifw-kiel.de/fileadmin/Dateiverwaltung/IfW-Publications/-ifw/Kiel_Working_Paper/2021/KWP_2192_Bayerlein_Boese_Gates_Kamin_Murshed_/KWP_2192.pdf

35 https://carnegieendowment.org/posts/2020/07/why-populism-can-survive-the-pandemic?lang=en&center=europe

36 https://www.asianage.com/opinion/columnists/030420/india-pays-the-price-for-acting-late-on-covid19.html

37 https://www.thehindu.com/news/national/pm-announces-21-day-lockdown-as-covid-19-toll-touches-10/article61958513.ece

38 https://www.youtube.com/watch?v=8aD9-Y4EHhc

39 https://www.indiatoday.in/india/story/pm-modi-speech-on-coronavirus-thank-corona-warriors-1657591-2020-03-19

40 https://www.news18.com/news/india/with-emphasis-on-self-reliance-pm-modi-used-atmanirbhar-19-times-in-economic-aid-speech-2617513.html

41 https://www.thehindu.com/news/resources/economic-stimulus-package-details-of-20-lakh-crore-package-announced-by-union-finance-minister-nirmala-sitharaman-in-five-tranches/article31606806.ece

42 https://timesofindia.indiatimes.com/india/centre-likely-to-retain-limited-role-and-allow-states-have-more-say-after-lockdown-4-0/articleshow/76092370.cms

43 https://theprint.in/opinion/pm-modis-speech-was-short-on-answers-that-indians-demand-of-him-during-second-covid-wave/643350/

44 https://www.bbc.com/news/world-asia-india-56771766

45 https://www.hindustantimes.com/india-news/didi-s-lessons-on-social-distancing-mamata-banerjee-takes-to-kolkata-streets-to-fight-covid19/story-oMNOulx2aPn1i2bbpjvwrO.html

46 https://www.youtube.com/watch?v=csmQqb75a30

47 https://www.youtube.com/watch?v=azMfZ4tdV5Q

48 https://www.timesnownews.com/kolkata/article/mamata-banerjee-to-resume-her-district-administrative-meetings-from-monday-first-since-covid-outbreak/640673

49 https://www.ndtv.com/india-news/coronavirus-row-over-centres-special-covid-19-teams-5-in-opposition-ruled-states-2215529

50 https://www.hindustantimes.com/cities/delhi-news/mohalla-clinics-a-waste-if-not-used-during-pandemic-delhi-hc-101620166912692.html

51 https://economictimes.indiatimes.com/news/politics-and-nation/bengal-spent-rs-4000-crore-on-covid-management-so-far-got-no-assistance-from-centre-tmc/articleshow/79465492.cms?from=mdr

52 https://www.ndtv.com/india-news/outright-false-statements-delhi-centre-blame-game-on-oxygen-crisis-2421754

53 https://www.indiatoday.in/india/story/oppn-fumes-as-pm-modi-blames-them-for-covid-spread-in-his-lok-sabha-speech-1910000-2022-02-07

54 https://www.indiatvnews.com/news/india/mamata-banerjee-denies-permission-to-central-teams-to-visit-covid-affected-areas-in-west-bengal-609500

55 https://www.indiatoday.in/law/story/supreme-court-communal-reports-media-tablighi-jamaat-coronavirus-1848329-2021-09-02

56 Catarina Kinnvall, “Populism, ontological insecurity and Hindutva: Modi and the masculinization of Indian politics,” *Cambridge Review of International Affairs* 32, no. 3: 283–302, DOI: 10.1080/09557571.2019.1588851

57 https://theprint.in/opinion/pov/indians-who-made-covid-muslim-virus-after-tablighi-jamaat-are-cheering-odishas-rath-yatra/447717/comment-page-1/

58 https://timesofindia.indiatimes.com/city/delhi/students-from-northeast-complain-of-racism-at-kmc/articleshow/74071475.cms

59 https://www.thestatesman.com/bengal/mamata-banerjee-blames-outsiders-spread-virus-1502963503.html

60 https://www.thehindu.com/news/cities/Delhi/delhis-hospitals-only-for-its-residents-says-arvind-kejriwal/article31771306.ece

61 https://scroll.in/latest/964352/cm-mamata-banerjee-claims-people-called-trains-carrying-migrant-workers-corona-express

62 https://theprint.in/india/governance/modi-image-on-covid-vaccination-certificate-is-self-projection-politics-some-parties-cry/612716/

63 https://www.bhimupi.org.in/donation-digitized-with-bhim-upi

# Index